STAND

FIRM

AND

FIRE

LOW

Private Journal
of the
Organization, March, and
Service of the
5th New Hampshire Regiment;
Colonel Edward E. Cross.

About the first middle of August
1861, the Governor and Council
of New Hampshire voted
to raise and equip the 5th
Regiment of Volunteers
for the existing war. On the
3d of August I arrived
in New York from Sonora
in Mexico, via San Francisco
& Panama Panama. At
Concord, on the 5th, I had an
interview with Hon N.S. Berry
Governor of N.H., at which time
he informed me of the manner in which the New Hampshire troops were raised and
put into the field. I had the
honor of offering some suggestions. The interview ended and
I proceeded to my home in
Lancaster.

            On the 17th of Aug.
I received a letter from Hon
Allen Tenny, Sec of State for
New Hampshire, inviting me
to visit Concord, the Governor
& Council "wishing to consult
with me upon military affairs."

First page from the "Private Journal" of Colonel Edward E. Cross. Edward E. Cross Papers, Milne Special Collections and Archives, University of New Hampshire, Durham, N.H.

The Civil War Writings of

STAND

Colonel Edward E. Cross

FIRM

EDITED BY

AND

Walter Holden, William E. Ross, and Elizabeth Slomba

FIRE

With a Foreword by Mike Pride and Mark Travis

LOW

University of New Hampshire

PUBLISHED BY UNIVERSITY PRESS OF NEW ENGLAND

HANOVER AND LONDON

University of New Hampshire

Published by University Press of New England, One Court St., Lebanon, NH 03766

© 2003 by the University of New Hampshire

Printed in the United States of America

5 4 3 2 1

Library of Congress Cataloging-in-Publication Data

Cross, Edward Ephraim, 1832–1865.
    Stand firm and fire low : the Civil War writings of Colonel Edward E. Cross /
edited by Walter Holden, William E. Ross, and Elizabeth Slomba ; with a
foreword by Mike Pride and Mark Travis.
        p.   cm.
Includes bibliographical references (p.   ) and index.
    ISBN 1–58465–280–2 (cloth : alk. paper)
        1. Cross, Edward Ephraim, 1832–1865. 2. United States. Army.
New Hampshire Infantry Regiment, 5th (1861–1865) 3. New
Hampshire—History—Civil War, 1861–1865—Personal narratives.
4. United States—History—Civil War, 1861–1865—Personal narratives.
5. New Hampshire—History—Civil War, 1861–1865—Regimental histories.
6. United States—History—Civil War, 1861–1865—Regimental histories.
7. United States—History—Civil War, 1861–1865—Campaigns.
8. Soldiers—Vermont—Biography. I. Holden, Walter. II. Ross, William E.
III. Slomba, Elizabeth. IV. Title.
E520.5 5th .C76 2002
973.7'81—dc21   2002012274

c l

Contents

Illustrations of people, places, and manuscript pages follow page 42

Foreword

In an army that often wanted for inspired leadership, Colonel Edward E. Cross met every challenge put before him. He was a fierce commander who molded a thousand volunteer soldiers from New Hampshire into one of the renowned infantry regiments in the Army of the Potomac. He led his regiment, the Fifth New Hampshire Volunteers, in some of the bloodiest battles of the Civil War. On the Peninsula, the Fifth built "the bridge that saved the army." On the march to Antietam, its division commander gave it the place of honor at the head of the entire column. At Fredericksburg, its discipline and courage took it close to the stone wall on Marye's Heights. At Chancellorsville and Gettysburg, after General Winfield Scott Hancock had referred to what remained of the Fifth as "refined gold," the regiment lived up to that compliment. Yet fame passed Cross by, at least the sort of fame won by his fellow northern New Englander, Joshua L. Chamberlain of the Twentieth Maine.

One reason for Cross's relative obscurity was that he did not make general. For good or ill, it was generals, not common soldiers or lower officers, whose names were remembered. Judged by his military deeds alone and the performance of his regiment, Cross had earned a brigadier's star. Hancock and many others recommended him for it. Cross commanded a provisional brigade at Chancellorsville, and when he was mortally wounded at Gettysburg, he was leading a brigade of Hancock's Second Corps. Had Cross been willing to put his Democratic politics aside and keep his judgments to himself, he would surely have been promoted before Gettysburg. But then he would not have been Cross.

The main reason Cross did not win more fame was that he died during the war. Unlike Chamberlain, he had no chance in the postwar years to mold a reputation for himself. He was a vain man with the writing talent to support whatever point of view he expressed. It is easy to imagine the brisk, opinionated prose that would have flowed from his pen after the war. He would have skewered those who deserved it (and some who didn't). He would have revered both the living and the dead among the common soldiers he called "my brave boys." And he would have left no doubt about his own determination never to retreat in the face of the enemy.

To suggest how Cross would have viewed the war in retrospect is not idle speculation. We know what he would have said because we know what he did say. He was always unbending in his opinions. Candid reflections animate his wartime reports and letters, and especially his journal. On the eve of the Battle of Fredericksburg, he spared no venom in writing of the commander of the Irish Brigade that in all the army there was not "another such a consummate humbug, charlatan, imposter, pretending to be a soldier, as Thomas Francis Meagher!" After Chancellorsville, he described Joseph Hooker, commander of the Army of the Potomac, as "completely outgeneraled; his magnificent army badly handled, his artillery not massed, not half of it used." To Franklin Pierce, the former president, he complained in a letter that the road to promotion in the Union army was paved not with courage or skill in battle but with political loyalty to Lincoln. "All the 2nd & 3rd rate officers, the sneaks, the malingerers, the cowards, have found this out, & cover their deficiencies by the cloak of Abolitionism," Cross wrote.

These quotations from Cross stress one key aspect of his character: Although he fully expected to give his life for the Union cause, he would not yield his freedom to speak his mind. Edward E. Cross let everyone know where he stood. He had been a political man since long before the war but never a politician. Even when his own interests were at stake, he could not bring himself to sacrifice his right to express his opinion for the purpose of playing politics.

Cross's wartime journal is far more than a catalog of the colonel's prejudices and opinions. Like his prewar writings, it combines wit, fancy, and joy in life. Cross spent many years before the war as an editor and writer, developing a good eye for detail and a fine ability to turn a phrase. He put these skills to use in the journal. Like all keepers of journals, he wrote his with posterity in mind. With the romantic flourishes of the Victorian age that produced him, Cross described the scenes that unfolded before him. He wanted readers of the future to see what he saw, on the march, in camp, on the battlefield.

And now many more readers will be able to do just that. The two of us were pleased to learn that, at long last, the journal, along with many of Cross's other wartime papers, would be made available to the public in the current edition. Walter Holden, who owned the journal for more than thirty years, agreed to donate his Cross papers to his alma mater, the University of New Hampshire, on the condition that they be published.

We met Walter on June 3, 1997. By then, we had been researching Cross and the Fifth New Hampshire for five years in hopes of writing a book someday. We were both newspaper editors and family men with an interest in the Civil War, so the research was a hobby. The book was taking on the aura of a pipe dream: We were eager to try it, but we had never written a history before and we hadn't progressed far.

We knew about Walter, and we knew he owned the journal, but despite our background as reporters, we had not been very clever about searching for him. Although we had heard he was in Virginia, West Virginia, and Texas, we had pursued none of these leads with any tenacity. Then one day, while working on a story for the *Concord Monitor* about a new effort to get Cross his posthumous brigadier general's star, we heard that Walter lived in Goffstown, fifteen miles south of the Monitor building. We looked him up in the phone book, and sure enough, there was his number.

We called and invited ourselves to his apartment. When we arrived, Walter had put a red trefoil, the Fifth New Hampshire's proud symbol, on the screen door just to be sure we found the right one. The man who greeted us was trim and square-jawed. His years as a teacher, writer, and editor had not slackened the bearing of the World War II combat infantryman he was in his youth. As we spoke that morning, we were aware that Walter was sizing us up. He is a cautious man and a stickler for accuracy, and he had devoted many years to his own study of the Fifth. Being a New Englander, he never told us what he thought of us, of course, but during a visit of about two hours, he provided the spark our book project needed. Before we were done, he had given us nearly all the material he had.

Walter gave us one other thing as well: our first taste of the joy of discovery that drives historians. Cross wrote his journal in a long notebook, eight and one-half by thirteen inches. The binding was crumbling, the ink brownish, the handwriting a challenge to modern eyes but ultimately readable. It was amazing to hold it in our hands. We could picture Cross writing it—on a travel desk in his tent or in an awkward posture on the way home to recuperate after he was shot at Fair Oaks and nearly blown up at Fredericksburg. Having in your hands history that few others know about is a deeply personal experience. At that moment we were closer than we had ever been to Cross, and we felt for the first time a responsibility to tell the story he had not lived to write himself. We had other similar moments during our research for *My Brave Boys*, our history of Cross and the Fifth, but this was the pivotal one.

We walked out of Walter's apartment that morning with his copy of a rare memoir written by a soldier of the Fifth and copies of several letters written by and about Cross during the war. Because Walter seemed a little stern and circumspect, we had not dared to ask for his typescript of Cross's journal. As we were about to get in the car, however, we summoned the courage to go back and knock on the door. Walter never let on whether our timidity had given him pause about our fitness for the task ahead, but he gave us the type-script. In retrospect, we have come to see that moment as the transfer of a sacred trust by one generation to the next. This was an act of generosity—and also a challenge. Walter had worked for three decades on a history of Cross's regiment, but now he had passed the duty on to us.

Cross's journal was essential to us in writing *My Brave Boys*, but because ours was a history of Cross's regiment, not a biography of Cross, there is a great deal more of the man and his adventures in this book than there is in ours. In New Hampshire and beyond, Cross, like Chamberlain of Maine, should be recognized as the epitome of the Union fighting man. He had grave differences with the Republicans who ran the war and many of the generals who commanded the Army of the Potomac, but his opinions never stayed him from his duty. Had Cross lived, he would surely have exercised a similar candor in creating for himself the kind of legend that grew up around other fighting generals who survived the war. He would have been a general, too; despite his politics, it would have been impossible to deny him his star had he not been killed at Gettysburg. Now, due to Walter Holden's generosity, Cross's principal wartime writing leading up to that fateful day near the wheat field will reach the audience the colonel so richly deserves.

Mike Pride and Mark Travis
Authors of *My Brave Boys: To War with Colonel Cross and the Fighting Fifth*

Preface

War promises much to many. In the swirl of battle's suffering and death, glory grows and promotions proliferate. A few years after the Civil War, Oliver Wendell Holmes, Jr., told a Memorial Day audience in Keene, New Hampshire: "Through our great good fortune, in our youth our hearts were touched by fire."

In the fire of that war, Colonel Edward E. Cross garnered glory as a top-notch leader of men in battle. In a letter to his friend Henry Kent, Cross claimed that thirteen generals had put his name in for promotion. General Winfield Scott Hancock, who called Cross's Fifth New Hampshire Volunteers as good as any regiment in the world, told the colonel at Gettysburg, "After this battle you'll get your general's star." Cross replied, "Too late, General," and rode out to his death.

The colonel's death was preceded by many near misses. He counted a dozen or so wounds received before Gettysburg and listed three duels before the war—one each with swords, pistols, and Burnside rifles. His survival until Gettysburg reminds us that history is a bundle of "ifs" and "whys." The biggest why in Cross's career was: Why didn't he ever receive his promotion? Pursuit of an answer to this question brought Mike Pride and Mark Travis to my door and propelled them on to the writing of *My Brave Boys*.

How close was Cross to being promoted to brigadier general? Scholars must exert caution: one contemporary history has his picture captioned "General Cross"; regimental histories styled him the same way. But it never happened, despite the fact that, as senior colonel in General O. O. Howard's brigade, he was in line for promotion even before fighting a battle; in December 1861 he wrote to Kent: "I command the brigade half the time." The following May—still before any important action—he and his men built the Grapevine Bridge, "the bridge that saved the Army," prompting one highly placed observer to write: "Any regular army officer would have immediately been promoted to general." In the battle that followed, Cross commanded the brigade after Howard was wounded; on through three more battles he commanded troops other than his own—thus, acting as a general.

All of which brings us to a related question: Could history be rewritten so that Cross would be given his star? Perhaps. Theodore Roosevelt was given the Medal of Honor over a century after his heroism as head of the Rough Riders in Cuba. This very week, November 2001, Acting Governor Jane Swift of Massachusetts officially exonerated Susannah Martin and four others executed during the Salem witch trials of 1692. Closer to the situation: one colonel, mortally wounded the same afternoon as Cross was, received a posthumous promotion to general.

One of the fascinating ifs of history is the thin thread that runs through. Outcomes of crucial events would have been totally different, had things been only a little different. George Herbert, with a little poetic license, shows how Richard III lost his final battle, his kingdom, and his life:

"For want of a nail the shoe was lost, for want of a shoe the horse was lost, for want of a horse the rider was lost."

How did I come to own the Colonel Cross journal and other papers? The story stems both from being in New Hampshire and being a history buff. The thin thread might easily have been cut at any number of times. For example, consider my historic ancestors. Had the Salem hysteria occurred some years earlier, Susannah Martin might have been hanged before she had any children. Susannah's contemporary, Hannah Dustin, was taken from her New Hampshire home by Indians, but escaped by killing her captors as they slept. If either of these women had met untimely deaths, I would not have been here to possess the colonel's journal.

More to the point is the fact that in the late 1950s I was teaching high school English in Keene and reading one of Bruce Catton's volumes on the Civil War. The teacher next door offered to lend me her history of the Sixth New Hampshire Volunteers. Hardly aware that regimental histories existed, I didn't expect much of it. I was surprised: the story of the Sixth was well written, full of important events and interesting people. Remembering that Catton was particularly high on a New Hampshire regiment, I checked back and found that Catton favored the Fifth New Hampshire and its colonel, Edward E. Cross. In his great trilogy about the Army of the Potomac, Catton made a dozen favorable references to Cross and the Fifth. Writing of the colonel's death, Catton quoted a tribute "in words which any troop commander in that war might have been proud of." The tribute came from a book by Thomas Leonard Livermore, a veteran of the Fifth: "He taught us to aim in battle, and above all things he ignored and made us ignore the idea of retreating. Besides this he clothed and fed us well, taught us to build good quarters, and camped us on good ground."

As soon as I could, I bought Livermore's *Days and Events* and Child's *History of the Fifth Regiment New Hampshire Volunteers*. Child quoted huge chunks from Cross's journal; other contemporary historians mentioned it. I was interested enough to begin my own book on the Fifth; but much as Mike and Mark found years later, I felt that research, no matter how deep, would be incomplete without Cross's journal. I checked sources in and outside of New Hampshire. As time passed, I became an editor in Boston, my office within walking distance of the Boston Public Library and its tremendous rare book collection. I gathered material from contemporary sources but found not even a hint about the journal. Apparently it had disappeared around the turn of the century.

I traveled to Lancaster, New Hampshire, where Cross was born and was buried. There I met Faith Kent, granddaughter of Cross's boyhood friend and most faithful correspondent, Henry O. Kent. Miss Kent was a mine of information and generously allowed me to copy dozens of letters that Cross had written her grandfather, but she had no idea where the journal might be. As head of the Lancaster Historical Society, she knew that it certainly wasn't in the town.

When I discovered an article written by a doctor with an interest in the war, the trail began to heat up. I called the man and asked about the journal. He said he had seen it. This was exciting news: in years of searching I had found no one who knew that the journal still existed—and here was a man who had actually seen it. When I asked who had it, the doctor, suddenly deciding he had revealed too much, would say no more on the subject. Still we were both Civil War buffs and admirers of Colonel Cross; over time we continued our discussions. He knew that I was writing a book on the Fifth and gradually became aware of the serious depth of my research. The doctor and I were to meet one Saturday morning in the fall to plan his approaching the journal's owner to see if I could be permitted a peek at it. When I called the morning of the expected meeting, the doctor was getting ready to go to a football game at Dartmouth; thoughts of the Big Green had driven me out of his mind. Feeling a need to compensate me, I suppose, or perhaps wanting to end my badgering, he said he would give me the name and address of the owner if I promised not to tell that he was the one who had told me. Of course I agreed. However, since both men have long since died, secrecy is no longer an issue.

Composing a letter to the second one—another doctor—I struggled to achieve the right mixture of special pleading and proof of need. The answer came back by phone, cautious and cautionary. For example, he couldn't tell me how he had acquired the journal, and I couldn't tell anybody he had it. I especially couldn't tell Faith Kent. After a good deal of backing and hauling, we set a time when I could get up to his northern New Hampshire town. This doctor, a short man in a tweed jacket and tartan tie, met me at his door.

Peering at me through thick glasses, he grudgingly let me in. The hall was dark and so was the parlor he took me into. Before showing me anything, he went over the stipulations again and added, as a further warning, that the journal was not for sale because he was leaving it to his daughters. Then he left the room. I waited uneasily until he returned, a large and tattered brown envelope clutched to his chest. "It's very fragile. I have to hold it myself." Without opening the envelope, he left again. This time he returned with a typescript in a green binder. He read me the title: "Private Journal of the Organization, March and Services of the Fifth New Hampshire Regiment, Colonel Edward E. Cross." I recognized the Cross touch; I was indeed in the presence of greatness.

Later he told me the story that I repeated in the foreword to *My Brave Boys*: "Years back he had gone to Lancaster to an auction of property belonging to either an uncle or a cousin of [Faith Kent's]. A stamp collector, he had bid on a barrel of old letters, gambling that he might find some valuable stamps. When he got home and dumped out the contents, there at the bottom of the barrel he found Colonel Cross's journal and other papers."

Maybe—but probably not. Faith Kent had no relative that fit his time frame. Cross's sister, Helen Denison, his last surviving sibling, willed her "papers of Colonel Cross" to the Lancaster Library. Nobody knows for sure what happened next. Although historians should not speculate, the logical assumption—based on the desire for secrecy—is that the "papers" were acquired from the library in some way the owner was not proud of. Two facts help the supposition: small local libraries were told in the sixties to clear their shelves of any material that wasn't moving, and it was said that there was in the Lancaster Library at that time "a young librarian who didn't care anything about history."

I was gullible, obviously. Time passed; we corresponded. He told me that "innumerable people wanted to see the journal"; but he could show it when he was "sure they did not have a hidden camera and only if certain they had a poor memory." I did get to see the typescript, but not the journal. Finally he called me one night. His daughters weren't interested in history, and he wanted to know if I would like to buy the journal and other Cross papers for three hundred dollars. I sure would, but as a young married man raising two small boys, three hundred dollars was a budget buster. Hoping not to insult him, I made a counteroffer of one hundred dollars, which he immediately accepted. As I look back, it does seem that he was suspiciously anxious to get rid of the very valuable materials. Incidentally, Faith Kent's sister worked in the same hospital as the doctor did and knew of his interest in Colonel

Cross; the two women were 90 percent sure right along who had sold me the journal and where he had gotten it.

I have held the papers for over thirty years, "until my book on Cross was published." Mike and Mark came along; I gladly handed them the guidon. And now, I hand the journal over to the University of New Hampshire, assured that, nearly 140 years after Cross closed the cover for the last time, these historic papers will be available for future generations to marvel at and enjoy.

Boscawen, New Hampshire   W.H.
March 2002

Editorial Notes

"Close up," cried the Colonel. "Close up and fire low."
If you fall, die like men with your hearts to the foe.
—From a poem by Edward E. Cross

Colonel Edward E. Cross was an excellent writer and, from his experience as a reporter, he had a keen eye for detail. However, he was not an objective observer. He clearly wrote his letters, his diaries, and his reports to reflect his opinions, and that is what makes his wartime writings so interesting. Whether from the force of his personality or from his background as an editorial writer, or both, the reader gets a clear idea of where Cross stands and what he thinks. To have written otherwise would not have been Cross. Cross's words, sometimes flowery, sometimes bitter, almost always straightforward, form the heart of this volume, and the editors' main goal was to let Colonel Cross speak for himself.

Unfortunately, Cross did not get a star for penmanship, consistency in formatting, spelling, or proofreading. That has been left to his editors, 140 years hence. Cross's handwriting was poor, and it appeared to worsen over the years. Although the editors achieved some mastery over the scribbled endings to his words, they were unable to decipher all words and proper names. Those instances are marked with the word "illegible," in brackets. Although these appear more frequently than the editors would like, they occur intermittently throughout the text. For the most part, the editors have worked hard to preserve Cross's words as they first appeared in letters or in print. His misspellings have been preserved, and his grammar has been left intact. On very few occasions, the editors placed bracketed additions within the text for the sake of clarity. Cross was also inconsistent in his use of punctuation and paragraph breaks. In the diary, the editors added some periods, but only when it was clear that Cross was moving on to another thought, line, or paragraph. The editors chose to leave the formatting as close to the original as possible, although Cross's indentations from the original have been standardized for the sake of readability. The letters provided a different challenge. In addition to the aforementioned problems, Cross was very inconsistent in placing dates, return addresses, and salutations in his letters. These have been standardized, but the texts of Cross's letters remain as true to the original as possible. Cross used underlining extensively in all his manuscript writing. However, italicization has replaced underlining in the published text.

When the editors began this project, they realized that footnotes would be needed to help illuminate Cross's writing. The casual reader may not be able to identify generals by their surnames, and even the Civil War buff is not able to identify the rank and file of a regiment. Notes are intended to place the people, locations, and events in the context of the diary entry, report, or letter. Full explanations have been repeated in places, but for the most part streamlined notes follow the first mention of a person, location, or event. Likewise, sources are provided in full the first time they are cited, but thereafter a short entry is used. The full initial entry of each source is meant to substitute for a full bibliography, although a brief bibliographical note follows the text.

Cross's writings have been separated by form. The diary, the cornerstone of this book, comes first. Those who have read and analyzed the diary marvel at Cross's candor, although it is clear that he intended it for posterity. Next come the reports, both manuscript and published. These contrast greatly depending on their intended audience. Cross's official, published versions are understandably restrained, while unpublished writings contain his hard-edged opinions and observation. All told, the reports are useful in providing a counterpoint to the diary and to supplementing the diary where Cross leaves off. The letters and poetry provide us with the clearest view into Cross's mind. His official letters range from deferential to sarcastic, but his private correspondence with Henry Kent and Franklin Pierce provide the reader with personal insights that are unavailable elsewhere.

Cross's diary was long in the hands of editor Walter Holden, but thanks to his generosity, it now resides in the Milne Special Collections Department of the University of New Hampshire Library. Text for the reports came from *Official Records,* published in the decades after the war; from those included in William Child's *History of the Fifth Regiment New Hampshire Volunteers;* and from Cross's own manuscripts. Once again, the latter now reside at the University of New Hampshire. The letters came from a variety of sources, but the largest number are used courtesy of Miss M. Faith Kent, granddaughter of Cross's best friend, Henry O. Kent. Additional letters came from other sources including The New Hampshire Historical Society in Concord, New Hampshire; the New Hampshire Division of Records Management and Archives, also in Concord; the Rauner Special Collections

Library at Dartmouth College, Hanover, New Hampshire; the Milne Special Collections and Archives Department of the University of New Hampshire Library, Durham, New Hampshire; and contemporary newspapers, particularly those in microfilm at the New Hampshire State Library in Concord, New Hampshire. The editors want to thank Charlotte Thibault for the use of her outstanding maps. Clearly, the editors are indebted to the artistry, effort, and generosity of donors, fellow researchers, librarians, archivists, artists, and photographers. They have contributed mightily to this work.

Closer to home, the editors wish to dedicate their efforts to the following: Walter Holden to Barbara; William E. Ross to the memory of his parents; and Elizabeth Slomba to Mom and Dad.

STAND

FIRM

AND

FIRE

LOW

Introduction

Edward E. Cross's Early Years

Edward E. Cross was born on April 22, 1832, in Lancaster, New Hampshire, the first son born to Colonel Ephraim Cross and his third wife, Abigail Everett. The elder Cross made his living as a hatter, but his leadership in the town militia earned him the title of "colonel." Cross's mother was the daughter of Judge Richard C. Everett, one of Lancaster's most prominent citizens.[1]

Cross grew up in this farming community of just over a thousand residents. The Connecticut River and the state of Vermont lay to the west. To the east and south, the White Mountains cast their long shadows over the wooded landscape. This land, north of the "notches," had been settled a scant three generations. There were plenty of fields for roaming, hills for climbing, and streams for fishing. By the time Cross reached adulthood, railroads and manufacturing were beginning to transform Lancaster's rural

1. Otis F. R. Waite, *New Hampshire in the Great Rebellion: Containing Histories of the Several New Hampshire Regiments and Biographical Notices of Many of the Prominent Actors in the Civil War of 1861–65* (Claremont, N.H.: Tracy, Chase & Company, 1870), 262, and Mike Pride and Mark Travis, *My Brave Boys: To War with Colonel Cross and the Fighting Fifth* (Hanover, N.H.: University Press of New England, 2001), 6.

economy. As an adult, Cross would leave Lancaster, but the rolling and rocky landscape of his birth would always be a part of him.[2]

Cross's maternal grandfather, Richard Everett, was a Revolutionary War veteran, and the oral traditions from that conflict likely influenced Cross and his young friends. When Cross was born, Andrew Jackson, the "Hero of New Orleans," was president of the United States. As a teenager, Cross watched his father recruit and organize young men from his community to march off and fight in the Mexican War. In spite of his peaceful and pastoral surroundings, Cross took careful notice of the world and adventures that lay beyond Coos County.[3]

Cross left school at the age of fifteen to become a printer with the *Coos Democrat*, the town newspaper. Over time, he would be joined at the newspaper by his younger brother, Richard, and his future brother-in-law, Dexter Chase. Cross's best friend, Henry O. Kent, also apprenticed at the newspaper, as did Charles Farrar Browne, who would later gain celebrity as humorist Artemus Ward. The editor of the *Democrat*, James Rix, was an unrepentant Jacksonian politician. In addition to running the *Democrat*, he also served as president of the New Hampshire Senate. The teenagers learned the newspaper trade and undoubtedly some politics from Rix. With such tutelage, Cross became a competent newspaperman, but he remained an adventurer at heart.[4]

In 1850, after about two years with the *Democrat*, Cross traveled with his father to Canada. From that day onward, although he periodically returned to Lancaster to visit family and friends, he would always call other places home. In June of 1850, Cross settled in Cincinnati, Ohio, where he became a printer for the *Cincinnati Times*. The pay was good, particularly by Lancaster standards. Over time, he became a reporter for the paper, a pursuit that helped Cross hone his writing skills but, more importantly, gave him an excuse to travel.[5]

Cincinnati served as a crucible for the melding of Cross's imagination and past experience with current political ideas. In between assignments, he wrote and published heroic tales about a pair of New England volunteers fighting in Mexico. Coincidentally, the two fictional heroes worked as printers in civilian life. Under Cross's spell, the two volunteers would tie handkerchiefs around their heads in preparation for battles that could be their last. In his day-to-day life, Cross became attracted to the American Party or

2. Pride and Travis, *Brave Boys*, 6.
3. Ibid., 6–7.
4. Ibid., and Waite, *New Hampshire in the Rebellion*, 262.
5. Pride and Travis, *Brave Boys*, 8–9.

Know-Nothings, an anti-Catholic, anti-immigrant movement that emerged as a national political force. For Cross, feelings of distrust for Catholics and the Irish would become stronger than any religious feelings of his own. As a result, he grew to embrace his Anglo-Saxon, Protestant roots and emerged a staunch supporter of the American Party.[6]

Cross traveled to Washington to serve as political correspondent for the *Cincinnati Times*. While in Washington, his abilities as a writer, coupled with his powers of observation, enabled him to publish newsworthy letters and columns in the *New York Herald* and other respectable periodicals. Cross used the byline "Richard Everett," in honor of his grandfather. As the issue of slavery threatened to divide the nation, Cross traveled south and witnessed firsthand the deleterious effects of the slave economy. Nevertheless, Cross remained leery of abolitionists and feared that their extremism would pull the nation apart. He opposed the election of those (particularly in his home state) whom he regarded as antislavery fanatics. His worst fears were realized during the election of 1856, when the issue of slavery split the American Party; it would not survive as a national political force. Finding himself unmoored politically, Cross worried that the Democratic Party was no longer the party of Jackson. However, it was far more palatable than the upstart Republican Party, whose leaders increasingly opposed the institution of slavery. Cross considered such a stance unconstitutional and reluctantly became a Democrat.[7]

Cross returned to Cincinnati to manage his newspaper's editorial staff, but the frontier and adventure beckoned. He left Cincinnati in 1857 to travel the northern plains. He sent columns back East about the lives of trappers and buffalo hunters and his encounters with the Sioux and Cheyenne. The columns documenting his adventures were popular, but in 1858 he set his sights on the Arizona Territory.[8]

Cross invested much of his savings in a mining venture and made the seventeen-hundred-mile journey across the Rocky Mountains into Arizona. He and his companions gained notoriety by transporting the first steam engine and first printing press across the Continental Divide. He sent regular accounts back to the *Cincinnati Times*, in which he described the backwardness of the Southwest, as well as sometimes tense encounters with the nearby Apaches. In January 1859, Cross and his small party reached Tubac, Arizona, where he became a shareholder in the local Santa Rita Mining Com-

---

6. Ibid., 9–11, 249–251.
7. Waite, *New Hampshire in the Rebellion*, 262, and Pride and Travis, *Brave Boys*, 12–13.
8. Waite, *New Hampshire in the Rebellion*, 262–263.

pany and edited Arizona's first newspaper, the *Weekly Arizonian*. Out of respect for his new surroundings, Cross adopted the pen name "Gila." The *Arizonian* served the few hundred white residents of the territory; however, Cross planned to make his fortune through his investments in local mining interests.[9]

While in Arizona, Cross grew accustomed to the lawlessness of frontier life. Most residents armed themselves for protection against Apaches, Mexicans, and outlaws. He also made the acquaintance of Captain Richard Ewell, U.S. Army, commander of the garrison at nearby Fort Buchanan. The army provided a necessary buffer between the settlers and the local Indians. Cross also learned to use his newspaper as a weapon. He wrote editorials in support of the annexation of the Mexican state of Sonora, which bordered Arizona to the south. He also employed his pen to ridicule Sylvester Mowry, a mine owner from Tucson. Cross contended that Mowry was exaggerating the mining and agricultural possibilities of Arizona in papers back East. Cross argued that these misrepresentations might enhance Mowry's short-term investments but that the end result of Mowry's publicity campaign would be a disservice to potential settlers. The war of words escalated into a duel with rifles. The two walked off their paces, but after a series of misses and misfires, Cross handed off his rifle, folded his arms, and dared Mowry to shoot. Mowry, either impressed by Cross's daring or persuaded by more peaceable spectators, put down his rifle. The controversy ended with a handshake, and Cross withdrew some of his more intemperate remarks.[10]

Cross returned to Lancaster in late 1859, both to look after his parents and to receive Masonic degrees from his hometown's North Star Lodge. He used some of his investment earnings to support his parents, who, partially due to his father's alcoholism, were having trouble making ends meet. Although he returned to the Southwest, the 1860 census listed Cross as a resident at his parents' address. The young entrepreneur also invested in a new silver-mining venture. Headquartered in St. Louis, Missouri, this enterprise would join competing interests in the Arizona Territory. When Cross returned to Arizona, he volunteered to join Captain Ewell on a scouting party to fight the Apaches. He would cite this experience years later during the Civil War, the story most likely inspired by his old friend's rise to corps command in Lee's Army of Northern Virginia.[11]

The election of 1860 confirmed Cross's decision to return to the Demo-

9. Pride and Travis, *Brave Boys*, 13.

10. Ibid., 19–21.

11. Ibid., 22, and William Child, *A History of the Fifth Regiment New Hampshire Volunteers, in the American Civil War, 1861–1865* (Bristol, N.H.: R. W. Musgrove, 1893), 214.

cratic Party. Although he had grown weary of Buchanan, he displayed great enthusiasm for Stephen Douglas, the Democratic presidential candidate from Illinois. He remained wary of mainstream Republicans and despised the abolitionist senator John P. Hale of his native state. The senator from New Hampshire would return the sentiment. Few, including Cross, would have predicted the nomination, much less the election, of Abraham Lincoln. It would turn the nation, as well as Cross's little corner of the republic, upside down.[12]

Beginning with South Carolina in December 1860, slaveholding states in the Deep South began to secede from the Union in response to Lincoln's election. As a direct result, many southern officers chose to leave the service and return to their native soil. The attrition weakened the frontier outposts, and the uncertain events back East led to the withdrawal of U.S. Army forces. The settlers tried to fill the void, taking part in several expeditions against the emboldened natives. Yet Apaches attacked the incipient mining venture from St. Louis, killing most of the settlers. The results of this attack threatened the local economy and devastated Cross's investments.[13]

During this unsettled period, Cross left Arizona and crossed over into the Mexican state of Sonora. There he served for several months as a garrison commander in Benito Juarez's Liberal Army. He had long supported Juarez's efforts to promote popular government, which Cross argued would reduce the influence of the entrenched elites, including the powerful Roman Catholic Church. The firing on Fort Sumter, however, would bring an end to Cross's crusade.[14]

Although California offered him a commission as captain in a regiment of mounted rifles, Cross decided to return to his native New Hampshire. He wrote the governor, offering his services on behalf of the Union. Cross left Arizona traveling overland to San Francisco. From there, he sailed to New York, where he landed on August 18, 1861. Within weeks, Cross had accepted a commission as colonel and commander of the Fifth New Hampshire Regiment of Volunteers. A new adventure had begun.[15]

12. Pride and Travis, *Brave Boys*, 22–23.
13. Waite, *New Hampshire in the Rebellion*, 264, and Child, *Fifth New Hampshire*, 311–12.
14. Pride and Travis, *Brave Boys*, 22–23.
15. Ibid., 23.

Part One

Private Journal of the Organization, March, and Services of the 5th New Hampshire Regiment[1]

Colonel Edward E. Cross

THE ORGANIZATION AND EARLY SERVICE
OF THE FIFTH NEW HAMPSHIRE

I at once entered upon my duty.

Private Journal
of the
Organization, March, and
Services
of the
5th New Hampshire Regiment;
Colonel Edward E. Cross

1. Edward E. Cross Papers, Milne Special Collections and Archives, University of New Hampshire, Durham, N.H.

About the first ~~middle~~ of August, 1861, the Governor and Council[2] of New Hampshire voted to raise and equip the 5ᵗʰ Regiment of volunteers for the existing war. On the 3d of August I arrived in New York from Sonora in Mexico,[3] *via* San Francisco & ~~Pannama~~ Panama. At Concord, on the 5ᵗʰ, I had an interview with Hon N. S. Berry,[4] Governor of N.H., at which time he informed me of the manner in which the New Hampshire troops were raised and put into the field. I had the honor of offering some suggestions. The interview ended and I proceeded to my home in Lancaster.

On the 17th of Aug. I received a letter from Hon Allen Tenney,[5] Sec. of State for New Hampshire, inviting me to visit Concord, the Governor & Council "wishing to consult with me upon military affairs." On the 20th I reached Concord. On the 22d in the Council chamber, Gov Berry offered me the command of the 5ᵗʰ Regiment. It was previously intimated to me that I could have the Lieut Colonelcy of the 4ᵗʰ Regiment, which post I determined to accept.

I stated to the Governor and Council that if I could organize and fit out the Regiment to suit myself, and appoint all the officers, I would take command. The terms were agreed to, & I cheerfully bear testimony to the fair & honorable style in which the authorities kept their faith. Just so far as was possible under the circumstances I had my own way in everything.

I at once entered upon my duty—my commission being dated Aug 27, 1861. On the 28th of September, Co A entered Camp near Concord, & was soon followed by other companies and detachments making in a few days over seven hundred men. The Camp was named "Camp Jackson"[6] in honor of the illustrious soldier & statesman who once occupied the Presidential

2. Beginning with the Constitution of 1792, the State of New Hampshire elected five executive councilors "for advising the governor in the executive part of government." State of New Hampshire, *Manual for the General Court* (Concord, N.H.: State of New Hampshire, 1999), 78.

3. The Mexican state of Sonora is located on Arizona's southern border. During the months before the Civil War, Cross sided with Benito Juarez in the Mexican civil war and commanded a garrison of troops in Sonora. Pride and Travis, *Brave Boys*, 19, 22.

4. Nathaniel S. Berry (1796–1894) was elected governor of New Hampshire in 1861 and 1862. During his two terms in office, Berry raised and equipped over 15,000 troops. Although a Democrat for 22 years, Berry left the party over the issue of slavery. He ran for governor five times on the Free Soil Party ticket prior to joining the Republican Party. *Granite State Monthly* 16 (May 1894): 382.

5. Allen Tenney, spelled variously as Tenny, served as secretary of state for New Hampshire from 1861 to 1865. See G. Parker Lyon, *New-Hampshire Annual Register* (Concord, N.H.: G. Parker Lyon) for New Hampshire government officials during the war years.

6. Camp Jackson, named after President Andrew Jackson, was located on Glover's Hill across the lower bridge from Concord, N.H. *History of Concord New Hampshire*, vol. II, James O. Lyford, ed. (Concord, N.H.: Rumford Press, 1903), 1175.

chair. Strict discipline was at once established. On the 1st of October I started for Washington to procure arms, & transact business for the Regiment. In the matter of arms I met with good success, but did not make out to procure leave of absence for Lieut Edward J. Conner[7] in order that he might take the post of Lieut Col of the Regiment.

Our term of service in the camp of organization was spent in drilling, whenever the weather permitted, but we had a great deal of rain and the men, not accustomed to camp life, were somewhat discontented. The first month of organization I had no one to assist me, and every contract for clothing or equipments required constant supervision.

Received orders to start with my Regiment for Washington. Not being ready in many respects, nor having my full complement of men I remonstrated, backed up by all my Regiment, and declared I should resign if pushed away in such a hurry. This movement secured a *reprieve* of 4 days.

During the time we were in camp Jackson, I had but little trouble with the men, and their quiet, sober, orderly behavior elicited praise from everybody in the city. I never saw men who sooner adapted themselves to military law. But the advantages of strict discipline at the outset were very apparent. The men found out that they *must* obey, or suffer the severest consequences. One slight mutiny occurred among some men from Portsmouth, which resulted in their entire defeat and humiliation before the entire Regiment.

On Monday, the 28th in the forenoon, the Regiment was paraded, and the Regimental colors presented — the Reg colors by Gov Berry, and the National by Gen Colby.[8] Speeches were made, and I did my best at a reply. The same evening at five o'clock we struck our tents, packed up and marched to Concord, where we spent the night, quartered in various halls and public buildings. Everything was quiet. At daybreak Tuesday morning, the line formed, & at ~~seven~~ half past six, with colors flying and our band playing "The Girl I left behind me," we marched to the depot & embarked. Many a

7. Edward J. Conner, of Exeter, N.H., never served in the Fifth New Hampshire. He remained in the U. S. Army, rising to the rank of captain prior to his retirement in December 1863. New Hampshire Adjutant-General's Office, *Revised Register of the Soldiers and Sailors of New Hampshire in the War of the Rebellion, 1861–1866* (Concord, N.H.: I. C. Evans, 1895), 1039.

8. Anthony Colby (1792–1873), of New London, N.H., was New Hampshire's only Whig governor (1846–47). A brigadier general in the militia, he served as state adjutant general from 1861 until his resignation in early 1863. *Biographical Dictionary of the Governors of the United States*, reprint edition, Robert Sobel and John Raimo, eds. (Westport, Conn.: Meckler, 1988), 956–957.

brave lad who that day followed his colors so gaily will never press his native heath again. For myself, I never felt better. That morning I bid farewell to my mother, & having been inured to partings, felt calm and happy. My face might have shown weariness but not sorrow.

We left Concord with 1012 officers and men. At Norwich[9] embarked on a steamer for Jersey City, which place we reached the next morning. At Jersey City took cars for Washington. Were hospitably entertained at Philadelphia & Baltimore. On the boat from Norwich to Jersey City the officer of the day discerned a man selling liquor to the troops. He was at once put in irons and when in the most desolate part of New Jersey, let loose with the irons on.

About one mile from the little village of Bladensburg,[10] on the evening of the 31st of October, our Regiment was set off, at the camp of the 4th Rhode Island Regiment, without tents or rations & some of the Companies without blankets. The Rhode Islanders, however kindly sent us hot coffee, & bread, which being issued, we bivouacked in the open air, & spent a comfortable, but rather cold night.

Next day our tents arrived, & we had scarcely pitched them when a storm of rain set in which continued two days rendering the soft soil on which we were encamped, a perfect bed of sticky mortar. On the evening of the second day, in the middle of the storm, we received orders to prepare for a forced march to Lower Marlborough[11] each man with 2 days rations in his haversack, and 40 rounds of ball cartridge. All night long in the cold rain & mud ancle deep, we were getting ready, cooking, packing & cleaning arms. We were to take no tents, & only three wagons to a Regiment. a 9 o'clock in morning the different Regiments marched out of camp. 1st the 45th Penn., 2d the 4th Rhode Island, 3d the 41st Penn, and one squadron of cavalry. The roads were in a wretched condition, every creek bank full of water & no bridges. We made very slow progress, the men being in full marching order, and unaccustomed to the route step; nevertheless we did well & had but few stragglers. At twelve o'clock stopped for dinner, one hour in an old field. The afternoon's march was harder yet, and we did not reach camp until 8 o'clock in the evening, completely tired out.

Our camp was in a second growth forest & there ~~afte~~ without supper we lay down like tired dogs, every man glad to close his eyes.

• • •

9. Norwich, Conn.
10. Bladensburg is located east of Washington, D.C., in Prince George's County, Md.
11. Lower Marlborough lies along the Patuxent River in Calvert County, Md.
12. Upper Marlborough is the county seat of Prince George's County, Md.

Monday Nov 3d. We were up and had coffee before any other Regiment, & led off on the march. Our route was through a good agricultural country, producing chiefly corn and tobacco. The town of Upper Marlborough which we entered about noon this day was a dilapidated place, although the shire town of Prince George's County.[12] Our noon camp we made at Ball's Ferry[13] over the Pautuxent river & our men were almost beaten out. The 5th, however, appeared to stand the fatigue as well as the Pennsylvanians and better than the Rhode Island Regiment.

The afternoon's march was in the county of Anarundel,[14] & the great farms showed wealth & comfort. This afternoon the march dragged badly, many of the men being foot sore, and all extremely tired. The men would lay down at the road-side at every halt, & it was hard work to start them up. I pitied the poor fellows very much, & often walked, carrying a musket, to let some ~~poor~~ tired soldier ride.

About nine o clock, we saw the camp fires of the advanced guard, glimmering through the trees. The band at once struck up a lively time and we marched into camp and a more wretchedly fatigued set of men it would have been hard to find. Down we lay, after kindling a few fires, with not a mouthful to eat, and but little water. However we got along somehow without much grumbling. The next day our rations did not arrive in camp and the men were half famished; but we made it up in the evening by a glorious supper of stewed beans.

Our mission was to disperse all armed bands of secessionists, and prevent any disturbance of the Election.[15] The Rhode Island Regiment was sent to ~~&~~ occupy the town of Lower Marlborough & the 5th stayed behind in camp, ready if called upon. The first night we had rain & I showed the men how to make small shelter tents with their blankets, for two men. The 2d day we drilled in the manual of arms, & filled the vacant places in our stomachs with plenty of fresh beef and coffee.

The men having rested 24 hours we marched home in pretty good style. All along the way the men behaved with the utmost order, & we received the written thanks of the General[16] in command for our good conduct.

· · ·

13. Not to be confused with Ball's Bluff or Balls' Crossroads in Virginia.

14. Anne Arundel County, Md.

15. Some thought Confederate sympathizers in southern Maryland would attempt to disrupt the November election, which went on without incident. Pride and Travis, *Brave Boys*, 47–48.

16. Oliver Otis "O. O." Howard (1830–1909) graduated from West Point in 1854. He led a brigade of New England troops at First Bull Run. Howard received his commission as brigadier general, United States Volunteers, on September 3, 1862, and was assigned a brigade under

Nov 6. Today we commenced to renovate & clean our camp and make everything comfortable. Our regular calls and drills were also instituted. The men soon recovered from their tramp, & its incidents & little episodes of fun and hardship furnished material for many a camp fire gossip.

On the 12th held our first Regimental court martial & tried two privates for small offenses.

On the 16th the Brigade was reviewed by Brig Gen Casey.[17] Maj Cook[18] placed under arrest.

On the 19th Brigade drill.

On the 22d, Capt Long[19] joined. This day had our first Regimental firing; and Lieut. Crafts[20] left on recruiting service, by orders from headquarters. Visited the camp of the Long Island Regiment, Lieut Col Cross, my brother.[21]

23d, Review by Gen Howard.[22] 81st Penn Regiment arrived.

24th Frank Heywood[23] died. He was an excellent young man, and a great

---

General Silas Casey. This brigade consisted of the Fourth Rhode Island and the Forty-fifth and Eighty-first Pennsylvania. Ezra J. Warner, *Generals in Blue: Lives of the Union Commanders* (Baton Rouge: LSU Press, 1964), 237, John A. Carpenter, *Sword and Olive Branch: Oliver Otis Howard* (Pittsburgh: University of Pittsburgh Press, 1964), 29, and Thomas L. Livermore, *Days and Events, 1860–1866* (Boston and New York: Houghton Mifflin, 1920), 29.

17. Silas Casey (1807–1882), best known for his *System of Infantry Tactics*, graduated from West Point in 1826. He received his commission as brigadier general, United States Volunteers, in August 1861. Soon thereafter, he commanded the Third Division of Erasmus D. Keyes's corps (Fourth Corps). Warner, *Generals in Blue*, 75.

18. William W. Cook, of Derry, N.H., was appointed major September 24, 1861. He was likely placed under arrest for appearing drunk at the review. Wounded at Fair Oaks, he resigned on July 17, 1862. Pride and Travis, *Brave Boys*, 50, and Child, "Complete Roster," from *Fifth New Hampshire*, 42. Child's history forms the first part of this book. A "Complete Roster" of the Fifth New Hampshire makes up the bulk of the second part and is numbered separately. Hereinafter, information from the first part will continue to be cited as *Fifth New Hampshire;* from the second, "Complete Roster."

19. Charles H. Long, a 28-year-old resident of Claremont, N.H., was appointed captain of Company G. Wounded at Antietam on September 17, 1862, Long resigned his commission in November 1862. Child, "Complete Roster," 114.

20. Welcome A. Crafts lived in Milan, N.H., and was first lieutenant in Company B. He would later serve as captain, major, and lieutenant colonel of the Fifth. He mustered out on June 28, 1865, as a brevet colonel. Crafts brought Cross's body back to Lancaster after the Battle of Gettysburg. Ibid., 44, and Child, *Fifth New Hampshire*, 212.

21. Nelson Cross (1824–1897) was Edward Cross's half brother. He served in the Mexican War and later enlisted in the Sixty-seventh New York, the "Long Island Regiment." He became its colonel and later was promoted to brevet brigadier general and brevet major general for distinguished service. Roger D. Hunt and Jack R. Brown, *Brevet Brigadier Generals in Blue* (Gaithersburg, Md.: Olde Soldier Books, 1990), 137.

22. General Oliver Otis Howard.

23. Francis (Frank) Heywood was from Lancaster, N.H., Cross's hometown. He mustered in as a 22-year-old private in Company B. Child, "Complete Roster," 87.

favorite of mine. I closed his eyes. He died just at reveille—the last bugle notes ushered his soul into the land of spirits.

Nov 26th Attended a grand review of regular troops, by Gen M'Clelland,[24] near Washington. Rode around the lines in the staff ~~escort~~ of Gen Casey. Stood close by Gen McClelland, while the troops marched past. They looked well, and were equipped in good style.

Nov 27. This afternoon, while we were making preparations to celebrate the New Hampshire Thanksgiving,[25] orders came transferring us to the Division of General Sumner[26] & instantly after orders to pack up, cook two day's rations and be ready to march at daylight the next morning across the Potomac. Instantly all was hurry & bustle. It was hard to leave our camp, & all the nice fixtures we had accumulated, but every body was elated at the thought of getting into the enemy's country, & we soon forgot about our Thanksgiving preparations in the joy of leaving the hated locality of Bladensburg.

Nov 28 Reveille at 1/2 past 3 this morning, & everybody on the alert. Coffee was soon served & then at 1/2 past 4 the "General" sounded, our tents fell & soon after we marched gaily off the ground with ~~much~~ colors waving & ~~pa~~ band playing. Our route led us through Washington City & as we passed along Pennsylvania Avenue the Regiment received many encomiums from hundreds of spectators, & the Band played splendidly. About noon we crossed the Long Bridge and entered the precincts of Virginia. In

24. George Brinton McClellan (1826–1885) ranked second in the West Point class of 1846. Lincoln chose him to command the Army of the Potomac after the First Battle of Bull Run, and he soon became the favorite of his men. A staunch Democrat, he feuded with members of the administration, but he brought order to and inspired the Army of the Potomac. His failure to seize the initiative, particularly following a Union victory, led to his removal as commander of the Army of the Potomac in August 1862. He was returned to command after the Union defeat at the Battle of Second Battle of Bull Run, but his dawdling after the Battle of Antietam proved the end of his military career. He ran for U.S. president as a Democrat in 1864 and served one term as the governor of New Jersey (1878–1881). *Historical Times Illustrated Encyclopedia of the Civil War*, Patricia L. Faust, ed. (New York: Harper and Row, 1986), 456.

25. The men of the Fifth planned to celebrate Thanksgiving with a large feast with food sent from their homes in New Hampshire. The expected food did not arrive until December 1861. Pride and Travis, *Brave Boys*, 50–51, 58.

26. Edwin Vose Sumner (1797–1863), who had come to the Army of the Potomac from his command in California, commanded a division within the Second Corps of the Army of the Potomac. In March 1862, he became commander of the Second Corps, and Israel B. Richardson took over command of the First Division. Howard replaced Richardson as commander of the First Brigade. The First Brigade included the Fifth New Hampshire, the Sixty-first New York, the Sixty-fourth New York, and the Eighty-first Pennsylvania. Warner, *Generals in Blue*, 237, 403, 489–490.

every direction could be seen the white tents of our army, & many of the hills were crowned with frowning batteries and strong forts. Our route led us through the ancient city of Alexandria. Here we made a short halt and our band entertained the good people ~~of the~~ with several fine pieces of music. Just at dark we encamped on an old camp ground lately occupied by a New York Regiment. During the night we had rain & a cold wind. I took supper with General Sumner, lately from California, an old and distinguished officer of the Regular Army. ~~In the~~ That night, sleeping out with a few blankets, and quite exposed, I took a violent cold & of course had one of my old fever and ague attacks, so severe that I was not able to march with the Regiment next day, much to my regret, and I remained at the home of some very kind people on the road. Nov 30th Joined the Regiment this morning at the new camp near Fort Worth.

Dec. 1st Paid off one month's pay, up to Oct 31st.

Dec 6 This day started out on picket duty, to the advanced lines, distance about four miles. Regimental line formed at 9 in the morning—816 rank and file. We received rousing cheers from the Rhode Islanders, the Penn & N. York troops. Gens Sumner, French,[27] and Howard accompanied us. At noon we reached Edsell's Hill,[28] and took possession, throwing out our pickets to fill up a gap between brigades of Gens. Sedgwick[29] and Blenker.[30]

I rode around personally, and posted the entire picket line, and each day of the five we were out I was at each post.

Made a reform in the "pass" system, and when we finished our tour of duty received the compliments of Gens Howard and Sumner.

Dec 12. Last night about 9 o'clock the Rhode Island Regiment got under arms and marched off, some said to the hill or to Camp Sumner, as I named the camp on Edsell's Hill. Soon after, just as I was going to ~~bed~~ bed, orders

---

27. William H. French (1815–1881) received his appointment as brigadier general in September 1861. He commanded the Third Brigade, First Division, of Sumner's Second Corps. Ibid., 161–162.

28. The Fifth was encamped at Camp California, named in honor of Sumner, who had previously commanded U.S. troops in that state. This camp was located 3 miles west of Alexandria. Edsall's Hill, a picket outpost that the Fifth frequented, lay southwest of Camp California near Springfield, Va. Pride and Travis, *Brave Boys*, 52, 62.

29. John Sedgwick (1813–1864) graduated from West Point in 1837. He became brigadier general, United States Volunteers, in August 31, 1861. He commanded the Second Division of Sumner's Second Corps. Warner, *Generals in Blue*, 430–431.

30. Brigadier General Louis Blenker (1812–1863) initially commanded a division in the Army of the Potomac, but later helped organize the defenses of Washington, D.C. Ibid., 37.

came to form the Regiment as soon as possible, without noise. General Sumner ordered me to report to him, & while Col Langley[31] was forming the Regiment I reported to the old Gen., whom I found just mounting his horse. He said, "Are you senior Colonel of Howard's Brigade?" "I am." "Then take command. March on towards Edsell's Hill, as soon as possible."

I formed the Brigade, marched off, and was soon joined by the General. Arriving on the Hill we took up positions, & with the Artillery which had also come up, waited until daybreak. I got an hour's sleep on the ground near a small fire.

At daylight we marched back, & were half way home when orders came to face about and march back again! This was rather hard, but back we went, without one mouthful to eat and the men very thirsty. At noon our wagons came up with bread and coffee. All day we remained under arms, & when night came marched back. Throughout the whole, the men behaved with great bravery, coolness, and discretion.

Dec 15. Had a visit from Mr. Grant & Dr Irwin.[32]

December 22. Spent all the past week at Brigade Drill under General Howard.

December 25th To-day celebrated Christmas with various games.

26th Commenced on our winter quarters.

Jan 1, 1862 Worked all day on our tents.

Jan 13. Regiment paid off. Total amount paid $36,000. Sent to NH over $23,000.

Jan 14 Regiment marched on picket duty under Lieut Col Langley, at Edsell's Hill. Being detailed on General Court Martial I did not go at first, but rode out to camp each day, and visited the pickets. Capt Barton[33] & forty men, my brother Richard[34] being rear guard with a part of the company. Scouted towards the enemy's lines & brought in one prisoner & ten cows. We encamped in the woods the snow and mud being ancle deep.

31. Samuel G. Langley, of Manchester, N.H., was appointed lieutenant colonel on October 26, 1861. He later resigned on December 1, 1862. Child, "Complete Roster," 108.

32. Both unidentified.

33. Ira Barton, a resident of Newport, N.H., was the son of a Republican politician, Levi Barton. Although Barton was appointed captain of Company E in October 1862, Cross did not have faith in his abilities as an officer, and Barton eventually resigned on September 6, 1862. Child, "Complete Roster," 13, and Pride and Travis, *Brave Boys*, 158.

34. Cross's brother, Richard E. "Dick" Cross (1834–1894), was appointed first lieutenant of Company H on October 12, 1861. He later served as captain of Company K, major, and lieutenant colonel but left the regiment on August 4, 1864, as a result of a court-martial verdict. The disability "resulting from dismissal" was removed January 16, 1865, and he returned to service. Child, "Complete Roster," 45, and Pride and Travis, *Brave Boys*, 264.

Tuesday, Feb 2 To-day Gov Berry & Hon. Allen Tenney, Secretary of State visited camp & stayed all day. The governor made a short speech.

Feb 3 [4 written over], Last evening received orders to be ready to march for the front with the Regiment — 2 day's rations & 40 rounds ammunition. Proved to be a false alarm.

Feb 22 Celebrated the day by listening to the Farewell Address of Gen Washington. In the afternoon drilled with the NH Battery,[35] which came to visit us.

Feb 23d. Read the order for promotions and appointments on parade.

~~March~~ Feb 28. Marched on picket. Lt Col Langley not present, sick.

March 1. Heavy snow storm all day and at night a terrible rain. March 3. Just as we were packed up to go home received orders to march to Springfield[36] mail station two miles distant, and support Gen Howard. Arrived at Springfield & bivouacked near the station. *March* 6 Received orders to move up to Burke's Station[37] near the enemy. Reached Burke's just before dark, after a hard march and camped in a piece of woods. March 8 About 11 o'clock at night was ordered to form the Regiment and march to the front. Long roll beaten & the Regiment under arms in five minutes. Marched two miles, one mile at "double-quick" — formed in a field and waited for the enemy, but they did not come up. Marched home. Regiment behaved nobly — officers & men cool and collected.

March 9 Marched home on the R R track 15 miles.

March 10th ~~19~~. Last night soon after 12 o'clock orders came to prepare to march at daylight next morning, with three days rations.[38] Made every preparation and soon after daylight Sumner's division moved, forming a portion of the grand advance of the Army of the Potomac. I commanded the advanced guard — two companies of the Regiment under Major Cook leading off. After the 5th came a battery of artillery, then one squadron of dragoons,

35. This was likely the First New Hampshire Light Artillery. This regiment was organized in Manchester in 1861. The regiment saw action mostly in northern Virginia and was later assigned to the Third Corps, Army of the Potomac, in the summer of 1862. It was later reassigned to the First Corps after Antietam and was mustered out in June 1865 as part of the Second Corps. Frederick H. Dyer, *Compendium of the War of the Rebellion* (New York: T. Yoseloff, 1959), vol. 3, 1346–1347.

36. Springfield is in Fairfax County, Va.

37. Located in Fauquier County, Va.

38. The Fifth New Hampshire would be involved in a series of skirmishes along the Orange and Alexandria Railroad during March 1862. The places mentioned in Cross's journal are located along this railroad, which ran from Alexandria to Culpeper, Va. Pride and Travis, *Brave Boys*, 68.

then the Brigades of Howard, French,[39] & Meagher.[40] Directly after the advanced guard came Gen Sumner, in command of the Division.

It rained all day and the roads were ancle deep with mud, but the troops marched well. Marched the 1st day to Brimstone Hill, & waited for night.

March 11th ~~17~~ In the morning the sun shone bright & clear—The whole division was encamped around, forming a grand and martial sight. At eleven o'clock started again and marched to Sangster's Station, on the Orange & Alex RR, where we camped for the night. After darkness set in the scene was grand, strange, and picturesque. Thousands of camp fires burning brightly, showed the line of battle, and the murmurs of the armed host sounded like the murmuring of waves upon the distant sea shore.

12th ~~18th~~ Started early and marched along the railroad track to Union Mills, where we came to the first fortifications of the enemy, very judiciously located on a range of high hills. They consisted of rifle pits, ditches, breastworks, & some batteries or rather works for batteries. Visited the works and camps, finding much property & abandoned stores.

~~19th~~ 13th Rode to Centreville[41] with Captain Sewall, a a gen[42] and examined the works. They were chiefly located on a long ridge, nine strong redoubts pierced for from 6 to 12 guns, very strong and so located as to command the entire country for miles around. Fine "[illegible]" of timber some open & some covered, ran from redoubt to redoubt, in several cases also fine rifle pits, and abattis in abundance. Behind the first, was a second line of defence of the same character.

Evidences were abundant that more than 50,000 men had been in the vicinity all winter. The quarters were of the most substantial and comfortable character, & from the appearances, the troops had an abundance of everything. Many dead horses lay around, I counted over 30 in one lot. Rode down among the camps on the left of the works, where we found abundant evidence of large numbers of men, with plenty of horses & military equipments. In the night we had a violent storm. 15th [9 written over] Marched to Fairfax County House[43] and camped. Had not been in camp more than one hour, having marched 9 miles in the rain, when orders came to break up and

39. Brigadier General William H. French.

40. Thomas Francis Meagher (1823–1867) organized the "Irish Brigade" in New York City after serving as major of the Sixty-ninth New York Militia. He was appointed brigadier general on February 6, 1862, and placed in commade of the "Irish Brigade," which had become the Second Brigade of Sumner's Division. Warner, *Generals in Blue*, 317–318.

41. Located in western Fairfax County, Va.

42. Frederick D. Sewall was acting adjutant general ("a a gen"), and later adjutant general, on Howard's staff. Carpenter, *Sword and Olive Branch*, 32.

43. The county seat of Fairfax County, Va.

march to the front. We were off in less than 15 minutes and marched until one o'clock in the morning, bivouacking on a hill side in a cold wind, not more than one mile from where we left in the morning. 16th Started early, crossed the celebrated stream of "Bull Run" and marched to an old rebel camp formerly occupied by Gen Earle's Brigade.[44] In the afternoon rode to the pa late headquarters of Gen Beauregard[45] and to Manassas Junction. Manassas Junction is located on a plain, & not fortified to any great extent. Here might be seen the evidences of the rapid and disorganized retreat of the Rebel Army. The depot was a mass of smoking ruins, as was the case with many other storehouses, while the earth around was covered with provisions and military equipments.

17 18th Went out foraging with a small party, & brought in 4 loads of corn. In the afternoon sent out 4 companies. This morning I spent much time in the quarters of Gen Ewell, formerly Captain Ewell, of the U S A one of my old frontier friends.[46] I also visited the quarters of Gens Smith[47] & Taylor[48] and brought away some of their tents and fixtures. All around we found first rate camps with evidences of every comfort. Also, some strong fortifications.

20th Rained all day. Rode out with Gen Richardson,[49] who a few days since relieved Gen Sumner in command of the Division, to examine the

44. Jubal Early (1816–1894), Confederate brigadier general and 1837 graduate of West Point, commanded a brigade under D. H. Hill in the Army of Northern Virginia at Yorktown. He was eventually assigned to a command under General Stonewall Jackson. Stephen H. Boatner, *The Civil War Dictionary*, revised edition (New York: McKay, 1987), 254–255, and Stephen W. Sears, *To the Gates of Richmond: The Peninsula Campaign* (New York: Ticknor & Fields, 1992), 364, 385.

45. Pierre Gustave Toutant Beauregard (1818–1893), a Louisiana native and West Point graduate, resigned as commandant at West Point in 1861 to accept a commission as brigadier general in the Confederate army. He commanded the bombardment of Fort Sumter and was second in command at the First Battle of Bull Run. *Encyclopedia of the Civil War*, 51–52.

46. Cross had met Richard Ewell in Arizona when Ewell was the commandant at Fort Buchanan. Ewell (1817–1872) was now a major general in the Army of Northern Virginia and commanded a division under Stonewall Jackson. Pride and Travis, *Brave Boys*, 19, and Boatner, *Civil War Dictionary*, 268–269.

47. Gustavus W. Smith (1822–1896) graduated from West Point in 1842. A major general in the Confederate army, he commanded the reserve wing of the Army of Northern Virginia at Yorktown. He later commanded the left wing at Fair Oaks and temporarily led the army until Robert E. Lee took over from the wounded Joseph Johnston. Boatner, *Civil War Dictionary*, 771–772, and Sears, *To the Gates of Richmond*, 366, 374, 386.

48. Richard Taylor (1826–1879), son of President Zachary Taylor, commanded a brigade in Ewell's division in Stonewall Jackson's command. Boatner, *Civil War Dictionary*, 827.

49. Israel Bush "Dick" Richardson (1815–1862) graduated from West Point in the class of 1841. A veteran of the Mexican War, he was appointed brigadier general on August 9, 1861. Richardson was assigned command of the First Division of Sumner's corps on March 13, 1862. Warner, *Generals in Blue*, 402–403, and Boatner, *Civil War Dictionary*, 697.

country. Charges placed against me by Capt E E Sturtevant,[50] and returned by Gen. Howard.

SKIRMISHING ALONG THE ORANGE & ALEXANDRIA RAILROAD

♣ ♣ ♣ ♣ ♣

This was the instant when we should have pushed on.

25th This morning, in the absence of Gen Howard I took command of the Brigade. The entire division moved. We marched about two miles beyond Manassas Junction & camped. Blenker's Division joined.

27th Started for Warrenton Junction. Encountered the enemy about 2 o clock, & drove in his mounted pickets.

28th Howard's Brigade was sent to make a reconnaissance to the Rappahannock River. I commanded the advance guard as follows

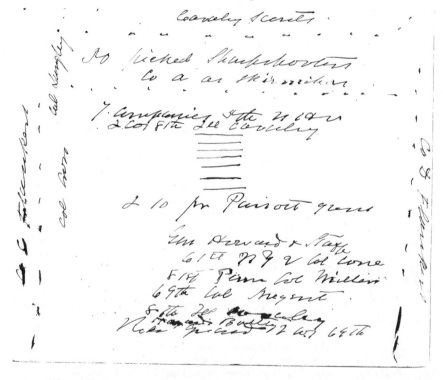

---

50. Edward E. Sturtevant, of Concord, N.H., was the first volunteer of the First New Hampshire regiment. He was appointed captain of Company A of the Fifth on October 12, 1861, and major in July 1862. The nature of charges mentioned is not known. Child, "Complete Roster," 175.

The mounted pickets of the enemy were discovered, & the[y] instantly commenced firing on our scouts & sharpshooters, who returned the fire whenever opportunity offered. In this way we marched for four hours, the enemy setting fire to hay & fodder stacks, corn, & barns full of grain, at the same time attempting to drive off the cattle and other stock. Our cavalry, however, captured a great deal. Several times I brought the two guns to the front & threw shell at the enemy, but do not know with what effect. About 4 PM our scouts came upon a large body of the enemy on the railroad near the Rappahannock Station. They were evidently loading cars and preparing to leave. I set the two guns at work on them & sent word to the General, who ordered up Hazard's Battery[51] & formed lines of battle. This was the instant when we should have pushed on. If we had done so, and made a vigorous attack, we might, with small loss have cut off a train of cars and five or six hundred of the enemy. When we did move, it was too late. Our skirmish line & sharpshooters had a brisk affair with the rear guard of the enemy as they retreated across the large Railroad bridge on the Rappahannock. As we neared and threw more shells the rebels blew up their bridge and set the fragments on fire, and instantly opened on us from a battery on the South bank of the river. The first ball, a solid 12 pn shot fell just inside our skirmish line—two others instantly followed—one striking between the two lead horses of ~~the~~ our guns, & the other just passing over company B. Our guns instantly limbered and moved to a hill close at hand where better range offered, my Regiment supporting them. At this moment the sharpshooters of the 5th were skirmishing with the enemy across the river. The solid shot and shell from the batteries of the enemy coming very thick, and as our guns seems short range we were moved up to the river's bank, near the burning bridge. ~~Arriving~~ On our way to that point no less than 15 cannon balls & three shells struck close to us—one spattering the dirt over me and my horse, yet no one was injured. The men were cool, marched steadily, kept well closed up, nor did the terrible screaming of the balls & the bursting of the shells seem to frighten them. The General sent word by one of his aids to "double-quick" until we were out of range but I did not do so, not willing to encourage the men in such ideas.

As we reached the bridge and formed on the bank we saw the lines of the enemy about three-quarters of a mile off—apparently about five thousand men—(we afterwards heard from a prisoner that Ewell's Division was there) but others were concealed in the woods.

51. George W. Hazzard was captain of the Fourth U.S. Artillery, the artillery unit of Howard's brigade. Hazzard would later be killed in the action at Glendale, Va. Sears, *To the Gates of Richmond*, 276, 289.

Hazard's battery having now come up, it was unlimbered directly in front of my Regiment, and commenced a rapid fire of 12 pn shells, which made a great scattering in the enemy's ranks, the cavalry moving off at a gallop, & the infantry at double-quick. The scene was now strange and exciting. The blazing bridge—the bursting bombs. The last rays of sunset falling on the vanishing lines of the enemy, made a picture long to be ~~forgotten~~ remembered. The enemy moving to the right a [illegible] distance, with one of their wings. The battery moved down opposite and again opened fire, supported by my Regiment. The enemy soon replied, but their shot flew high & no one was injured. We remained at our post until after dark, then withdrew and marched two miles back to ~~camp~~ a camp in the woods—all hands tired, literally worn out, without waiting for supper, laid down in leaves and soundly slept.

29th This day marched back to Warrenton Junction, capturing on the way 400 head of cattle. I forgot to mention that in our skirmish the other day we captured a Lieutenant of the Black Horse Cavalry and five privates.[52]

30th & 31st Back in camp—weather cold and wet. Mud a foot deep—short rations and a large number of sick men.

April 1 Marched 14 miles to ~~M~~ a camp near Manassas Junction—forded three streams, & camped without a mouthful to eat.

April 2d Marched to the Junction & camped. 3d Rode in the cars to Alexandria, arrived about eight o'clock in the evening, & camped in an old field. Major Cook, Lt Col Langley and the Adjutant[53] all absent in town. Had command of the Brigade, and had a hard time getting the men comfortable, providing them wood and water. On my feet nearly all night.

THE FIRST PART OF THE PENINSULA CAMPAIGN

♣ ♣ ♣ ♣ ♣

It was well for them that they retreated, as they could not have withstood the fire of our tremendous batteries for half a day.

52. The Black Horse Troop was the nickname of Company H of the Fourth Virginia Cavalry. During the last half of March, the Black Horse Troop was serving General Joseph E. Johnston as guides and scouts and was harassing the Union scouting parties along the Orange and Alexandria Railroad. Kenneth L. Stiles, *4th Virginia Cavalry* (Lynchburg, Va.: H. E. Howard, 1985), 1, 9.

53. Charles Dodd, of Boston, Massachusetts, was 25 years old when appointed adjutant on September 24, 1861. He resigned on June 13, 1863. Child, "Complete Roster," 52.

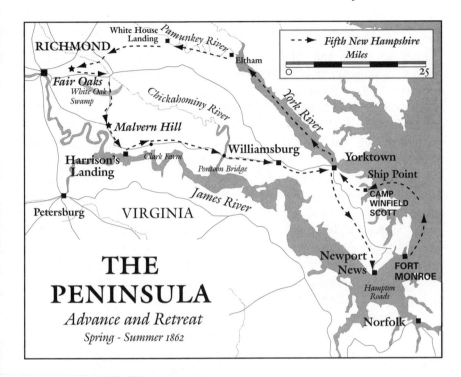

White House Landing · *Pamunkey River* · RICHMOND · Eltham · *Fifth New Hampshire* · Miles · 0 · 25 · Fair Oaks · White Oak Swamp · *Chickahominy River* · *York River* · Malvern Hill · Williamsburg · Yorktown · Harrison's Landing · *Clark Farm* · *Pontoon Bridge* · Ship Point · CAMP WINFIELD SCOTT · Petersburg · VIRGINIA · *James River* · Newport News · FORT MONROE · THE PENINSULA · *Advance and Retreat* · *Spring - Summer 1862* · *Hampton Roads* · Norfolk

April 4th. Made my arrangements and at 9 o'clock embarked on board the steamer Donaldson, with six companies & the band. The other 4 companies went on the Croton with Lt Col Langley.

April 5th On our way to Hampton, or Fortress Monroe. Weather cold and dismal.

6th Reached Fortress Monroe. Saw the celebrated Monitor and the Fortress. Sailed same evening for Ship Point.[54]

7th Reached Ship Point—deserted works of the rebels. Rough weather. Worked all day landing the Regiment. The men waded ashore. The works at this point were quite strong.

8th Finished landing the stores & horses. We lay at Ship Point for four or five days. During this time the Regiment furnished from 400 to 500 men each day to work on the roads.

We then moved up to ~~H~~ward the front and centre of the line & joined the other Divisions of our Army Corps under General Sumner. At this point large numbers of troops were concentrated.

54. Ship Point was located 12 miles upriver from the mouth of the York River in Virginia.

. . .

April 20. Rainy and cool. On the 18th we had our first Division Drill under General Richardson.[55] April 25th Received orders detaching us from Howard's Brigade and placing the Regiment temporarily in the Engineers Brigade of Gen Woodbury,[56] of NH. We were sent out to make Gabions and facines.[57] While on this work I often visited the trenches and batteries of our line and saw the vast labors of our troops. By order of Gen M'Clelland[58] we furnished a detail of 75 men to build a signal tower near Gen Headquarters. The heavy bombardment shook the earth near us, and the bursting shells were continually resounding. While visiting the works several large shells burst near me—one killed a mule near where I was ~~standing~~ sitting on my horse. Scenes and Incidents of the siege—the sharpshooters & the great mortar battery. About 1 ~~12~~ o'clock in the morning of May 1st I was awakened & had orders to march to the Brigade quarters 3 miles distant. The night was dark & the road in a very bad condition, nevertheless we made the march in good season. Arriving in camp & just getting ourselves comfortable, we received order to march *instanter*, and resume our old labors at the old place. We did so, as usual going over our ground a second time. We continued our labor of making gabions until Sunday morning, May 4. The night previous there was a very heavy bombardment, which ceased about 2 o'clock in the morning. Sunday morning, soon after breakfast I received word from one of my Lieutenants in the Signal Corps that the enemy had evacuated Yorktown. I at once started for Gen Hdqr's & found the rumor fully confirmed. Joining a party of officers I rode into Yorktown. Near a big shady tree on the road to the main entrance to the fortifications, the enemy had buried large shell with percussion fuses[59] which exploded on being trod upon. One of these went off not far from me, killing two men and wounding

55. Brigadier General Israel Bush Richardson.

56. Daniel Woodbury (1812–1864) was a native of New London, N.H. He graduated from West Point in 1836 and served in the Engineer Corps, rising to the rank of captain in the prewar army. Despite immense pressure from his wife's Southern family to join the Confederate army, he remained loyal to the Union. He was promoted to brigadier general, United States Volunteers, March 19, 1862, and commanded the Volunteer Engineers Brigade under McClellan. He died of yellow fever in August 1864, after being assigned to command of the District of Key West and Tortugas. Warner, *Generals in Blue*, 570–571.

57. Gabions are open-ended baskets made of wood or metal, and fascines are bundles of brush or stakes. Both were used in building retaining walls in field fortifications. Boatner, *Civil War Dictionary*, 276, 320, 693.

58. Major General George B. McClellan.

59. These percussion fuses, called torpedoes by Civil War soldiers, were rudimentary land mines devised by Confederate General Gabriel Rains to slow down the federal army advance. McClellan estimated that four or five men were killed and about a dozen wounded by these shells when the federal soldiers moved into Yorktown. Sears, *To the Gates of Richmond*, 66–67.

several others. I found more than a dozen of these dangerous engines of war and marked their locality with red flags. The fortifications of Yorktown were very formidable and beautifully constructed. In their haste the enemy left many guns and a vast quantity of ammunition. It was well for them that they retreated, as they could not have withstood the fire of our tremendous batteries for half a day. On Monday the 5th we marched, in the midst of a rain storm, to Yorktown and bivouacked near the walls. About nine o'clock the booming of cannon was heard giving indication of a~~l~~ battle in our front. The sounds increased at times & then died away, until about 5 o'clock in the afternoon when, the cannonading was very heavy. Soon after this we received orders to march. It rained heavily—a cold soaking rain, and darkness set in before we were past Yorktown. My Regiment led the Division, & we blundered on, the mud perfectly awful, & mixed up with ~~dirt~~ tree tops, logs, brushwood, with now and then a deep hole full of water. Through this state of things we toiled along, officers and men covered with dirt and wet to the skin. About two o'clock in the morning we received notice that we were not needed, so turning off into an old cornfield, we lay down, the most tired & miserable of men. Howard's Brigade was the only one of the Division in any sort of shape the two others, French's and Meagher's, were greatly demoralized. In the morning we got off soon after day break, and marched about three miles. The main road being impassable, I cut a new road for a long distance through the woods. Camped about 5 miles in the rear of battle field of Williamsburg.

May 8th Marched back to Yorktown & camped on a high bluff overlooking the York river. Here we remained until Sunday, ~~tot~~ the 11th. I had just paraded the Regiment for inspection about 9 o'clock, when orders came to pack up for embarkation. We did so & about dark the same evening reached a locality known as "Eltham" four miles above West Point,[60] and not over 25 miles from Richmond. On the 12th we moved into camp on the road to Richmond. On the 13th we had Brigade Drill, Inspection & received orders to cook three days rations.

On the 15th we marched to a point near Cumberland Landing,[61] where we were crowded into a small space in the woods—the weather rainy & warm. While in this camp, Mr Liscomb,[62] the State Agent, came & brought the commissions of the officers of my Reg't who had been appointed by me. From this point we were marched over a beautiful country, to a locality

---

60. Eltham's Landing was located near the junction of the York and Pamunkey Rivers. West Point was on the York River downstream from Eltham and was the terminus of the Richmond and York River Railroad.

61. Cumberland Landing was located farther up the Pamunkey River from Eltham's Landing.

62. Unidentified.

known as St. Peter's Church. Here we camped in a lovely and picturesque spot—our Division lying all around on the crest & sides of the sloping hills, with the trains parked in a vast & beautiful amphitheatre below. The old church was near—a venerable and singular edifice situated in a grove of fine trees. At night the scene was lovely and strange—a thousand gleaming camp-fires—the low hum of thousands of brave men, and at 8 o'clock the clear sweet notes of the bugler & anon the rolling drums, added inspiration to the scene. At evening parade the view was one to warm a soldier's heart. On the far crest of the highest range of hills was camped the "red artillery,"[63] their parti colored guidons fluttering in the breeze—the grim cannon frowning on the host beneath. On each hill the different Regiments under arms, music playing, colors waving & the bright arms glittering in the declining sunbeams. It was a picture of the "Romance of War."

THE GRAPEVINE BRIDGE AND THE BATTLE OF FAIR OAKS

♣ ♣ ♣ ♣ ♣

Of all the party I alone knew of the critical necessity of having the bridge done as early as possible.

21st Marched to and across the Richmond & York Rail Road, and soon after moved up very near the Chickahominy River. The country here though low, possessed many beauties besides a rich soil, free from stones & very productive. Many evidences of ancient settlements exist—the remains of houses, old gardens, fruit trees now blooming in forests and the almost obliterated roads.

On the 26th inst received orders to report to Gen Sumner, for duty, with my Rg't for fatigue purposes. Marched at daybreak next morning. Found that we were ordered to build a bridge passable for artillery, across the Chickahominy river and swamp. At first f view the job seemed impossible. The 1st Minnesota Rg't had commenced, and made a temporary bridge over the main stream, but the approach to their work was a deep morass into which they had thrown a few logs. I rode into the swamp accompanied by Lieut. Chas Howard,[64] at at the imminent risk of our horses' lives and our own, we selected a route for the bridge. The channel of the stream, proper, was only about 40 yards wide, but all through the swamp, the dark, almost

<hr/>

63. Quote from the poem "Hohenlinden" by Thomas Campbell (1777–1844), a Scottish poet known for his patriotic poems. Robertson, *The Complete Poetical Works of Thomas Campbell* (London: Oxford University Press, 1907), iii, xix–xx, 196–197.

64. Lieutenant Charles Howard, General Oliver Otis Howard's younger brother, served on Howard's staff. Carpenter, *Sword and Olive Branch*, 2, 23.

thick, water, was from two to six feet in depth. The swamp itself was a mass of sorry vegetation, huge trees, saplings, bushes, grape vines & creeping plants. Beneath the water lay a thick bed of rich, soft earth, about the consistency of mortar. Such was the scene of our labors. Here we were to build a heavy bridge sufficient to support field guns, in two days. It seemed impossible.

The Rg't stacked arms and the men were quickly divided into gangs, some to chop, some to carry timber, and some to place the bridge. Officers were placed over each party and the work began. ~~w~~ At each end of the bridge and at its centre I rode into the swamp on my horse "Jack" & personally directed the labors of my men. Cribs of heavy timber were constructed from 20 to 25 feet apart, and sunk in the water—on these "cribs" were placed large "stringers" & the whole being firm, logs were laid crosswise instead of plank. In some few cases the stringers laid on top of the ground. Where the water was very deep—say six feet we built two large cribs and placed stringers across. To do all this work the men were obliged to labor in the water—sometimes up to their arm pits. Many large logs were floated to the bridge from a distance of half a mile or a mile. On the second day my detail of laborers was increased by 250 men of the 64th New York and 150 of the Irish Brigade. The water rose during night so as to impede our operations to a great extent, but we persevered. Of all the party I alone knew of the critical necessity of having the bridge done as early as possible. About noon the second day, Gen Sumner sent me a barrel of whisky which was at once issued to my wet and tired men, and the labor pushed on with renewed vigor until at sundown. I had the happiness of sending word to Gen Howard that the bridge was ready for inspection. Mounting my horse I gallopped across first, & found the job solid and well done.

May 30th. Last night there came a heavy rain. As I lay at night and heard the water splashing down in torrents, I thought of my bridge—of its vast importance, & wondered if it would stand the pressure. Breakfast over off I rode accompanied by Adjutant Dodd. Found the Bridge all safe, and so reported to Gen Sumner.

Saturday May 31st The dreadful hour of battle drew near. Silently the angel of death hovered over our camps. The lives of thousands drew near their end. But all unconscious were the victims. The laugh, the song, the soldier's story all were prevalent in our camp, when from far across the river came the roar of battle. This was about eleven o'clock. Fortunately my men had their dinners ready and plenty of provisions in their haversacks. At first we heard only the artillery—but soon the vollies of musketry & the rattle of the small arms could be distinctly heard. For once I felt that we were wanted, and without waiting for orders directed the men to roll their blankets and prepare for marching. Our preparations were just completed when

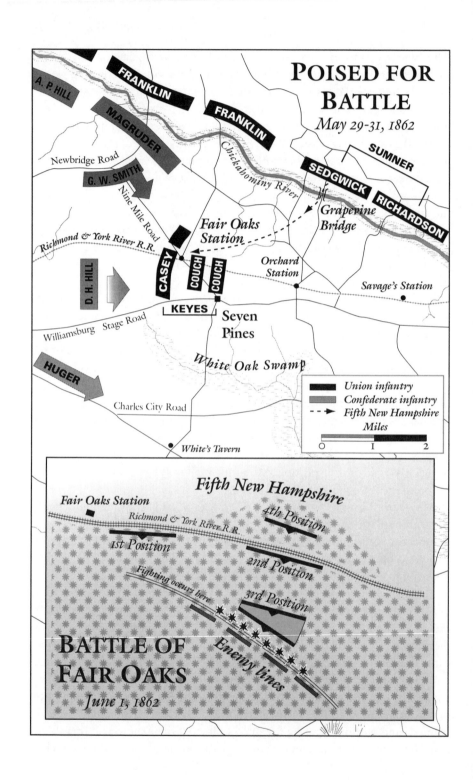

POISED FOR BATTLE

May 29-31, 1862

A. P. HILL

FRANKLIN

MAGRUDER

FRANKLIN

G. W. SMITH

SUMNER

SEDGWICK

RICHARDSON

Newbridge Road

Nine Mile Road

Chickahominy River

Grapevine Bridge

Richmond & York River R.R.

Fair Oaks Station

D. H. HILL

CASEY

COUCH

COUCH

Orchard Station

Savage's Station

KEYES

Seven Pines

Williamsburg Stage Road

White Oak Swamp

HUGER

Charles City Road

White's Tavern

Union infantry
Confederate infantry
Fifth New Hampshire
Miles

0   1   2

BATTLE OF FAIR OAKS

June 1, 1862

Fifth New Hampshire

Fair Oaks Station

Richmond & York River R.R.

4th Position

1st Position

2nd Position

Fighting occurs here

3rd Position

Enemy lines

orders came to be ready to march at 10 minutes notice. I instantly formed my Regimental line and reported the 5th "ready." "As usual," said the General[65] "the 5th is always first!" "Thank you, General" I answered as I rode to my post. Gallopping along the line I told my men that it was our march to the battle field & every man must keep in his ~~pos~~ place. The brave boys answered with a cheer, and off we started. Sedgwick's Division of Sumner's Corps led off over our bridge, and Richardson's Division marched to Miller's Bridge, which was built by the 81st Penn Vols, Col Miller.[66] The 2d Brigade, Gen French, had the advance, and succeeded in passing over the bridge, but the fast rising waters prevented the other brigades from crossing, so we had to march up the stream two miles until we came to the Bridge built by my Reg't. Sedgwick meanwhile pushed on & reached the battle field in time to assist checking the onward tide of the rebels.

With the roar of battle in our ears we pushed on across the bridge over the muddy & trampled fields beyond until we gained the high ground, and halted for a few moments in a broad and beautiful field of wheat which was almost ready for the sickle. Here the division closed up. The rapid volleys of musketry & booming of cannon was now incessant, & the change of sound indicated to a soldier's ear the advance or retreat of the opposing hosts. The afternoon was dark and rainy. When the column again moved evening was close at hand. An hour's rapid march, through mud and water, brought us close to the battle field—but for some time the din of the fight had slackened, and only a few ~~scattered~~ dropping shots were heard. In thick darkness our columns formed, and the whole Division, passing Sedgwick's tired and blood-stained force, marched across the battle field to take position in front of the enemy ready for the next morning.

~~nine o'clock~~ It was now after nine o'clock—very dark, and nothing could be heard but the groans of the wounded & smothered words of command, as we moved into position. The field was covered with wounded men. Some begged for water, some that their wounds might be dressed, and some for blankets as the night air of the neighboring swamps chilled their wounded bodies. As I rode along one poor fellow said—["]Don't tread on me, sir— I am badly wounded and very cold!" Another—"Stranger, for God's sake give me a little water—I'm a Mississippian, shot through both legs." Another—"Gentlemen, for Heaven's sake help us to the hospital—we are freezing here." And so it was, from all sides—enough to move the most

65. General Oliver Otis Howard.
66. Colonel James Miller, commander of the Eighty-first Pennsylvania Infantry. Francis Amasa Walker, *History of the Second Army Corps in the Army of the Potomac* (New York: Charles Scribner's Sons, 1886), 4.

hardened heart to sympathy. We halted. "Where's Col Cross" asked Gen
Howard. "Here, sir" said the Col riding forward into the darkness towards
the voice. "March your reg't forward and report to Gen Richardson," was
the order. The Reg't was in close columns of divisions right in front. Lt Col
Langley brought forward the men, while I reported to the General, who said
"Col Cross, I'm going to give you the advanced guard. Hold your position
until you are whipped or relieved." He then gave me some general directions
& information about the lines of battle, & left me with one of his staff, who
was to show me the ground. I advanced some 200 paces beyond the first line
of battle and deployed the column—then moved forward until I was about
300 paces from the first line. I then detached two companies, namely, A & C
as skirmishers, & posted them myself. The order of battle was as follows—

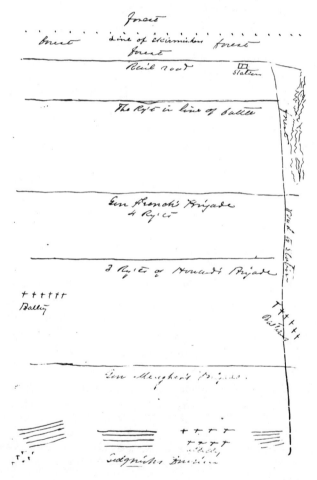

Such was the order of battle on Saturday night.

May 31 after one day of bloody strife during which the Confederates had driven Casey's Division[67] from its camp and captured a large amount of property. The arrival of Sedgwick's Division alone saved the army from disastrous defeat, and be it remembered Sedgwick's Division crossed the Chickahominy swamp on the bridge of logs 70 rods long, built by the Fifth New Hampshire Regiment! Let the impartial historian remember this. My men laid down in line of battle their arms loaded and by their sides I requested all the officers that could do so, to keep awake and watchful. Sentinels were posted in front of each company. The horses stood close by ready saddled. It was at eleven o'clock before all the arrangements were made— the night very dark and cloudy. Col Langley and Major Cook laid down to sleep, and I spread my cloak on the ground and laid down, but not to close my eyes. My Regiment was the alarm clock of the army, and the responsibility upon my mind of that position I had no desire to sleep. One fact I here desire to note, namely, that Gen Thos F. Meagher of the Irish Brigade was *drunk* on the march to the battle field, and while the army was being posted behaved in a very disgraceful style, shouting and riding about in a manner highly unbecoming an officer and a gentleman, especially on such an occasion.

Dr. L. M. Knight,[68] surgeon of my Regiment sat up with me, and in a low tone we talked of the impending battle, while the men slept the deep sleep of worn and tired men. Poor fellows! To many it was the last of earthly slumber—their last sweet dream of home & friends—for the end of their days was at hand—for hundreds of others the next night was to be one of wounds and suffering—and yet they slept!

About one o'clock in the morning I resolved to ascertain the meaning of many lights which for some time had been moving about in the woods on our right flank. On coming on the field I had been told that they belonged to our men—a part of Gen Couchs Division,[69] but it did not seem possible. Still, as the information came from a staff officer I supposed it to be correct. Torches were moving around in the woods, and now & then voices could be heard. These lights were not more than 300 yards from my line, & a singular

---

67. Silas Casey was now commanding the Third Division of Keyes's corps (Fourth Corps). He received a commission as major general, United States Volunteers, and a brevet commission for brigadier general in the regular army for his action at Fair Oaks. Warner, *Generals in Blue*, 75.

68. Dr. Luther M. Knight came from Franklin, N.H. He was appointed regimental surgeon on September 13, 1861, and resigned on May 28, 1863. Child, "Complete Roster," 106.

69. Darius Couch (1822–1897), a 1846 graduate of West Point, was then commanding the First Division of Keyes's corps (Fourth Corps). An impatient but effective commander, he led the Second Corps at Fredericksburg and Chancellorsville. Following the Battle of Chancellorsville, he requested a transfer from the Army of the Potomac so that he would no longer have to serve under Joseph Hooker. Warner, *Generals in Blue*, 95–96.

suspicion crossed my mind that they were carried in rebel hands. Accordingly I woke up Major Cook, and sent him with Company B to reconnoitre. He soon returned with the information that to the best of his belief the enemy were in the woods. In order to be sure I scouted forward alone, picking my way among the stumps & over the bodies of the killed & wounded. I crossed a road which ran to the left toward the railroad depot, when suddenly I heard the sharp click of a rifle lock, & a sharp voice said "Who comes there?["] The accent was unmistakably Southern, so I promptly answered "Wounded man of the 5th Texas"—who are you?["] ["]Pickets of the 2d Alabama," was the reply. "I want to get to your fires, said" I. "Pass around by the depot,["] ~~said~~ answered the voice, ["]& you will find the Doctor." I backed off into the darkness, & joined my Reg't. It being thus ascertained that the enemy were on our flank, a change of front became necessary. While preparing to execute this several prisoners were brought in, who stated that the pickets of the enemy were close upon us, but not aware that we were in the field. One of the prisoners was captured by Lieut Larkin[70] of Co. A. The man came out the woods into the open fields to pick up some sticks to make a fire. All at once he stumbled on my line. The men being on the ground & all quiet. Lieut L said "What do you want?" supposing the fellow to be one of our boys. "I want some wood to make a fire." ["]Who ordered a fire made," said Larkin, rising up. "Why, Col Terry, of the 5th Texas."[71] The words were no sooner out of his mouth than Larkin had him by the throat & a pistol at his ear. From this prisoner we learned that the enemy were in large force in front of us, with strong pickets on our right flank. Other prisoners brought in about this time confirmed the statements of the first. Besides this the Confederate troops could be heard forming their lines in the woods—even the words of command issued by the Colonel were distinct in the stillness of the night. My Reg't now executed a partial change of front, & French's Brigade did the same. Also Howard's. By the time these movements were executed day was breaking—the morning wet and misty. Then was the time my Reg't should have been pushed into the woods on our flank to attack & cut off the pickets of the enemy, but although I asked leave of Gen Richardson to advance he would not allow me permission & the

70. James E. Larkin, of Concord, N.H., was 29 years old when he became first lieutenant of Company A on October 12, 1861. He went on to serve as captain of Company A, major, and lieutenant colonel and was discharged October 12, 1864. Child, "Complete Roster," 108.

71. The Fifth Texas was part of John Bell Hood's Texas Brigade, which was part of Gustavus W. Smith's command. James Archer was the colonel of the Fifth Texas; Colonel Terry is unidentified since there were no officers of that name in the regiment at the time. Harold B. Simpson, *Hood's Texas Brigade: A Compendium* (Fort Worth: Landmark Publishing Co., 1999); Boatner, *Civil War Dictionary*, 23; and Sears, *To the Gates of Richmond*, 85.

enemy, seeing our heavy lines of battle fled back at double-quick. I promptly threw out skirmishers to pursue them—killed half a dozen & wounded others—captured 7 or 8 prisoners. In this affair I lost two men badly wounded. The first man hit was Stephen Avery[72] of Co D—shot through the body by a rifle ball. To the surprise of everyone he lived, & after he had been left for dead, arose & walked into camp. When the battle began, the line was as below

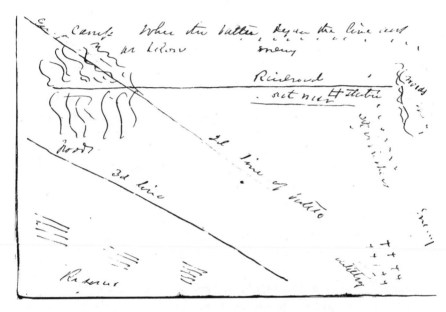

~~The battle~~ Just before the battle commenced on our left wing a horseman rode out of the woods from the direction of the confederates, and came slowly towards our lines. I saw he was an orderly belonging to the enemy. My Reg't was at that time laying down & the colors were not displayed. He did not therefore see that we were federals. I dismounted and passing my line walked up to him. Pulling up his horse a few paces the man asked—"Where's Gen Pryor?" "Here he is" said I "close by—have you dispatches?" "Yes—from Gen Pryor to Gen Anderson."[73] Said I, "give them to me." As he put his hand in the breast pocket of his jacket to get the papers, I stepped forward

72. Stephen Avery was a 28-year-old private from Rochester, N.H. He was discharged as disabled in October 1862. Child, "Complete Roster," 10.

73. Roger Pryor (1828–1919) had been appointed brigadier general, Confederate army, in April 1862. He commanded a brigade under James Longstreet. Richard Anderson (1821–1879) graduated from West Point in 1842, was a brigadier general, and also commanded a brigade under Longstreet. Boatner, *Civil War Dictionary*, 14, 674.

quickly & grasped his horse by the bit saying—"You are a prisoner!" "What ~~you~~ do you mean?" "I mean that you are in the federal lines, and a prisoner of war." "Then I surrender" and I led his horse quietly to the rear. His dispatches proved very valuable, & were at once sent to Gen ~~Richardson~~ Sumner. From this man we learned the locality of the enemy & found that Huger's Division[74] was in front of us. I took possession of the prisoner's mare a beautiful animal, which afterwards proved very valuable.[75]

Soon after this the battle commenced on our left, with some skirmishing along the front of my line, & on my left. The sharpshooters of the enemy came very near killing me—shooting one ball through my coat & another within an inch of my nose. We remained in the woods near the railroad track some time. A Regiment of the rebels, 6th Virginia, advanced on us slowly through the woods. When near us we poured in a volley which broke their line & the men straggling in, we took many prisoners. The battle meanwhile increased, & Howard's Brigade was sent in. The 81st Penn Vols of this Reg't broke at the first fire and ran, leaving their Colonel dead on the field. Colonel Miller[76] was a good soldier, & the only field officer who ~~cold~~ could hold his Regiment, which [was] partly Irish & part American. The Brigade of Gen French was pressed very hard & the 53d Reg't[77] gave way in disorder. Gen Howard, with the 61st New York & the 64th entered the woods—his two Reg'ts together did not muster over 800 fighting men, but they engaged the enemy with great fury. Howard led his men with the greatest gallantry close up to the enemy & the heavy firing told that the storm of the battle was at its height. The General lost two horses killed & a third wounded—a ball struck him in the right arm below his elbow but he continued to cheer on his men, until hit by another ball in the same arm, which shattered the bone in a shocking manner. Word was at once sent to me that the General was disabled, & at the same time I received orders to move my Reg't into the fight. Being ~~lead~~ senior Col of the Brigade the command devolved upon me. I left the woods & moved down the railroad double-quick, until I came opposite the point where Howard's Brigade were engaged. By Adjutant Gregory[78] of the 61st I sent orders for the remainder of the Brigade to clear my front, &

74. Benjamin Huger (1805–1877) graduated from West Point in 1825. He was appointed brigadier general in June 1861 and major general in October. He commanded a division under James Longstreet. Ibid., 416, and Sears, *To the Gates of Richmond*, 119.

75. This was the black "Rebel" mare that Cross had sent back to Lancaster, N.H. Child, *Fifth New Hampshire*, 90.

76. Colonel James Miller.

77. The Fifty-third Pennsylvania was part of French's brigade, First Division, First Corps. Sears, *To the Gates of Richmond*, 359.

78. Unidentified.

form in the rear. While this was being done the Irish Brigade came up yelling & charging—the enemy at least 200 yards off not in sight. The 69th formed on my right & the 88th[79] surging up on my left in a *perfect mob*, began to fire. This whole movement was a farce—~~but~~ & it was some time before they were got into any sort of shape. The bullets of the enemy now came quite thick, & finding Howard's Brigade out of the woods I prepared to advance & open fire. At this moment we were posted as follows

General Meagher not being present nor any other general officers to be found I ordered an advance—"Forward in line, guide centre!" & my Reg't stepped off in noble style. The "Irish" Reg'ts however stood still, greatly to my surprise. The 5th kept on—both colors fluttering the men steady. I gave orders for none to fire without the word, & though the bullets flew thick & struck down many a brave fellow on we pressed, until in plain view of the enemy's line among the trees. That day the confederates wore white bands around their hats—so that ~~their~~ they were easily distinguished from our men.

When about 30 ~~rods~~ paces from the enemy I ordered a halt, "Kneel down" to be sounded—& a fire by Battalions. At the close range we were the effect was awful. I could hear the balls strike with a tearing sound into the close ranks of the rebels. Instantly moving forward—the 1st rebel line gave way &

79. Sixty-ninth New York and Eighty-eighth New York of Meagher's "Irish Brigade." Sears, *To the Gates of Richmond*, 359.

we encountered another—the 6th Alabama—the first line was the 2d Ala. Again we moved up close & fought at short range—my men behaving nobly —only two or three showing the white feather. At this instant the Irish Brigade fired a volley into the backs of my men—killing and wounding several. There was no excuse for this murderous act only stupidity of the grossest kind. Fortunately the aim was high or my Reg't would have been annihilated. This act and the charge up to the rear of my Reg't was all that the Irish Brigade did at the battle of Fair Oaks. Gen Meagher was not present to command, nor did I see any mounted officers

Finding many of my men were being wounded by the buck shot of the enemy, I ordered another advance, and while in the act of shouting "Forward in line," received a Minie ball in the left thigh, which made a very severe wound. However, I kept on my feet for a few moments, & even after I fell rose up & gave orders, sustaining myself by a tree. While in this position three buck shot struck me on the left temple—a p-ball passed through my hat, and one through the sleeve of my blouse—in all seven balls struck my person. Several officers & soldiers came to me, but I sent them away at first[80] until the fire slackened, after which Lieut Parks[81] & Corporal Towne,[82] assisted by some others carried me to the railroad track. Here we found the Irish Brigade just where we left them, & Lieut Col Kelly[83] sent some men to carry me to the rear. The fire of the enemy soon slackened & Lieut Col Langley took out the Reg't in good order—the men bringing most of their wounded Comrades, who were not able to walk. Thus ended the Battle of Fair Oaks—the fifth firing the first and last shots.

In this battle the Generalship on the part of the federals was wretched. Instead of shelling the woods with 30 pieces of artillery, as we could readily have done—we allowed the rebels to choose their own ground—ambush themselves and wait for our attack—nothing but the indomitable bravery of our rank & file and line officers, saved us from defeat. Early in the morning I sent word to Gen Richardson that the artillery could be employed to great advantage in shelling the woods. He sent for me & desired me to point out the exact locality of the enemy. I did so, but nothing was done. Our lines of

80. According to Captain John W. Bean, Cross received a severe wound to the upper thigh. He was struck just behind Bean's Company I. Two of Bean's men rushed to aid the colonel, but Cross reportedly raised himself on his elbow and ordered: "Never mind me, men, whip the enemy first, and take care of me afterwards." Child, *Fifth New Hampshire*, 89.

81. James W. Parks came from New York City. He enlisted as a sergeant in Company D and became second lieutenant of Company B on February 18, 1862. He later became first lieutenant in Company C, but he resigned in January 1863. Child, "Complete Roster," 141.

82. Matthew T. Towne, of Claremont, N.H., enlisted as a 36-year-old corporal in Company E. He was later discharged as disabled on December 24, 1862. Ibid., 184.

83. Lieutenant Colonel Patrick Kelly of the Eighty-eighth New York Infantry. Walker, *Second Corps*, 50.

infantry ought, also to have been formed back from the woods in order to draw the enemy out. As it was we entered a regular trap set for us the night before. I believe an Apache warrior would have arranged our men better. We had no advantages—everything was on the side of the enemy—position numbers—and knowledge of the ground. It ~~may~~ was a wonder that we were not defeated.

Howard's Brigade did nobly. The General was the only Brigadier that I saw on the field who led his men into battle & handled them there — He acted with a bravery bordering on rashness & nobly sustained his reputation as a brave & efficient officer. Great injustice was done to him by somebody, in detaching his two largest Reg'ts on the day of battle & leaving him only two. His Brigade went into battle with less than two thousand men, & had 713 killed, wounded, and missing—double the loss of any Federal Brigade on that day. ~~Of~~ Of the field officers ~~ea~~ there was killed, Col Miller & Lieut Col Massett;[84] wounded Gen Howard, Col Cross, Lieut Col Bingham,[85] Major Cook,[86] Lieuts Howard[87] & Miles[88] of the General's Staff.

In my own Regiment I lost 30 killed dead on the field & 170 wounded— 11 prisoners. My best men were taken—also my best non-com officers. In this respect fate seemed against me. When the Regiment entered the woods, it was an anxious moment for me. I did not know whether they would stand or not. But they did stand in the most heroic style never faltering, & firing with a rapidity which astonished the rebels, ~~& to wh~~ made them give way.

Being carried to a farm house in the rear where the Doctors were at work my wounds were dressed, and I lay under a tree until morning. On Tuesday, the 3d I was moved to Savage Station placed on the cars & sent to White House Landing[89]—placed on the steamer Spaulding and carried to Phila-delphia.[90] At the US Gen Hospital, corner 5th & Baltimore, I lay for two

84. Lieutenant Colonel W. C. Massett of the Sixty-first New York Infantry. Ibid., 49, 52.

85. Lieutenant Colonel Daniel G. Bingham of the Sixty-fourth New York. Ibid., 52, 396.

86. Major William W. Cook.

87. Lieutenant Charles Howard.

88. Nelson Miles (1839–1925) was serving on Howard's staff. Afterward, he commanded the Sixty-first New York and won the Medal of Honor for service at Chancellorsville. He rose to command the Second Corps of the Army of the Potomac. Boatner, *Civil War Dictionary*, 550.

89. Cross refers to Savage's Station on the Richmond and York River Railroad, site of the battle on June 29, 1862. White House Landing, site of a plantation owned by William "Rooney" Lee, son of Robert E. Lee, was located where the Richmond and York River Railroad crossed the Pamunkey. Sears, *To the Gates of Richmond*, 103–104, 273.

90. In all, 1,500 wounded made the 6-day voyage to Philadelphia. Cross was joined on the *Spaulding* by his brigade commander, General Oliver Otis Howard, and his major, William Cook. Howard would recuperate in Maine and return to action at Antietam in September minus his right arm. Cook, with a minié ball lodged near his sciatic nerve, would return to New Hampshire for the duration of the war. Child, *Fifth New Hampshire*, 89, and Pride and Travis, *Brave Boys*, 90–91.

weeks—thence to New York to the Ladies Home for wounded soldiers where I received the kindest treatment. Thence to Concord, NH, where I arrived on the 4th of July.

After I left my Reg't it took part in the labors and battles in front of Richmond, & acted as a portion of the rear guard ~~at~~ on the retreat of the right wing. During all this time it behaved with the greatest gallantry.

After remaining in Lancaster a short time I came to Concord & commenced enlisting men for my Reg't, and on the 10th of August started once more to the wars, with some thirty recruits for the 5th. My wound was painful and troublesome, but I resolved to bear it, though my endurance was severely taxed. I took ship with my party at New York & landed at Fortress Monroe. Here I learned of the evacuation of the Peninsula, which in my opinion was a bad move. The point to attack Richmond effectively is on the James River and from Petersburg side is my opinion.

With Cross and Major Cook injured, and Lieutenant Colonel Samuel Langley intermittently ill, Captain Edward E. Sturtevant assumed command of the Fifth New Hampshire for much of June. Over the next few weeks, the Fifth dug in not far from the Fair Oaks battlefield. Near abandoned Rebel entrenchments, they cleared brush and built barricades to protect themselves from enemy pickets. However, nothing could spare them from the heat and humidity. Apart from sniper fire and the occasional artillery shell, the greatest danger came from disease. In the weeks since their landing at Fort Monroe, twenty-five members of the Fifth had died from disease. Nearly double that became sick enough to return home for good. Unfulfilled expectations for a battle and boredom likely took their toll as well.[91]

During the last week of June, the two great armies converged again. By this time, the new Confederate commander, Robert E. Lee, had determined to push the Union force away from Richmond; on the other hand, Major General George McClellan was clearly losing his will. On June 25, McClellan tested the Confederate right at Oak Grove. For the next few days, the men of the Fifth heard the roar of cannons and crackle of gunfire, but they saw little action. Major battles at Mechanicsville and Gaines's Mill led many in the Fifth to think that the final push toward Richmond was on, but McClellan failed to press his numerical advantage. Instead, following the bloody confrontation at Gaines's Mill, Union forces began streaming away from Richmond toward Harrison's Landing on the James River. On June 29, five days after the start of the Battle of Oak Grove, the Fifth joined the retreat as part of the rear guard of

91. Pride and Travis, *Brave Boys*, 94–97, and Livermore, *Days and Events*, 73–77.

McClellan's army. The Fifth dug in around Savage's Station to slow Rebel pursuit of the Army of the Potomac. The rear guard burned supplies and tried to evacuate the Union wounded, but that evening they received orders to withdraw, leaving three thousand sick and wounded soldiers to the advancing Rebels.[92]

Lee's army maintained contact with the rear guard throughout the night and into the next day, June 30. Confederate artillery rained down on the retreating army, and several members of the Fifth died as a result. They moved to aid a Union force near Glendale and, by the end of the day, withdrew to an encampment on an open piece of land named Malvern Hill. The heat and proximity of Lee's army made rest difficult. The following morning, July 1, Confederate artillery opened up on the exposed Union force. Sturtevant ordered the Fifth away from the open hilltop to support a line of Union artillery. That line would receive and repulse several Confederate attacks during the day. By holding the high ground, McClellan held a strategic advantage, and Confederate losses were considerable, but he soon forfeited his position. That night, McClellan renewed the Union retreat and began withdrawing from Malvern Hill. The Fifth did not receive an order to withdraw and, as a result, was the last regiment to leave Malvern Hill. Rebel artillery fire rained on the Fifth for most of its withdrawal to Harrison's Landing. McClellan's army would remain encamped along the north shore of the James River for the next six weeks.[93]

While the Fifth slogged dejectedly across the Peninsula, Cross was recovering from his wounds. After receiving treatment in Philadelphia and New York, Cross returned to his home in Lancaster on the Fourth of July. His warhorse, "Jack," and the recently captured "Rebel mare" were shipped back to Lancaster as well. While recuperating back home, Cross toured the White Mountains accompanied by local friends, including Henry Kent. During that trek, Jack pulled a red wagon containing the tourists to the top of Mount Washington. Cross also used the time both to recruit and to boost the war effort. On August 4, Cross joined his brigade commander, O. O. Howard, in Concord, New Hampshire, for a war meeting. They were joined by future New Hampshire governor Walter Harriman, newly commissioned colonel of the Eleventh New Hampshire Regiment. The purpose of the meeting was recruitment, and Cross mistakenly thought that the new draft would bring 350 new men to his regiment. Instead, he returned to Virginia with 61 men, including 17 returning soldiers.[94]

Cross left Concord with his recruits on August 13. Joining them was William Child, a Dartmouth graduate who would serve as the regiment's assistant

---

92. Pride and Travis, *Brave Boys*, 98–101.
93. Child, *Fifth New Hampshire*, 97, and Livermore, *Days and Events*, 86–108.
94. Pride and Travis, *Brave Boys*, 111–112.

surgeon. The party went by train and boat to New York and by steamer from there to Fort Monroe. Cross and his men reached Newport News, Virginia, on August 23. There they found the rest of the regiment, waiting to be shipped out for a return to northern Virginia. Child recalled that at Newport News he and the other recruits "were at once introduced to active campaign life" in the Fifth Regiment. "The romance departed in just two minutes," he added.[95]

SECOND BATTLE OF BULL RUN AND THE MARCH INTO MARYLAND

I cannot imagine why the enemy did not attack us.

On the 23d inst I joined my Regt and received a hearty welcome. I found everything in a very disorganized state—discipline broken, and a general confusion. Ten minutes after my arrival I had commenced reforms and in ten days things were in much better condition. We soon embarked and after a very tedious voyage landed at Acquia Creek[96] with orders to march & join Burnside at Frederick.[97] Now witness the uncertainty of military affairs. We had marched in the dust and heat about two miles, when orders came to go back and get on board the transports. We did so, and landed at Alexandria. Thence we marched to our old camp, where we spent the winter. Things were greatly changed, but we received a warm welcome from our old friend, Mr Richards.[98] Here we remained one day, when orders came to march to the relief of Gen Pope's Army.[99] He was evidently being badly handled, as the road was crowded by stragglers, spreading absurd stories & long trains of wagons rolling in towards Washington. It was a shameful sight

We first marched to Arlington Heights, where we found the 9th NH Reg't.

95. Child, *Fifth New Hampshire*, 98.
96. Aquia is located on the Potomac River north of Fredericksburg.
97. Cross probably means Fredericksburg here. Ambrose Burnside (1824–1881) had now joined the Army of the Potomac after his expedition in North Carolina and promotion to major general, United States Volunteers. He commanded the Ninth Corps. Reinforcements for General John Pope from the Army of the Potomac were expected to arrive at Aquia and Fredericksburg at this time. Burnside had arrived in Northern Virginia in early August. Boatner, *Civil War Dictionary*, 23; Warner, *Generals in Blue*, 57–58, and John J. Hennessey, *Return to Bull Run: The Campaign and Battle of Second Manassas* (New York: Simon & Schuster, 1993), 27, 60.
98. Unidentified.
99. John Pope (1822–1892) was about to confront Confederate forces near the old Bull Run battlefield. Pope's Army of Virginia, with limited support from McClellan, would lose the battle and be forced back toward Washington, D.C. Warner, *Generals in Blue*, 376–377.

Its long line reminded us of the day when our ranks were one thousand strong. We had scarcely formed our camp when orders came to march with all possible haste, & the deep booming of guns towards Centreville told that a battle was raging. On we pushed, all the afternoon—the sun scorching hot and the roads dusty. The men, greatly worn by long hardships on the Peninsula, had not the strength for such efforts. We marched until about midnight, when we lay down in the road, without blankets, and a sharp rain falling. In the morning we started on, and marched until within sight of Centreville when we halted, & stood 3 hours in a heavy rain. Every indication of a great battle, but we were too late. We found, however that Pope had been terribly whipped, & his Army badly scared. Sumner's Corps was sent to the front and a large detachment including my Regt placed on picket. Here we remained all one day and night & the next day. From the moment we arrived Pope's Army commenced a retreat, which continued without intermission. The evening of the 2d day a furious storm of rain came on which wet us to the skin. By this time the larger portion of the whole Army had left— Richardson's Division forming the rear guard. I was placed in command of the 64th New York Regt and my own, and in the darkness of the night sent out to picket in a sort of swamp or "filled piece"—a perfect jungle. I had orders to connect with pickets of Kimball's Brigade,[100] but in the darkness it was impossible to find anybody. More than three hours were spent stumbling about among fallen timber & brushwood; at length I found myself near some troops. At first, I took them for rebels, & was on the point of firing, when the name of the Regt & its commanding officer were announced.

The night was bitter cold, & as the men had no blankets nor overcoats, they suffered severely besides they were much exhausted by the march from Arlington to Centreville. We remained expecting relief until almost daylight. The pickets of the rebels could be heard in front, & we expected a strong attack on our rear, every moment. At-The entire Army had now gone except the three Reg'ts on picket which were—14th Ind., 5th N H & 64th N.Y. Gen Kimball came & advised us to march at once. By the time we had disengaged ourselves from the swamp it was broad day. Thousands of stragglers on foot and horseback, were scattered about, many were stretched on the ground fast asleep. Tents, boxes, broken wagons, and piles of ammunition were scattered around in every direction. My Regt never passed a worse

100. Nathan Kimball (1822–1898) served in the Mexican War and received his commission for brigadier general on April 18, 1862. He commanded the First Brigade of French's division (Third) of Sumner's Second Corps. After recovering from wounds received at the Battle of Fredericksburg, he commanded a division in the Sixteenth Corps, taking part in the Vicksburg campaign. Ibid., 267–268.

night on picket, nor did we ever see a ~~scene~~ greater waste of material, or worse straggling. We pushed on at our most rapid rate expecting every moment to be attacked by the cavalry of the enemy or shelled. I cannot imagine why the enemy did not attack us. They certainly missed one of the best chances of the war.

We reached Fairfax Court House and found a scene of inextricable confusion. The streets were blocked by wagons & artillery—the fields so full of infantry that it was almost impossible to force a passage—swearing, shouting & jamming in every direction. Here again was a splendid opportunity for an attack. We rested one hour and I seized some provisions from a passing train to supply my men. We then moved on some two miles near the village & halted; the entire corps in order of battle. Here we remained till about two o'clock in the afternoon, when we moved on, the enemy, at the same time commencing to shell our rear guard. One shell burst a few feet from Gen Sumner's headquarters, but without damage. This was another hard march—long after darkness had set in, we pushed on & after we were beyond the reach of the enemy's Artillery the straggling became fearful. Whole companies of Sigel's men[101] were to be found camped by the side of the road or sound asleep. Luckily the moon shone bright so that we had no difficulty in finding our way. The troops marched in three lines—one column in the road & one each side. We were obliged to make chain bridge that evening. I was so worn with watching & anxiety, & my limb pained me so that I could not ride, so I tried walking. Very soon I became sleepy and absolutely fell asleep and tumbled down several times, flat on my face. Several of my officers and men did the same. At length we halted & all hands laid down, having marched 26 miles that day, without one wink of sleep the night before! Such was our retreat from Centreville, after covering the withdrawal of that humbug, Gen Pope who came near ruining the federal cause. McClellan was sent for to Save the Army. In this disastrous campaign Gen Pope lost even his own headquarters & private effects to say nothing of millions of private property. He proved himself incapable of conducting a great army, and disgraced himself before the country—"*Pope* told a flattering tale." On the [3d] day of September we crossed Chain Bridge, evacuating Virginia in a most inglorious manner!

Gen Lee's Army of rebels was now threatening to invade Maryland. The federal Army had been compelled to take refuge behind the fortifications of

101. Franz Sigel (1824–1902) was commissioned brigadier general in August 7, 1861, and promoted to major general in March 1862. He replaced John C. Frémont as commander of the First Corps of John Pope's Army of Virginia. Ibid., 447–448, and Boatner, *Civil War Dictionary*, 761.

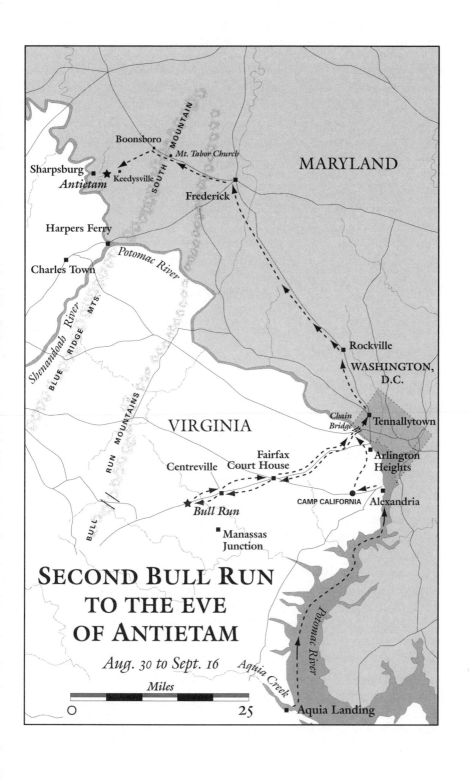

Boonsboro

Mt. Tabor Church

SOUTH MOUNTAIN

Sharpsburg
Antietam Keedysville

Frederick

MARYLAND

Harpers Ferry

Charles Town

Potomac River

Shenandoah River

BLUE RIDGE MTS.

BULL RUN MOUNTAINS

Rockville

WASHINGTON,
D.C.

VIRGINIA

*Chain
Bridge* Tennallytown

Fairfax
Court House

Centreville

Arlington
Heights

CAMP CALIFORNIA Alexandria

Bull Run

Manassas
Junction

BULL

SECOND BULL RUN
TO THE EVE
OF ANTIETAM

Aug. 30 to Sept. 16

Aquia Creek

Potomac River

Miles

0   25   Aquia Landing

Washington. McClellan was stripped of his command. The prospect was dark indeed. But the emergency of the case caused the President to act on his own responsibility. He sent for Gen McClellan & tendered him command of the Army for the defense of the Capitol. Pope was sent off to the frontiers. This move was received by the Army with unbounded enthusiasm. All had confidence in Gen Mc—always had, knowing his plans, whenever thwarted, were by the buffeteers of the Administration. In three days there was a change. The immediate necessities of the men were supplied, & full of hope & confidence we set out, 75,000 of the veterans of the campaign to drive Lee out of Maryland. No one in the Army doubted the result.

On our second days march we found that the enemy had crossed the Potomac & were at Frederick in strong force. F Toward this ancient city we marched, and about noon came in full view of the beautiful valley in which Frederick is located. The booming of cannon & puffs of smoke from the far off hill side showed where the rear of the enemy was covering the retreat. We passed through Frederick in fine style The—the fifth with bugles blowing drums beating, & our faded and tattered colors flaunting bravely. As the old writer said, "verily it was a stately and gallant sight."

THE BATTLE OF ANTIETAM

♣ ♣ ♣ ♣ ♣

We must conquer this day or we are disgraced and ruined.

The next day—Sept 15 [Sept. 14]—we followed the enemy to Middleton Heights where they made a stand, & a severe battle was fought.[102] Our Corps was held in reserve, taking no active part. Towards evening after the firing had pretty much ceased, we were ordered up to the Battle field & lay on our arms all night. 16th [15th] Early in the morning we formed in line of battle and started over the mountain where the rebels had been stationed the day before. We passed over their dead, & some wounded. I saw seventeen dead in awful group—all from an Alabama Regt. The rebels had a very strong position, in the slopes of a rocky, wooded mountain, commanding the gorges and hollows in every direction. The struggle appeared to be fierce & bloody, but our brave troops finally drove the rebels over the crest & down the hill—giving them a tremendous defeat. The road was strewn with their clothing & equipments & their wounded.

102. The Battle of South Mountain had been fought the day before. Middleton, Md., is to the south of the Catoctin Mountains and 4 miles east of South Mountain. Stephen W. Sears, *Landscape Turned Red: The Battle of Antietam* (Boston: Houghton Mifflin, 1983), 117, 127.

Left, Colonel Edward E. Cross, Fifth New Hampshire Regiment. Carte-de-visite from late 1861 or early 1862. Milne Special Collections and Archives, University of New Hampshire, Durham, N.H.

Right, Henry O. Kent, Cross's best friend and most frequent correspondent, shown here as colonel of the Seventeenth New Hampshire Regiment. Photograph from Charles N. Kent, *History of the Seventeenth Regiment, New Hampshire Volunteer Infantry, 1862–1863* (Concord, N.H., 1898).

Left, Nathaniel S. Berry, the New Hampshire governor (1861–1863) who appointed Cross as colonel of the Fifth. From an engraving by George E. Perine. Photograph from Otis F. R. Waite, *New Hampshire in the Great Rebellion* (Claremont, N.H., 1870).

Right, Anthony Colby, the former New Hampshire governor who served as adjutant general for the state from 1861 until 1863. Photograph from *A History of the Town of New London* (Concord, N.H., 1899).

Above, rendering of the "Grapevine Bridge," built over the Chickahominy River prior to the Battle of Fair Oaks. Photograph from William Child, *A History of the Fifth Regiment* (Bristol, N.H., 1893).

Below, photograph of what has been identified as the Fifth New Hampshire's "Grapevine Bridge." Photograph by D. B. Woodbury. Library of Congress, Washington, D.C.

Left, Thomas L. Livermore rose through the ranks of the Fifth and commanded the Eighteenth New Hampshire during the last months of the war. His memoir, *Days and Events* (Boston, 1920), is one of the finest and most reliable sources on the Fifth. Photograph from William Child, *A History of the Fifth Regiment* (Bristol, N.H., 1893).

Right, Reverend Elijah R. Wilkins was a printer before becoming a Methodist minister. He served as chaplain of the Fifth from its organization until shortly after the Battle of Fair Oaks. Photograph from William Child, *A History of the Fifth Regiment* (Bristol, N.H., 1893).

Cross's favorites. *Above left,* General Oliver Otis Howard, Cross's brigade commander through the Battle of Fair Oaks. In his account of Fair Oaks, Cross reported that Howard "acted with a bravery bordering on rashness & nobly sustained his reputation as a brave & efficient officer." *Below left,* the old veteran, Major General Edwin "Bull" Sumner, was Cross's division and, later, corps commander. He was one of a number of generals to write in support of Cross's promotion to brigadier general. *Below right,* General Winfield Scott Hancock commanded Cross's division at Fredericksburg and Chancellorsville. Hancock wrote several letters on Cross's behalf. Of Hancock, Cross recalled that at Fredericksburg his division commander was as "cool & brave as a Lion." Brady photographs. Library of Congress, Washington, D.C.

Subjects of Cross's scorn. *Above left*, of the Irish Brigade's Thomas Francis Meagher, Cross wrote, "there is not in the United States, certainly not in the Army of the Potomac, another such consummate humbug, charlatan, imposter, pretending to be a soldier." Photograph from Francis A. Walker, *History of the Second Corps* (New York, 1866). *Below left*, men of the Fifth claimed that Brigadier General John Caldwell spent the early stages of the Battle of Antietam behind a haystack. Cross's recollection was slightly less harsh: "I had seen Gen Caldwell only once, & then far in the rear of his Brigade. His conduct was very singular." Brady photograph. Library of Congress, Washington, D.C. *Below right*, in assessing Major General Joseph Hooker's leadership of the Army of the Potomac at Chancellorsville, Cross wrote, "Hooker has not the amount of *brains* necessary to manage a vast army." Brady photograph. Library of Congress, Washington, D.C.

Left, Colonel Edward E. Cross. From an engraving by George E. Perine. Photograph from Otis F. R. Waite, *New Hampshire in the Great Rebellion* (Claremont, N.H., 1870).

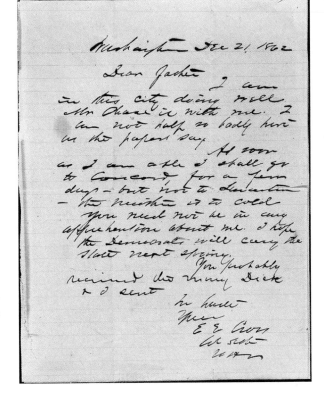

Right, letter, Edward E. Cross to Ephraim Cross, December 21, 1862. While recovering from wounds received at Fredericksburg just days before, Cross still managed to inject his political feelings into this letter to his father. Edward E. Cross Papers, Milne Special Collections and Archives, University of New Hampshire, Durham, N.H.

Above, the Everett Homestead in Lancaster, home of Edward E. Cross. Cross's funeral took place on the front porch. Photograph by Mrs. P. F. Chase, 1899. Photograph from A. N. Somers, *History of Lancaster, New Hampshire* (Concord, N.H., 1899).

Below, erected by the State of New Hampshire and dedicated on July 2, 1866, the Fifth New Hampshire monument at Gettysburg rests on the spot where Cross was mortally wounded. Photograph from William Child, *A History of the Fifth Regiment* (Bristol, N.H., 1893).

Expecting a fight every instant, & full of confidence, we hurried along, Richardson's Division in the advance—the 5th forming rear guard. About half a mile from the little village of Boonsboro,[103] the Division suddenly halted, and an order came for the 5th Rg't to get to the front double-quick. With a cheer the boys started off—all the other troops breaking to the right so as to let us pass. "There goes the fighting fifth" "Give 'em hell, boys" ["]Hurrah for Richardson's Cavalry" was shouted to us on all sides by the German & Irish troops of the Division. As I rode up to Gen Richardson to report he said, "Col we have no cavalry nor artillery your Rg't must act as both. Deploy & sweep the sides of the road."

In a few moments I had four companies deployed on each side the road in this manner

We swept quickly through the town & captured several prisoners, & the 8th Illinois cavalry coming up pursued the enemy on the Williamsport road while Richardson's Division took the Sharpsburg Turnpike. The cavalry of the enemy had just left. One little bridge was smoking & in flames but we put out the fire. The wounded of the enemy came out of the fields to meet us, & from the houses. The main body of the Army followed on consisting solely of Richardson's Division without cavalry or artillery. This was a great oversight, as the rear of the enemy might have been greatly annoyed. We kept on for a couple of miles, passed the little village of Keedysville, my skirmish line constantly exchanging shots with the cavalry of the enemy, whom we drove easily before us. One of their balls passed through the National Colors of my Rg't. About noon my picket line came in full view of the enemy drawn up in order of battle—their line appearing about one mile long with plenty of Artillery. They did not keep us long in suspense, but opened with shell & solid shot. That afternoon was when the enemy should have been at-

103. Boonsboro, Md., is located on the western side of Turner's Gap in South Mountain. Ibid., 127.

tacked. My skirmishers drove the rebels across the Antietam River & a brisk fire commenced across that stream. This was the ~~16th~~ 15. Our artillery now came up & soon a fierce cannonading commenced, which was kept up until dark. During the afternoon my men killed and wounded not less than 12 of the enemy and took 60 prisoners. We might have taken more but I had not sufficient force to scout my flanks as we marched & there was no cavalry.

On the morning of the 16th a battery of 16 20 lb guns came up & took position, & all day we had a fierce Artillery duel, which resulted in our Division losing about 125 men killed and wounded. Our damage to the enemy must have been greater as we used heavier guns, & fired at longer range. The day before I had one officer & 2 men wounded, & for my own part a ball cut my blouse near the left shoulder strap. My men remained on duty till 9 o'clock at night. The next day I was ordered to send four companies of my Reg't to prevent the enemy from burning a small bridge over the river, and to drive off the sharpshooters. This we effected. Two companies were also sent to destroy the dam over the Antietam River, but did not succeed for want of tools. The firing from the artillery continued until late at night. Just at dark Hooker's Corps[104] which had crossed the river commenced an attack on the enemy. The flashes of the cannon could be seen reminding me of the lines in Campbell's celebrated poem, "Far flashed the red artillery." [105] I never until that moment realized the truth & power of that bit of poesy.

Just at evening 80 rounds of ammunition was issued to each man. Heavy reinforcements had come up & we all expected a great battle on the morrow. In the night our brigade was awakened and marched to Gen McClellan's Headquarters. I grumbled a great deal at this order for I feared it would deprive us of our share in the battle.

Sept 17

The morning of the great struggle dawned pleasant and calm. About 8 o'clock I went up to the House occupied by Gen McClellan, & while there had an

---

104. Joseph Hooker (1814–1879), a graduate of West Point, had been commander of the Second Division of Samuel Heintzelman's corps (Third Corps). He was then promoted to major general in May 1862 and commanded the First Corps of the Army of the Potomac at the time of South Mountain and Antietam. Warner, *Generals in Blue*, 233–234, and Boatner, *Civil War Dictionary*, 409.

105. Quote from the poem "Hohenlinden" by Thomas Campbell. Stanza reads: "Then shook the hills with thunder riven, / Then rushed the steed to battle driven, / And louder than the bolts of heaven / Far flashed the red artillery." Robertson, *Poetical Works of Thomas Campbell*, 196–197.

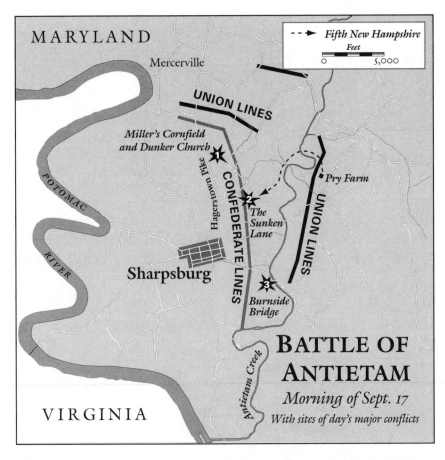

MARYLAND

Mercerville

- - -► *Fifth New Hampshire*
Feet
0   5,000

UNION LINES

*Miller's Cornfield
and Dunker Church* ⭐1

Hagerstown Pike

POTOMAC

CONFEDERATE LINES

⭐2 *The
Sunken
Lane*

•*Pry Farm*

UNION LINES

Sharpsburg

⭐3

*Burnside
Bridge*

RIVER

Antietam Creek

**BATTLE OF
ANTIETAM**
Morning of Sept. 17
With sites of day's major conflicts

VIRGINIA

introduction to the General. He seemed in good spirits though thin and careworn. A messenger came from the signal station with dispatches from
Hooker. The General read, turned to the group of officers and said, "All goes
well. Hooker is driving them." I soon left, and on going to the hill top, attracted by the cheers of the men, found that we could see the enemy retreating with Hookers men in fast pursuit. Thousands of scattered rebels were
seen breaking from the woods and scudding across the plowed fields now &
then turning to fire. Pressing after them came the long dark lines of Hookers
gallant corps. Sometimes there was a brief halt & a struggle but the rebels
always fled. All this time Sumner's Corps was on the march, crossing the
river. Sedgwick's ~~Corps in~~ Division in the advance, then French, then Richardson. Sedgwick had got into action & by the time we ~~French~~ was over the
river. French was also engaged. As the 5th crossed the Antietam the roar of
the battle was awful 50 cannon on each side were booming at once, while

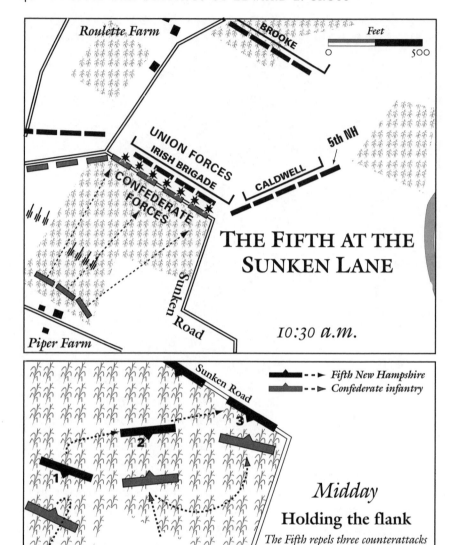

Roulette Farm

BROOKE

Feet

0   500

UNION FORCES
IRISH BRIGADE

5th NH

CALDWELL

CONFEDERATE
FORCES

THE FIFTH AT THE SUNKEN LANE

Sunken Road

Piper Farm

10:30 a.m.

Sunken Road

━━◆- - - ▶ *Fifth New Hampshire*
━━◆- - - ▶ *Confederate infantry*

Midday

Holding the flank

The Fifth repels three counterattacks aimed at the vulnerable Union left

the shouts of the combatants could be heard above the contiuous vollys from the small arms. Sumner's corps formed the center of the line, Hooker on the right, Burnside the extreme left. Porter's corps,[106] about 16000 men, was the sole reserve.

Richardson's Division crossed the river in the following order: 1st the

106. Fitz-John Porter (1822–1901) was born in Portsmouth, N.H., and graduated from West Point in 1845. Appointed brigadier general, United States Volunteers, in August 1861, he commanded a division in the Third Corps and then the Fifth Corps during the Peninsula

Irish Brigade, about 2000 men, 2d the Brigade of Col Brooks,[107] 3d the Brigade of Gen Caldwell.[108] My Regt was the extreme left & of course last. As soon as the Brigade was over the river it halted; I ordered the rolls to be called in order to see exactly who was present. This call showed 301 bayonets, and 18 commissioned officers, not counting the surgeons. The roll being called I ordered attention and spoke to the men as follows. "Officers and soldiers, the enemy are in front and the Potomac river is in their rear. We must conquer this day or we are disgraced and ruined. I expect each one will do his duty like a soldier and a brave man. Let no man leave the ranks on any pretense. If I fall leave me until the battle is won. Stand firm and fire low. Shoulder arms! Forward march" On the way to the fight about half a mile I encouraged the boys all I could, telling them we had a fair field and ought to whip the enemy—they all seemed in good spirits, and I never felt better in my life. We now began to meet the wounded, limping or crawling from the field, & the bullets whistling over the field in front of us struck around our feet, knocking up the dust in fine style. The Brigade formed in line of battle, under the brow of a hill and waited for a few moments. Coming down the slope behind us several men were hit—the first one a private of Company A.

Some orders came for us to move by the right flank. We did so, until we came very near the line of battle. We then marched by the left flank which brought us face to face with the enemy. We had marched only a few paces when the balls began to fly around us like hail & several men were hit. I quickly advanced to the front & centre of the Rg't to lead it on. At this moment Major Gen Richardson came suddenly around my left flank.[109] I halted for an instant and ordered "three cheers for Gen Richardson." They were given & the boys added three more for the Col. Said Gen R. "Where's Gen-

campaign. He became a major general for his service at Malvern Hill. When his corps left the Peninsula, he was attached to the Army of Virginia. His corps was reunited with the Army of the Potomac after Second Bull Run. Warner, *Generals in Blue*, 378–379.

107. John R. Brooke (1838–1926) was appointed colonel of the Fifty-third Pennsylvania in November 1861. He was commanding the Third Brigade, First Division, Second Corps, during the Battle of Antietam. Boatner, *Civil War Dictionary*, 88, and Sears, *Landscape Turned Red*, 361.

108. John Caldwell (1833–1912) was appointed brigadier general in April 1862 after serving as colonel of the Eleventh Maine. He took command of the First Brigade, First Division of the Second Corps, on June 4, 1862, briefly commanding the First Division at Gettysburg, and would remain with the Second Corps until March 25, 1864. Warner, *Generals in Blue*, 63–64, and Boatner, *Civil War Dictionary*, 112.

109. "right—T.L.L." (Correction in journal by Thomas L. Livermore, who served as an officer in the Fifth New Hampshire and wrote one of the best histories of the Fifth New Hampshire, *Days and Events*. He and Child both made use of Cross's journal.) It is more likely that Richardson approached on the left, in accordance with Cross's account. The First Brigade consisted of the Fifth New Hampshire, Seventh New York, Sixty-first New York, Sixty-fourth New York, and the Eighty-first Pennsylvania. Pride and Travis, *Brave Boys*, 132–133, and Sears, *Landscape Turned Red*, 360.

eral Caldwell?" I answered "in the rear." Some body called out "He's behind the hay stacks." The General then called in a loud voice "Gen Caldwell, come up here, sir & take command of your Brigade" & then added "Go on Col & do all you can—relieve that Reg't.["] All the time previous to this I had seen Gen Caldwell only once, & then far in the rear of his Brigade. His conduct was very singular. I-At the moment Gen Richardson left me I was hit by a couple of pieces of shell. One struck me in the left cheek and another over the right eye making slight, but painful wounds. My hat was also knocked off. My Reg't marched bravely up to the line of battle under a heavy fire without faltering in the least. As we marched by the right flank to gain proper distance the enemy opened on us with shrapnel and cannister shot at short range. One discharge of cannister killed and wounded eight men in one company (G.) & tore the state colors of my Reg't in two pieces. I was also hit on the right arm. When [I] took post and opened fire our position was as below:

W̶h̶e̶ We had only been firing for two or three minutes when Lieut George A. Gay[110] came to me & catching me by the arm S̶a̶i̶d̶-said, "Col, the enemy are out-flanking us." "Impossible," said I. "They are—come & see, quick." I ran with him to the left of the Reg't and sure enough the enemy were coming—a whole Brigade. I counted five battle flags & one large stand of colors. Their movement was as below

110. George A. Gay was a resident of Newmarket, N.H. He enlisted in Company K, was appointed sergeant in April 1862, and then promoted to sergeant major. He was promoted to second lieutenant of Company D on September 11, 1862. Child, "Complete Roster," 70.

I instantly changed front forward on the 1st Company,[111] by filing part of the Reg't & bringing the remainder for ward into line. The movement was made just in time to save the entire Division from being outflanked. Their centre (enemys) came directly opposite to us, & at not over 100 yards distant as they were advancing in line of battle, ~~we~~ yelling horribly, we met them with an awful volley, which smashed the Reg't in front of us, (4th NC) all to tatters. ~~The~~ My men raised ~~an awful~~ a terrible howling & pressed forward; at the same instant ~~sent~~ I sent for reinforcements, & also sent two Serg'ts to find Gen Caldwell, but he was not to be seen. The 81st Penn vols & the 7th New York came to my aid while the 2d Line moved up & took their places. We now had sharp work for about ten minutes, both sides firing & cheering, but at length the enemy, broken by the close shooting of the federal troops wavered & fell back in disorder. In our first rush towards the enemy Corporal George Nettleton[112] was injured by a piece of shell, but he gallantly remained on the field, & brought off the State Colors of the 4th North Carolina Reg't, showing great bravery & endurance. When the infantry of the enemy fell back their artillery instantly opened with round shot & shell, knocking over large numbers of our men, until our own artillery came into play. My Regt moved slightly back so as to have a little shelter behind the rising ground. I then had the roll called & found 125 men and ~~eleven~~ ten officers missing. Some of the men soon came up—so that our total loss was 7 killed 106 wounded of the enlisted men, and of officers one killed & ten wounded. Poor Gay—only 4 days a Lieutenant—a young gentleman of extraordinary talent, cheerful, diligent—beloved by his entire circle of acquaintance—was struck in the top of his head by a fragment of shell. His brain was instantly paralyzed—though his body continued the vital principle for some hours. Before his body could be rescued from the field it had been robbed of sword, watch & other articles, by some of the federal troops. When the body was brought out, I sat for a long time & held the hand of my young friend—hoping that he might yet evince some consciousness. But in vain. The night waned, & he still lay in the stupor of death. "After life's fitful fevers he slept well.["][113] All his young hopes & the bright dreams of his youth had ~~bad~~ been scattered by the ruthless hand of the Angel of Death. Long shall his memory be cherished!

About 4 o'clock in the afternoon the enemy commenced an attack on the

111. "10th—T.L.L." (Correction in journal by Thomas L. Livermore.)

112. From Claremont, N.H., George Nettleton mustered in as a sergeant of Company G. He was promoted to second lieutenant of Company E November 10, 1862. Wounded at Fredericksburg on December 13, 1862, Nettleton died ten days later. Ibid., 135.

113. From Shakespeare's *Macbeth*, act 3, scene 2: "After life's fitful fever he sleeps well." *Oxford Dictionary of Quotations*, third edition (New York: Oxford University Press, 1979), 461.

left of our centre & we sent skirmishers forward to meet him. The rifles of my men were very dirty, in some cases the rammers could scarcely be forced home—still we were not relieved for the reason that there were no fresh troops to spare. For the next three hours there was a terrible roar of Artillery our line working from 80 to 100 pieces all the time until dark. Shells were flying & bursting all around us—while every now & then rifle balls came whistling over our heads or striking close at hand. Gladly did we see the sun go down upon the field of battle, & the dull clouds of war roll away to the west. Firing ceased. In place of the din of arms we now heard a perfect chorus of groans and cries of pain and distress from the thousands of wounded that covered the ground in front of our lines. It was impossible to go on the field on account of the sharpshooters of the enemy; at the same time our sharpshooters kept the rebels from venturing on the battle ground. At night part of my Reg't was sent out as far as possible to picket & prevent surprise, while the remainder laid on their arms.

Sept 18th Early this morning we saw fresh troops pressing towards the field in every direction—artillery and cavalry. The Division of General Couch formed in the rear of Richardson's Division. Everybody expected an instant attack—the skirmishers were firing constantly. No large force of the enemy could be seen—nor any dust, indicating reinforcements. A few of the wounded that could be reached without great danger, were carried off. The rebels took many of their disabled men under cover of the darkness, and also carried away a few of ours. One Captain of an Alabama Reg't sent out a Masonic letter. It came to me. In company with some other free Masons of my Reg't I crossed into the corn field where he lay—saw our wounded brother & brought him off the field. He was shot through the thigh. The scenes on the Battle field were awful beyond any power of mine to describe them. The rebel dead lay in long lines, & literally, in some cases, in piles. To the best of my judgement we killed 3 or 4 rebels to every *one*, of our men dead. We had more men wounded than the confederates, owing to the fact that they used many smooth bore guns—the cartridges having a ball & three buckshot. As usual, in this battle the cavalry did nothing beyond driving in a few stragglers. The Artillery, on the contrary was splendidly worked, especially that portion of the force stationed on the opposite bank of the Antietam—the shells from these guns damaged the rebels very much.

To-day we were hardly able to renew the battle for want of fresh troops— & the rebels were withdrawing. This we did not know certain at the time, but everybody expected it. Their artillery practice was not as good as ours but their infantry fought splendidly. Many of their troops marched double-quick for several miles in order to get into battle. My Reg't was not withdrawn from the field, but furnished the picket & a large detail to bury the dead. A party of recruits joined me on the battle field, the evening after the action. I had them marched to the field and equipped from the bodies of the slain.

From the battle field, in that portion of it where we were encamped we marched to the ground occupied by a part of Hooker's column where we remained one day. Before leaving the subject of the battle of Antietam I must chronicle my opinion of some of the chief actors in the eventful scene. Gen Richardson behaved gallantly—leading & ordering his men until he was struck by a piece of shell in the breast. Gen Meagher was drunk as usual. Gen Caldwell did not show himself either brave or skillful; & he lost the confidence of his soldiers. Col Brooks, of the 7th New York Vols,[114] did nobly—in command of the old brigade of Gen French. My own Regt—& in fact, the entire Brigade did nobly—worthy of a better General over them.

We next marched to Harper's Ferry. A long dusty march—& camped one cold bleak evening on Bolivar Heights. Here we remained doing picket duty to the front, until the day of the reconniorsance under Gen Hancock[115] when the 5th formed a portion of the skirmish line. We remained out all night.

Oct 26 One year ago to-day, at 9 o'clock in the evening I was mustered into the service of the United States, and the 5th became a Reg't. It has been an arduous year for me—much hard labor—much anxiety—much hardship. The *material* for the Reg't was good, but very raw. Nearly all my commissioned officers were strangers to me—and untried, inexperienced men. From first to last I had the Regiment to make—officers and men, and I found it far more difficult to make officers than soldiers. Volunteer officers do not have that sense of military responsibility felt by regulars, and they require constant watching to remind them of their duty to the Reg't and the government. I had the advantage of being a stranger in the State, which circumstances aided me greatly.

I made up & sent my yearly report to the War Department, also a lengthy report to the Gov of the State.

Oct 28 Marching orders came about sundown. At dark we left just as we had made our camp comfortable. We had a large brick oven all done, big

---

114. "53 Pa.—T.L.L." (Correction in journal by Thomas L. Livermore.) Cross may have confused Brooke with George W. Von Schack, colonel of the Seventh New York Infantry.

115. Winfield Scott Hancock (1824–1886) graduated from West Point in 1844. He originally commanded the First Brigade, Second Division, of Keyes's corps (Fourth Corps) during the Peninsula campaign but was transferred to the First Division, Second Corps, during the Battle of Antietam on September 17, 1862. Warner, *Generals in Blue*, 202–204, and Boatner, *Civil War Dictionary*, 372.

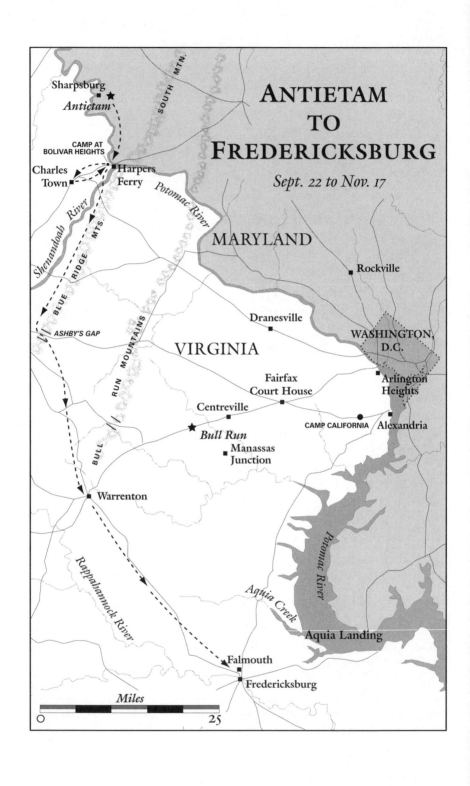

enough to bake for the whole Reg't. Marched about five miles & camped. On the 2d of Nov ~~we~~ I commanded the advanced guard of the Division & my skirmish line under Major Sturtevant drove in the enemy at Snicker's Gap. My not having any cavalry was a great annoyance, & prevented the capture of the only gun the enemy had in the Gap. We then moved along the base of the mountains to Ashby's Gap, & so on to Warrenton. Here we heard of the removal of McClellan from command of the Army—at this time an ill-advised operation. We were going on well, & two days more would have brought us to the enemy. The troops turned out & bid him a glorious farewell. It was a grand sight. All along his path the way was lined with serried ranks of ~~bay~~ bayonets glistening in the sun—artillery posted in the intervals. The General rode along the line with a shade of sadness ~~of~~ on his noble face. He carried the heart of the Army with him.

From Warrenton we marched to Fredericksburg. Gen Burnside's great error was in not crossing the river and taking possession of the City at once. We had abundant force. If we had even crossed any time within the next three days it would have ended well enough; but the enemy soon appeared in strong force, commenced throwing up earthworks, which each morning saw more formidable and well mounted with artillery. Our own army, meanwhile made itself comfortable in the well wooded and watered country opposite Frederickburg, and perfected its organization & equipment by numerous inspections. ~~In~~

On the occasion of Gen Sumner's reviewing Couch's Army Corps,[116] when the old General came to my Reg't he paused with his entire escort, & looked steadily along the ranks. He then rode *twice* up and down my front & greatly complimented the Reg't for its fine appearance and its important services.

Soon after this there came an inspection and review by Gen Hancock, in which the 5th carried off the palm for soldierly appearance.

THE BATTLE OF FREDERICKSBURG

♣ ♣ ♣ ♣ ♣

As God is my witness it seemed to my heart that it was a failure.

I was one of those who did not believe that Gen Burnside intended to cross the river opposite Fredericksburg, and storm the heights in the rear of the City. After carefully examining the ground several times, such a plan

---

116. Couch had been promoted to command of the Second Corps after Antietam. Warner, *Generals in Blue*, 95–96.

seemed to me totally impracticable, and attended with great risk to the whole army. It seemed better to cross the river 10 or 12 miles further down where we could have the aid of the gun boats, and the level nature of the country, gave us an equal chance with the enemy. In addition to these advantages, our powerful artillery could be brought into action effectively. Most of us were inclined to believe that if any attack ~~were~~ was made on the works in the rear of the city it would only be a feint to cover the real movement. We also had reason to believe that Sigel's forces would cross the river some miles *above* Fredericksburg, and attack the enemy's left flank. We were sadly, bitterly disappointed.

On the 10th of Dec, it became evident that the hour of battle drew near. That day cooked rations and extra ammunition was ordered, and I carefully inspected the Reg't — finding everything in good order.

That evening there was a convivial gathering at my camp. Some of the officers who had lately been commissioned contributed the necessary "materials" for drink, and at the quarters of Capt Cross there was assembled a merry party. We all expected battle — well we knew that some must fall, but all joined gaily in song and cheer & the jovial repartees of camp life. One of the editors of the Cincinnati Commercial[117] was present.

All the colonels & most of the mounted officers of the old 1st Brigade were there. Von Schack of the 7th NY,[118] Brown of the 145th Pa,[119] Miles of the 61st NY[120] & McKean of the 81st Pa.[121] Capt Moore[122] was master of ceremonies. Many a toast we drank — many a kindly sentiment we pledged

117. Cross had met Murat Halstead in Cincinnati when Cross worked for the *Cincinnati Times* as printer, reporter, and then editor from 1850 to 1857. Pride and Travis, *Brave Boys*, 8, 13, 165.

118. George W. Von Schack (died 1887), from Prussia, became major of the Seventh New York in July 1861 and colonel in February 1862. He left the regiment in May 1863 but returned as lieutenant colonel in July 1864 and was appointed colonel in November 1864. He received a brevet appointment to brigadier general. Boatner, *Civil War Dictionary*, 881.

119. Brown is likely Hiram Loomis Brown (died 1880), who originally served in the Eighty-third Pennsylvania. Brown was promoted to colonel of the 145th Pennsylvania and received a brevet appointment to brigadier general in September 1864. Ibid., 90–91.

120. Lieutenant Colonel Nelson Miles.

121. Henry Boyd McKeen had just been appointed colonel of the Eighty-first Pennsylvania. Sumner commanded the Right Grand Division of the Army of the Potomac; Darius Couch commanded the Second Corps and Winfield Scott Hancock the First Division. The First Brigade now contained the Fifth New Hampshire, Seventh New York, Sixty-first New York, Sixty-fourth New York, Eighty-first Pennsylvania, and 145th Pennsylvania. Walker, *Second Corps*, 144, 172.

122. William A. Moore, from Littleton, N.H., mustered in as second lieutenant of Company C and later received an appointment as first lieutenant of Company E in February 1862. He was promoted to captain of Company H in November 1862, but died at Fredericksburg. Child, "Complete Roster," 130.

each other. We carried our merriment into the late hours. I had barely gone to bed when an order came to repair to the headquarters of the General. It was after midnight. Gen Caldwell had just come from Gen Sumner's head-quarters, where he had been to receive instructions about the battle. All the Colonels were present. Gen Caldwell then stated plan of the battle. Six pontoon bridges were to be put down that night. Franklin[123] was to cross three miles below and endeavor to turn the right wing of the enemy. Sumner was to attack the centre and left. Hooker was to be held ready to strike where occasion offered. We had 140 pieces of artillery in position on the river's bank & 180 pieces ready to cross. Such was the plan. As God is my witness it seemed to my heart that it was a *failure*.

By this time my Captains were all in bed and asleep. I went to them personally—told them to prepare their troops for battle & be ready to march at daybreak.

Dec 12th

The 1st Brigade marched from camp soon after daybreak a little over 2000 strong. Early in the morning I was up—overlooked every arrangement, and tried to eat breakfast. Being quite sick, however, the idea was a failure. Some how I had an impression that I was to be killed or badly wounded, so I made my will, and an inventory of my property packed everything in my trunk, and gave my key to the chaplain. I also gave my boy Mike, every necessary direction about my horses. Although greatly prostrated by physical weakness, and my mind overshadowed by the sense that we were marching to disaster, I believe I never performed my duty with more earnestness, and the Reg't marched off in fine order, though our numbers were small. Our Brigade headed the Division, and we marched to the general gathering place of the corps—near the headquarters of Gen Sumner. Heavy firing commenced on our side early in the morning, and we moved to the front to the deep booming of our batteries. Forming into closed columns, out of range of the shells of the enemy, we sat down to rest. Several hours passed away. A terrible cannonading was opened on the City of Fredericksburg, in order to drive out the sharpshooters of the enemy so that the Pontoon Bridges could be laid, but without effect. Again, later another furious bombardment took

123. William B. Franklin (1823–1903), an 1843 graduate of West Point, had commanded the Sixth Corps since the Peninsula campaign. During the Battle of Fredericksburg, Burnside named him commander of the Left Grand Division, which included John Reynolds's First Corps and his own Sixth Corps. Warner, *Generals in Blue*, 159–160.

place, to which the enemy made no reply. Their continued silence was by some interpreted that they had fallen back—others that they were short of ammunition, but the latter reason did not seem to prevail after they once got good range on our Columns. Towards evening a bold push was made by a party of our troops in boats, a landing effected—the bridges laid down & in a few moments our men were pouring across—Howard's Division having the lead. Hancock's Division went into bivouac for the night. During the day we expended tons of ammunition to no purpose, while we lost several brave officers and not less than 40 or 50 men.

Dec 1̶2̶ 12
The disastrous day dawned bright and warm. We marched early from our bivouac. On all sides, & from all directions troops were pouring towards the bridges—four of which were across near the city. We marched over, turned down the river a short distance, and then formed in close Columns near the water's edge. Here we remained until evening—the men amusing themselves by fishing up tobacco which had been thrown into the river in boxes by the rebels. The town was plundered—carpets, books, furniture, & all lay in every direction—a perfect sense of havoc & desolation. A little up from the river lay the dead bodies of some confederate soldiers, who had been killed in the assault on the city.

That night the Reg't bivouacked in the street. Being very unwell, the Major, Adjutant and myself slept in a house. We expected an attack during the night, but with the exception of some little picket firing all was quiet. In the streets the soldiers rioted in all sorts of plunder and although on the eve of a bloody contest lost nothing of their gaiety or fun. Every body seemed cheerful. Major Sturtevant slept with me that night—the next, the stars looked down on his bloody corpse! Such is what men call the "fortunes of War!"

Dec 13 Early in the morning I was among my brave boys. I found them cheerful & full of hope. Hardly able to sit on horseback—dizzy, weak, suffering acute pain—still I kept as brave a front as my physical condition admitted—Thank God my soul was strong and bright.

The battle opened by Franklin on our left. His guns thundered & the rattle of musketry could anon be faintly distinguished. Our Brigade formed along the street in its projected order of battle. The forenoon wore away, but soon after 12 we received notice to prepare for the attack. Gen Hancock, accompanied by Gen Meagher rode along the ranks of the Irish Brigade & the latter addressed his troops one of those frothy, meaningless a̶ speeches peculiar to the man. And here let me record the opinion formed after more than one year's observation in the field—that there is not in the United States, certainly not in the Army of the Potomac, another such a consummate humbug, charlatan, imposters, ~~an~~ pretending to be a soldier as Thos Francis Meagher! Nor ~~I do b~~ do I believe him to be a *brave* man, since in every battle field he has been *drunk* and not with his Brigade. x x x I venture the prediction that the drunkenness & incompetence of Gen Meagher will sooner or later be exposed. Gen Hancock sent for the Colonels of the 1st Brigade, and explained to them the plan of attack, which was to form columns of Brigades and endeavor to storm the hill.

I went to my Reg't counted my files, found that I had 249 rifles, and nineteen officers—line, & field, & staff. I passed along the ranks and spoke to the ~~men~~ officers and men—told them it was to be a bloody strife—to stand firm & fire low—to close on their colors—be steady—to the officers I only said that they were expected to do their duty. I then took my place at the head of my men & we started—following the Irish Brigade. As we marched up the streets towards the batteries of the enemy—they opened on us with solid shot and shell, and before we had reached the open fields several men were disabled. However, my Reg't kept up in fine style, & we formed line of battle on the ground selected, under heavy fire of shell, grape and cannisters. Gen Caldwell and staff, & Gen Hancock and staff were present, the latter on horseback—cool & brave as a Lion. While taking up our position, it came necessary to cross a canal or deep ditch filled with water. This scattered the men some, but we came "forward into line" in fine style. Meantime the Irish Brigade had formed and moved forward, but instead of charging the works of the enemy, faltered, commenced firing, & finally laid down. It soon became our turn to move forward. The Reg't rose up as one man and started forward, a little ahead of the line, in complete order. We were thus advancing when a shell exploded in the air directly in front of me and about the height of my head. A large fragment hit me on the breast, a smaller piece knocked out two of my teeth—& filled my mouth with sand; another bit struck me on the forehead, making a slight wound, another bit over the eye, and still another along the back of my hand. I was knocked clean off my feet, & lay insensible until roused by a violent blow on the left leg—made by a piece of shell which hit me there. Getting on my hands & knees, & spitting the sand, stones & blood out of my mouth I looked around. The tattered colors of my Reg't thank God were in the van! I tried to get on my feet, but could not stand. I then tried to crawl, but the balls came so thick & tore up the ground so spitefully that I could not go it—besides a ball struck my ~~ser~~

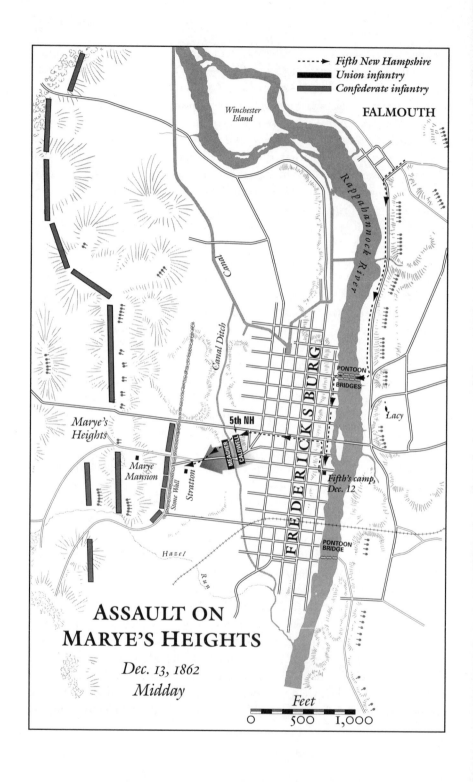

Fifth New Hampshire (dashed arrow legend)
Union infantry
Confederate infantry

FALMOUTH

Winchester
Island

Rappahannock River

Canal

Canal Ditch

PONTOON
BRIDGES

Lacy

Marye's
Heights

5th NH

MEAGHER
CALDWELL

Marye
Mansion

Stone Wall

Stratton

FREDERICKSBURG

Fifth's camp,
Dec. 12

Hazel

Run

PONTOON
BRIDGE

ASSAULT ON
MARYE'S HEIGHTS

Dec. 13, 1862
Midday

Feet
0   500   1,000

sabre scabbard, knocking me over. After that warning I concluded to lie still. So placing myself on my back feet to the foe, I awaited death. The failure of the rear lines to come up & their firing at long range on the enemy—placed me between two fires, not only of musketry, but of shell, and for more than an hour I lay in expectation of instant death or a mortal wound. I employed most of my thoughts about my Reg't. Some times when the shot came particularly strong & thick I covered my face & counted rapidly from one to one hundred! Thus I lay while the awful battle raged. Some of the troops— new Regt's *marched* over me on the advance, & *ran* over me a few moments after, in their retreat. Some of the new Reg'ts behaved well, but a majority of them, wavered, scattered, fired wild, & broke. The rebels managed their part of the battle with great skill—their rifle pits were well filled with men, but not too much so—their artillery was well served, & fired with great rapidity. Opposite where my Reg't stood—on the side hill, running for several hundred yards was a stone wall about 4 feet high, with a rifle pit at the base. Behind the wall was another pit—thus forming a double line of intrenchment. Our Column of attack was not long enough, instead of Brigade front it should have been by division.

After my fall Major Sturtevant took command, & led my Reg't up to the enemy. My brave boys never faltered, & had they been supported would have carried the first rifle pit and wall. Of this there is no doubt. Not being supported the 5th held its ground until nearly destroyed. Six times the bearers of the colors were shot down. Most of my officers fell. The brave Major was shot dead. Capt Murray[124] was pierced through the brain and dropped instantly. The gallant Captain Perry[125] was shot mortally with the National Colors in his hand. On all sides men fell like grass before the scythe, but especially in the old ~~new~~ Reg'ts—the veterans of Fair Oaks, Malvern Hill and Antietam. Most of the new Reg'ts acted very cowardly—straggled, wavered & ran away. Their fire was also very wild.

I lay on the ground for nearly three hours—part of the time between two fires—momentarily expecting death, when I was discovered by Lieut Dan K Cross[126] of my Reg't—then on Gen Caldwell's staff, who bringing some of

124. John Murray, a resident of Newcastle, N.H., mustered in as captain of Company D on October 12, 1861. Child, "Complete Roster," 134.

125. James B. Perry, of Lebanon, N.H., was captain of Company C. Perry and James Larkin had just been found innocent of Cross's charges against them stemming from events during the march to Warrenton in November. Ibid., 192, and Pride and Travis, *Brave Boys*, 159–162.

126. Daniel K. Cross, a resident of Hanover, N.H., was a cousin of Edward Cross. At the time he was serving on General Caldwell's staff. Cross enlisted as a sergeant major of Company G and rose through the ranks to become first lieutenant in that company. He was discharged on November 14, 1863. Child, "Complete Roster," 45, and Pride and Travis, *Brave Boys*, 175.

my brave boys—they carried me from the field. While lying there on the ground I saw many acts of cowardice & bravery. Many officers and men ran shamefully from the field without a scratch—others counterfeited wounds—other skulked behind & lay down. It was a sad and shameful sight!

Capt Larkin brought off all that remained of the Reg't that night. I was carried to the house of the mayor of the city which was used as a hospital. Here I remained all night & in the morning was carried to my old camp. On the 16th inst., I started for Washington on leave of absence taking the colors of my Reg't. On the 17th I reached Washington. Here I remained until able to travel; then started for Concord, NH which city I reached on the evening of Dec. 31, 1862.

On Jan 1st 1863 I was invited to attend the Convention which assembled on behalf of the Republican party to nominate a candidate for Governor. The State & National Colors of my Reg't & the Colors of the 4th North Carolina Vols were taken into the Convention amidst great enthusiasm. The remarks I then made may be found in this book.

About the 25th I submitted to the Governor & Council the names of officers & sergeants that I desired promoted, & everything was arranged to my satisfaction. Soon after Lieut Col Hapgood[127] started for the Reg't.

On the 5th of ~~March~~ Feb. I started for my Reg't but was unable to proceed farther than Boston, on account of my wounds—for nearly two weeks. When I did feel able to travel rode to Washington & remained there until March 16, when I again joined my Reg't I found only 150 men for duty.

> Cross's manuscript ends with this entry. For Cross's account of the Chancellorsville campaign, see his manuscript in part 2 of this volume. That report, which Cross titled "Hooker's Campaign," accompanied the manuscript journal, but because it was physically separate and formatted differently, it has been treated as a report. It likewise serves as a substitute for Cross's official report, which was either never written or never published.

> Despite several wounds, Cross was able to leave Fredericksburg on December 16; he reached the nation's capital the next day. Following a period of convalescence, Cross traveled to Concord, New Hampshire, where he arrived on

127. Charles E. Hapgood, a 30-year-old resident of Amherst, N.H., served as captain of Company I. He was appointed lieutenant colonel on December 14, 1862, and assumed command of the regiment on July 3, 1863, the day after Cross died. He was wounded at the Battle of Cold Harbor in June 1864 and discharged the following October. Child, "Complete Roster," 82, and Daniel F. Secomb, *History of the Town of Amherst, Hillsborough County, New Hampshire* (Concord, N.H.: Evans, Sleeper & Woodbury, 1883), 889.

December 31. Ironically, Cross attended the Republican State Convention on New Year's Day. Those gathered to nominate their party's candidate for governor cheered as Cross stood before them holding his regiment's flag along with that captured from the Fourth North Carolina. Cross no doubt swallowed his animus for many of those in attendance; moreover, he masked what he considered Burnside's disastrous leadership of the Army of the Potomac. Instead, he used the forum to praise the men of his regiment—brave, well-trained men who did not know the meaning of retreat, men who under the withering fire above the town of Fredericksburg advanced closer to the stone wall on Marye's Heights than any other regiment. According to Captain Charles Hapgood, who was in New Hampshire recruiting for the Fifth, Cross appeared to be in improving health. While in Concord, Cross sought and received Hapgood's promotion to lieutenant colonel of the Fifth. Hapgood returned to Falmouth in February and assumed command of the Fifth until Cross's return. Nevertheless, Cross's own promotion to brigadier general languished in spite of his performance before the Republican convention and the open campaigning of several general officers, most notably Hancock.[128]

While Cross recuperated and politicked in New Hampshire, two events occurred that would change the course of the war. First, Lincoln's Emancipation Proclamation went into effect on January 1. Many men in the Fifth, including Cross, did not like that the fight to preserve the Union had become a war to end slavery. Few in the Fifth regarded slaves as equals, and many felt that the proclamation weakened the resolve and purpose that many had held from the beginning of the war. While soldiers in the Fifth debated the issue, the 1863 gubernatorial election in New Hampshire quickly became a referendum on the issue of slavery. Only Republican intrigue kept the Democratic nominee from achieving a majority of the vote, thus leaving the Republican-controlled House to decide the election in favor of Republican candidate Joseph Gilmore. At the same time, Burnside's days as commander of the Army of the Potomac were numbered. In mid-January, he ordered two of his corps to move westward from Falmouth. In the midst of the worst rainstorm of the winter, the Fifth waited for orders to leave. The thousands of men who had left became mired in the mud and were ordered to return to Falmouth through the ruts and mire. Shortly after the infamous "Mud March," Major General Joseph Hooker replaced Burnside as commander of the army.[129]

128. Pride and Travis, *Brave Boys*, 182–183. Confederate soldiers substantiated Cross's claims about Fredericksburg. They reported that the Union soldiers who fell closest to the wall on Marye's Heights were from the Fifth New Hampshire, Sixty-ninth New York, and Fifty-third Pennsylvania. Douglas Southall Freeman, *Lee's Lieutenants: A Study in Command*, vol. 2 (New York: Charles Scribner's Sons, 1943), 367–368.

129. Ibid., 183–194.

Before leaving Concord, Cross visited Jenny Larkin, wife of Captain James Larkin. Although Cross and Larkin's disagreements were well documented, Cross had made amends with Larkin before leaving the Fredericksburg battlefield. Cross now took his campaign to smooth things over to the home front. During the visit, Cross extolled Larkin's virtues and claimed to share an interest in Mrs. Larkin's spiritualism. Although relieved that his relationship with Cross had improved, Larkin remained somewhat skeptical of his commander's actions. Cross also visited his friend Henry Kent, whose Seventeenth New Hampshire was forming at Camp Ethan Allen, near Concord. While there, Cross attended a concert by the regimental glee club and met with Charles Long, formerly of the Fifth, who was lieutenant colonel of the Seventeenth.[130]

Cross set out from New Hampshire on February 1, but it grew apparent that his wounds had not yet healed. He remained in Boston for two weeks before leaving for Washington. While there, Cross renewed his campaign for promotion and watched the conscription debate from the Senate gallery. In letters to former President Franklin Pierce, a new confidante, Cross decried the politics surrounding promotions. Cross's outspoken political views and the Senate's growing conservatism in approving such appointments made Cross's task increasingly difficult. By the time he returned to Falmouth in mid-March, Cross was forced to accept the fact that no promotion was forthcoming.[131]

130. Ibid., 195–197.
131. Ibid., 197–198.

Part Two

Regimental Reports of
Colonel Edward E. Cross

MANUSCRIPT REPORT OF THE BATTLE OF FAIR OAKS,
JUNE 2, 1862[1]

*The fire was now very close and deadly, the opposing lines
being several times not over 30 yards apart.*

Headquarters 5th NH Vols
Camp at Fair Oaks Station, June 2, 1862

Captain

I have the honor to report to you the part taken by my Regt in the Battle of June 1st.

On the evening of May 31st the Fifth Regiment was posted as advanced guard in front of the brigade of General French.[2] Being very near the enemy

---

1. Edward E. Cross Papers, Milne Special Collections and Archives, University of New Hampshire, Durham, N.H.

2. William H. French (1815–1881) commanded the Third Brigade, First Division, of Sumner's Second Corps. Boatner, *Civil War Dictionary*, 316.

we took several prisoners, and soon after daybreak an orderly, bearing a dispatch from Gen Pryor of the Confederate Army to Gen Anderson was taken, & sent to Headquarters.[3] Soon after this my regiment moved across the Railroad & took post in the edge of the woods. Here, being fired upon by the enemy's pickets, we had one man killed & two wounded. We returned the fire and the pickets retreated. We were then ordered back to a position in the front line of battle, but soon after advanced into the woods again, where we took fifteen or twenty prisoners, members of the Virginia Rgts, who came suddenly upon our line. The battle had now raged violently for nearly one hour, when I received orders from Gen Richardson[4] to move to the support of French's Brigade. While moving along the railroad I received notice that Gen Howard[5] was severely wounded, & command of his brigade devolved upon me. Finding that the 81st Penn, 64th New York & 61st New York—the other regiments of the brigade—had been severely handled, I sent word to them to file out of the woods & reform in the van of Meagher's Brigade.[6] While I advanced my Rgt to occupy the ground [against] vastly superior force & under a fire seldom experienced by troops in battle, the lost of my Rgt in killed wounded & missing is about 185 men, & five officers wounded namely, Col Cross, Major Cook,[7] Capt Sturtevant,[8] Lieut Reed[9] & Lieut Cummings.[10]

I am very truly

3. Roger Pryor (1828–1919) and Richard Anderson (1821–1879) both commanded brigades under General James Longstreet. This incident is described further in Cross's journal. Ibid., 14, 674.

4. Israel Bush "Dick" Richardson (1815–1862) was assigned command of the First Division of Sumner's corps on March 13, 1862. Warner, *Generals in Blue*, 402–403, and Boatner, *Civil War Dictionary*, 697.

5. Oliver Otis Howard (1830–1909) commanded the First Brigade under Israel B. Richardson. His command included the Fifth New Hampshire, Sixty-first New York, Sixty-fourth New York, and Eighty-first Pennsylvania. Warner, *Generals in Blue*, 237, 403.

6. Brigadier General Thomas Francis Meagher (1823–1867) organized and commanded of the Irish Brigade, the Second Brigade of Richardson's division. The brigade consisted of the Sixty-third New York, Sixty-ninth New York, and Eighty-eighth New York. Ibid., 317–318, and Boatner, *Civil War Dictionary*, 427.

7. William W. Cook, of Derry, N.H., was appointed major on September 24, 1861. Wounded at Fair Oaks, he resigned his commission on July 17, 1862. Child, "Complete Roster," 42.

8. Edward E. Sturtevant was appointed captain of Company A on October 12, 1861, and replaced Cook as major in July 1862. Ibid., 175.

9. Dexter G. Reed, a native of Newport, N.H., mustered in as a second lieutenant in Company E in October 1861 and rose to the rank of first lieutenant. He resigned in November 1862. Ibid., 150.

10. Albert G. Cummings, of Enfield, N.H., mustered in as an 18-year-old sergeant in Company A. By March 1863, he had risen to the rank of captain. He was wounded at Fair Oaks, Fredericksburg, and Chancellorsville. Ibid., 46.

Edward E. Cross
Col 5th NHV
Capt Morrill[11]
A A General

PUBLISHED REPORT OF THE BATTLE OF FAIR OAKS, JUNE 2, 1862

No. 8.

Report of Col. Edward E. Cross, Fifth New Hampshire Infantry.[12]

HDQRS. FIFTH REGIMENT NEW HAMPSHIRE VOLS.,
Camp near Fair Oaks Station, June 2, 1862.

CAPTAIN: I have the honor to report the part taken by my regiment in the Battle of June 1 near this place:

On the evening of May 31 the Fifth Regiment was posted as advance guard in front of the brigade of General French. Being very near the enemy we took several prisoners, and soon after daybreak an orderly, bearing a dispatch from Gen. Pryor, of the Confederate Army, to General Anderson, was taken and sent to headquarters. Soon after this my regiment moved across the railroad and took post in the edge of the wood. Here, being fired upon by the enemy's pickets, we had several men wounded. The fire was promptly returned and the pickets retreated. We were then ordered back to a position in the first line of battle, but soon after advanced into the woods again, where we took quite a number of prisoners.

The battle had now gone on nearly an hour, when I received orders from General Richardson to move to the support of General French. While marching along the railroad I received notice that Brigadier-General Howard was severely wounded, and the command of the First Brigade devolved upon me. Finding that the three other regiments of the brigade had been some time in action and severely handled, I directed that they should move out of the woods and reform in the rear of Meagher's brigade while I advanced my regiment to occupy the ground. We moved forward in line of battle through a thick woods, and about 300 yards from the railroad track encountered the

---

11. Probably Captain J. M. Norvell, who was the assistant adjutant general of Richardson's division. *War of the Rebellion: Official Records of the Union and Confederate Armies*, series I. (Washington, D.C.: Government Printing Office, 1884), vol. XI, pt. 1, 770. Hereinafter cited as *OR*.

12. *OR*, vol. XI, pt. 1, 771–772.

rebel line of battle, and a fierce fire commenced on both sides. Twice my line advanced in the most gallant style, and each time the enemy fell back.

The fire was now very close and deadly, the opposing lines being several times not over 30 yards apart. When about ordering another charge I was struck by a rifle-ball in the thigh and disabled. Lieutenant-Colonel Langley[13] then took command of the regiment, and the rebels endeavoring to flank us, he brought off the regiment in excellent order, carrying most of our wounded.

I cannot speak too highly of the coolness, bravery, and good conduct of the officers and men of my regiment in the face of a largely-superior force and under a fire seldom experienced by troops in battle.

The loss of the regiment in killed, wounded, and missing is about 185 men and 5 officers wounded.*[14]

       Yours, very respectfully,
           EDWARD E. CROSS,
       Colonel Fifth New Hampshire Volunteers.

ASSISTANT ADJUTANT-GENERAL,
Howard's Brigade.

PUBLISHED REPORTS OF THE ANTIETAM CAMPAIGN, SEPTEMBER 18, 1862[15]

♣ ♣ ♣ ♣ ♣

In this severe conflict my regiment captured the State colors of the Fourth North Carolina Regiment, Corpl. George Nettleton, of Company G, although wounded, bringing them off the field, displaying great bravery and endurance.

No. 43.
       Reports of Col. Edward E. Cross, Fifth New Hampshire Infantry, of skirmish at Boonsborough and Battle of Antietam.

HEADQUARTERS FIFTH NEW HAMPSHIRE VOLUNTEERS,
       Camp near the Battle-field, September 18, 1862.

CAPTAIN.: I have the honor to report the operations of my regiment on the march in pursuit of the enemy from Middletown Heights on the 15th instant:

13. Samuel G. Langley, from Manchester, N.H., was appointed lieutenant colonel October 26, 1861. He later resigned on December 1, 1862. Child, "Complete Roster," 108.

14. This reference is to casualty report, which lists aggregate losses of 180 for the Fifth New Hampshire. *OR*, vol. XI, pt. 1, 757.

15. *OR*, vol. XIX, pt. 1, 287–288.

On arriving within 1 mile of the village of Boonsborough,[16] my regiment, which formed the rear guard of the division, suddenly received orders to march to the front as soon as possible. We passed the division at double-quick, and on reaching the front received orders from Major General Richardson to deploy as skirmishers and cover the advance. I therefore threw four companies on each side of the road, keeping two companies in the center. We advanced through the village, taking quite a number of prisoners, and proceeded on the track of the enemy along the road to Sharpsburg. The cavalry of the enemy were soon encountered, and our line advanced, skirmishing briskly, until the enemy were driven over Antietam Creek, and their line of battle discovered. During the day my regiment held the front, exposed to the fire of the enemy's artillery and sharpshooters. The latter we several times drove from their lurking places. We held our ground until 9 o'clock in the evening, when we were relieved, having lost during the day 1 officer and 3 men wounded—all slightly. We killed and wounded at least 12 of the enemy and took 60 prisoners. More might have been taken, but I could not spare the force to pursue them.

The next day four companies of my regiment were sent, under Major Sturtevant, to drive away the enemy's sharpshooters from the upper bridge and prevent the bridge from being burned. Two companies, under Captains Cross[17] and Long,[18] were sent to destroy a dam which backed up the waters of the creek, but were unable to perform this duty for want of tools.

I beg leave to mention particularly Major Sturtevant,[19] Captains Pierce,[20] Murray,[21] Long, Cross, Perry[22] and Crafts,[23] for excellent and skillful con-

16. Boonsboro, Md., is located on the western side of Turner's Gap in South Mountain. Sears, *Landscape Turned Red*, 127.

17. Richard E. "Dick" Cross was appointed first lieutenant of Company H on October 12, 1861. He later served as captain of Company K, major, and lieutenant colonel of the Fifth New Hampshire. Child, "Complete Roster," 114.

18. Charles H. Long, 28-year-old resident of Claremont, N.H., was appointed captain of Company G. Wounded at Antietam on September 17, 1862, Long resigned his commission in November 1862. Ibid., 192, and Pride and Travis, *My Brave Boys*, 264.

19. Major Edward E. Sturtevant.

20. Horace T. H. Pierce was a 37-year-old resident of Keene, N.H., when appointed captain of Company F in October 1861. Cross later accused Pierce of tardiness in organizing a detail for guard duty and asked for his resignation. Pierce complied on January 29, 1863. Child, "Complete Roster," 145.

21. John Murray, from Newcastle, N.H., was appointed captain of Company D on October 12, 1861. Ibid., 134.

22. James B. Perry, of Lebanon, N.H., was appointed captain of Company C on October 12, 1861. He survived court-martial charges brought by Cross stemming from an alleged mutiny during the march to Warrenton in November 1862. Ibid., 143, and Pride and Travis, *Brave Boys*, 158–162.

23. Welcome A. Crafts, of Milan, N.H., was first lieutenant in Company B. He would later serve as captain, major, and lieutenant colonel of the Fifth before he mustered out on June 28,

duct while commanding their skirmishers, as they were under fire from a concealed foe for more than ten hours, and they report the conduct of their men as excellent throughout.

Very respectfully,

E. E. CROSS,

Colonel Fifth New Hampshire.

Captain CALDWELL,

Assistant Adjutant-General.[24]

HEADQUARTERS FIFTH NEW HAMPSHIRE VOLUNTEERS,
On the Battle-field, September 18, 1862.

CAPTAIN.: In reference to the part taken by my regiment in the Battle of the 17th instant, I have the honor to report that, on arriving at the scene of action, I was ordered forward to relieve one of the regiments of the Irish Brigade, which was done under fire. We then advanced in line of battle several hundred yards and entered a corn-field. While marching by the right flank to gain our position in line of battle, we received a heavy fire of shell and canister-shot, which killed and wounded quite a number of officers and men, a single shell wounding 8 men and passing through the State colors of my regiment.

I had scarcely reached my position on the left of the first line of battle and opened fire, when it was reported that the enemy were cautiously attempting to outflank the entire division with a strong force concealed behind a ridge, and in the same corn-field in which I was posted. They had, in fact, advanced within 200 yards of the left of our lines, and were preparing to charge. I instantly ordered a change of front to the rear, which was executed in time to confront the advancing line of the enemy in their center with a volley at very short range, which staggered and hurled them back. They rallied and attempted to gain my left, but were again confronted and held, until, assistance being received, they were driven back with dreadful loss. In this severe conflict my regiment captured the State colors of the Fourth North Carolina Regiment, Corpl. George Nettleton,[25] of Company G, although wounded, bringing them off the field, displaying great bravery and endurance.

My regiment remained on the battle-field all the remainder of the day,

---

1865, with a brevet colonelcy. Crafts brought Cross's body back to Lancaster after the Battle of Gettysburg. Child, "Complete Roster," 44.

24. Captain George H. Caldwell of General John Caldwell's staff.

25. George Nettleton, a native of England and resident of Claremont, N.H., mustered in as a 29-year-old private. He was appointed sergeant of Company G soon thereafter. Child, "Complete Roster," 135.

under fire of shot and shell, and picketed the field at night. Throughout the whole time my officers and men exhibited all the qualities of good soldiers, steady, brave, and prompt in action, although the forces of the enemy were more than three to one.

Major Sturtevant, Adjutant Dodd,[26] Captains Pierce, Long, Murray, Cross, Perry, Randlett,[27] and Crafts deserve especial mention for their gallant conduct; also Lieutenants Graves,[28] George,[29] and Bean,[30] each commanding companies, and Lieutenants Livermore,[31] Ricker,[32] and Goodwin.[33]

The following officers were wounded: Colonel Cross (slightly); Captains Long and Randlett; First Lieutenants Graves and Parks;[34] Second Lieutenants Bean, George, Twitchell,[35] Little,[36] and Hurd.[37] Lieut. George A. Gay,[38] a gal-

26. Charles Dodd, the regiment's adjutant, was from Boston, Mass. He was appointed adjutant on September 24, 1861, and resigned June 13, 1863. Ibid., 52.

27. Nathan H. Randlett came from Lebanon, N.H., and served as first lieutenant of Company C and was appointed captain of Company E. He was wounded at Antietam and was discharged as disabled in March 1863. Ibid., 149.

28. Janvrin W. Graves, of Tuftonborough, N.H., mustered in as a second lieutenant in Company H and rose to the rank of captain by December 1862. He was wounded at Antietam and Fredericksburg. Ibid., 75.

29. George W. George, of Amherst, N.H., originally mustered in as first sergeant of Company I and was appointed second lieutenant in August 1862. Wounded at Antietam, he was discharged as disabled in March 1863. Ibid., 70.

30. John W. Bean from Danbury, N.H., mustered in as second lieutenant of Company I in October 1861. He became first lieutenant of Company A in July 1862, but returned to Company I as captain in December. Ibid., 14.

31. Thomas L. Livermore, of Milford, N.H., mustered in as first sergeant, Company K. He was appointed second lieutenant in June 1862, first lieutenant in December 1862, and captain of Company E in March 1863. Ibid., 113.

32. John S. Ricker, of Milton, N.H., mustered in as a 20-year-old sergeant in Company D. He rose to the rank of major by the end of the war. Ibid., 153.

33. George F. Goodwin enlisted from Lebanon, Maine, as sergeant of Company D and was promoted to second lieutenant of Company F in August 1862, to first lieutenant of Company D in December 1862, and to captain in March 1863. He was wounded at both Fredericksburg and Chancellorsville. Ibid., 73.

34. James W. Parks was a resident of New York City. He enlisted as a sergeant in Company D before being promoted to second lieutenant of Company B on February 18, 1862. He was first lieutenant in Company C when he resigned in January 1863. Ibid., 141.

35. O'Neil R. Twitchell, of Dummer, N.H., enlisted as a sergeant in Company B. He was promoted to second lieutenant in September 1862, to first lieutenant of Company I in December 1862, and captain of Company A in October 1863. Ibid., 186.

36. Samuel B. Little was a 33-year-old recruit from Claremont, N.H. He served in Company G as first sergeant and was appointed to the rank of second lieutenant in August 1862. He died at the end of December 1862 from wounds received at Fredericksburg. Ibid., 113.

37. Sumner F. Hurd, of Newport, N.H., enlisted in Company E and was appointed sergeant in December 1861. He rose to the rank of first lieutenant by November 1862. Wounded at Fredericksburg, he resigned May 27, 1863. Ibid., 94–95.

38. George A. Gay was a resident of Newmarket, N.H. He enlisted in Company K and was appointed sergeant in April 1862 and later sergeant major. He was promoted to second lieutenant of Company D on September 11, 1862. Ibid., 70.

lant young officer, was killed. Sergeant-Major Liscomb[39] was also wounded. Of enlisted men, as far as can be ascertained, 107 were killed and wounded. Our wounded were attended to by Drs. Knight,[40] Davis,[41] and Child[42] as rapidly and as well as possible, and were all made very comfortable.

Very truly,

EDWARD E. CROSS,
Colonel Fifth New Hampshire Volunteers.

Captain CALDWELL.

FIRST ANNUAL REPORT, OCTOBER 31, 1862[43]

♣ ♣ ♣ ♣ ♣

In whatever position placed, in battle or in march, enduring hunger, cold or heat, the regiment has never faltered, never failed to do its duty.

HEAD-QUARTERS FIFTH NEW HAMPSHIRE VOLUNTEERS,
CAMP ON BOLIVAR HEIGHTS, October 31, 1862

Governor Berry:—[44]

The Fifth New Hampshire Volunteers has now been in service one year, and it seems proper that I should present you with a statement of the services of the regiment and its present condition.

The regiment completed its muster on the evening of October 26, 1861, and left Concord on the 28th, numbering one thousand and ten, officers and men. On the 31st we reached Bladensburg, where we encamped. On the 3rd of November, in the midst of a rain and the roads in a very bad condition, we formed a portion of Howard's Brigade, ordered to Lower Marlborough, Md. The distance—about fifty miles—was made in two days, after remain-

39. Charles F. Liscomb was a resident of Lebanon, N.H. He mustered in as corporal of Company C and was appointed sergeant major on September 11, 1862, and served on the non-commissioned staff. He achieved the rank of first lieutenant in December 1862. Ibid., 112.

40. Dr. Luther M. Knight came from Franklin, N.H. He was appointed the regiment's surgeon on September 13, 1861, and resigned May 28, 1863. Ibid., 106.

41. Unidentified.

42. William F. Child, of Bath, N.H., wrote the first regimental history of the Fifth New Hampshire. He was appointed assistant surgeon on August 13, 1862, and surgeon on October 28, 1864. Child, "Complete Roster," 35.

43. Printed in Child, *Fifth New Hampshire*, 134–143, as well as in several New Hampshire newspapers.

44. Nathaniel S. Berry (1796–1894), governor of New Hampshire from 1861 to 1863.

ing one. No more severe march has been made by any regiment of the Army of the Potomac. On the 27th of November the regiment marched across Long bridge into Virginia, and was assigned, with the remainder of Howard's Brigade, to the division of General Sumner. A great deal of hard labor was here expended in rendering habitable a bad location for a camp but we afterward had the satisfaction of having the neatest and most comfortable quarters in the division. The regiment soon commenced doing picket and outpost duty at the front, and established the first line of pickets on the line fronting the enemy at Fairfax Court House. In the intervals between picketing and scouting, whenever the weather would allow, the men were thoroughly drilled, not only in regimental but brigade tactics, also in the bayonet exercise. The commissioned officers also were also drilled in the practical part of the duty. Schools were established by the colonel and lieutenant-colonel for the instruction of officers and sergeants during the winter evenings. A "common school," for such of the boys in the regiment as needed instruction in the elementary branches, was also put in operation, the necessary books being donated by the Sanitary Commission.[45]

All through the winter my regiment furnished heavy details to build roads, repair bridges and cut timber. The pioneers were also instructed to make gabions, fascines,[46] and other engineering work. The good effect of the drill and instruction has been apparent in officers and men on trying occasions.

Measles and mumps prevails in my regiment to an extraordinary extent, but at no time up to the Battle of Fair Oaks did the regiment fail to turn out more men for duty than any other in the entire division. All through the winter we averaged from six hundred and fifty to eight hundred men for duty daily. Several times while the regiment was out on duty at the front, it was exposed to severe storms of rain and snow, without tents, for five or six days at a time.

On the 1st day of March, while on picket, received orders to move up and join the remainder of Howard's Brigade, then on a scout to the front. While on this expedition the regiment was called out in the night to meet the enemy. In less than seven minutes from the time the long role commenced beating, the whole regiment was on the march.

On the 10th of March my regiment, under its commanding officer, formed

---

45. The U.S. Sanitary Commission was created by citizens in June 1861 to help care for sick and wounded Union soldiers. During the war, the Sanitary Commission raised over $7 million and handed out donated supplies valued at $15 million. *Encyclopedia of the Civil War*, 656.

46. Gabions are open-ended baskets made of wood or metal, and fascines are bundles of brush or stakes. Both were used in building retaining walls in field fortifications. Boatner, *Civil War Dictionary*, 276, 320, 693.

the advance guard of Sumner's Division,[47] when it marched from Camp California[48] on Manassas, Major Cook commanding my skirmish line. On the march to Warrenton Junction the entire force were obliged to ford creeks and rivers, some waist deep—five of these fords in one day. Guard and picket duty were severe; the weather cold and rainy; the roads almost impassable; often the men could not build fires; often the ground was so wet and muddy that they could not lie down; no tents; not cooking utensils but tin cups; and no wagons; in this state for thirty-one days. Yet the men were cheerful, and we averaged seven hundred men for duty daily.

On the 28th of March General Howard commanded a reconnaissance in force, from Warrenton Junction to the Rappahannock River, eight miles, for the purpose of forcing the enemy to cross the river, and burn the railroad bridge. I had the honor again to command the advance guard, Lieutenant-Colonel Langley commanding the skirmish line. The enemy were driven all day, the bridge and railroad depot burned, and the rebel force shelled out of their position. Here the Fifth Regiment first came under fire—the skirmish line from the enemy's riflemen, and the main body from shot and shell.

The behavior of the regiment in this expedition, and its important service, gained great praise from the commander of the forces. While on this campaign to Manassas the regiment marched one day, in rain and mud, sixteen miles on the railroad track, from Union Mills to Fairfax Court House; and, having less than an hour's rest, marched back the same night. The exigency of the case required this severe toil, and the men cheerfully did their duty. It is worthy of note that during this thirty-one days' campaign, without tents, wet, cold, hungry, severely fatigued, we had scarcely any sick men, sometimes not one. It is in camp where soldiers are sick to the greatest extent. Without returning to Camp California, where our tents and regimental property were left, the regiment proceeded to Alexandria, and on the 4th of April embarked for the peninsula. The weather was cold and wet when we reached Ship Point,[49] and the men were obliged to wade ashore from the vessel, and camp in the water-soaked earth, with no tents. My regiment was at once set to work, making corduroy road through a swamp, and building bridges. Our daily detail was about five hundred men for this purpose. Added to this hard labor in mud and water, the locality was very unhealthy.

47. Edwin Vose Sumner (1797–1863) came to the Army of the Potomac from his command in California. He commanded a division that became part of the Second Corps and in March 1862 was appointed commander of the Second Corps. Warner, *Generals in Blue*, 489–490.

48. Camp California, named in honor of Sumner, was located 3 miles west of Alexandria. Pride and Travis, *Brave Boys*, 52.

49. Ship Point was located twelve miles upriver from the mouth of the York River in Virginia.

Our brigade commander[50]—as he always did—performed his duty for our comfort, and no pains were spared by the regimental officers to look out for the health of the men. To this may be attributed the fact that we had less in hospital at Ship Point than any other regiment in the brigade. In building roads and bridges the men showed their usual good qualities; so much so as to be greatly complimented by the general over us. When the siege of Yorktown opened the Fifth was sent to join the Engineers' Brigade under General Woodbury.[51] While with this brigade, we constructed two thousand five hundred gabions and a large number of fascines. The regiment also built a tower, one hundred feet high and forty feet base, of heavy timber, for an observatory at general headquarters. This labor was about completed when the enemy evacuated Yorktown.

The march of our regiment to Williamsburg was a day to be remembered. We started just at dark, in the midst of a severe rain. The road was horrible. Fifty thousand men with all their wagons and artillery had passed along that day. The track was bordered by thickets most of the way and in the center was a sea of mud, in some places absolutely knee deep. The night was pitch dark, and the whole brigade plunged along in the most wretched condition imaginable, halting toward morning in an old corn-field for rest. In a few days we marched back to Yorktown, and on the 11th of May embarked for West Point on the Pamunkey river. From this place we marched to the Chickahominy river, near the enemy. Here the regiment was at once put in fighting order.

On the 25th of May received orders to report to General Sumner with my whole regiment for fatigue duty. We marched early in the morning, and I was informed by General Sumner that the work was to build a bridge over the Chickahominy swamp and river sufficiently strong for artillery and wagons. On reaching the locality the labor seemed impossible. The swamp was flowed from one to four feet with water, and nearly half a mile wide. On the borders was the channel of the stream, some thirty yards wide and quite deep. Here a Minnesota regiment had commenced work the day before, but had been ordered away. The swamp was a mass of huge trees, vines, brushwood and wrecks of old trees and shrubbery. The labor was commenced, and with some assistance from the Sixty-fourth and Sixty-ninth New York Volunteers—small detachments—the bridge, built on piers, all of heavy logs, seventy rods long, was completed at sundown on the evening of May 30, just

50. General Oliver Otis Howard commanded the First Brigade.
51. Daniel Woodbury (1812–1864) came from New London, N.H., and had graduated from West Point in 1836. He served in the Engineer Corps before the war and commanded the Volunteer Engineers Brigade under McClellan. Warner, *Generals in Blue*, 570–571.

in time for Sumner's Corps to cross the next day in season for Sedgwick's Division[52] to check the enemy that evening. Richardson's Division did not arrive until later. How much depended upon that bridge, called the "Grapevine bridge," can now be seen. In this great labor the officers and men labored together, often in water waist deep, with slimy mud and thick brush under foot and around them. Well may it be pronounced one of the most important and arduous labors of the Peninsular campaign.

Reaching the field of battle in the evening, the Fifth was pushed ahead, and formed the advance guard and skirmish line of the army. During the night we discovered the enemy within three hundred yards of us, and took several prisoners. At daylight the commanding officer of the regiment captured a rebel courier with important dispatches. The Fifth fired the first and last shot of the great battle of June 1, and alone met and drove back a strong column of the enemy, fighting them at thirty yards' range; and although outflanked by the greatly superior numbers of the rebels, caused them to break and retire. Our loss was severe, but we had the proud satisfaction of having performed our duty without flinching, and added another enduring laurel to the military glory of our state. The colonel and major of the regiment being severely wounded, the command fell to Lieutenant-Colonel Langley.

After Fair Oaks the regiment was at once placed in the front line, constantly picketing and skirmishing; losing quite a number of men, killed and wounded, until the movement to Harrison's landing commenced. Nearly all the military property was saved or secured, and the regiment fell back with its brigade, fighting at Savage Station, Peach Orchard, White Oak swamp, Charles City and Malvern Hill—being the last regiment that marched off the battle-field. Lieutenant-Colonel Langley being sick most of the time on this march, Captain, now Major, Sturtevant had command. Being in hospital at the time, it was not my fortune to be present with the regiment during the retreat; but I have since heard good accounts from many sources of the patience, courage and excellent conduct of officers and men.

From Harrison's landing the regiment marched to Newport News, where I again assumed command and we soon after sailed to Alexandria, landed, and marched to our old locality—Camp California.

Nearly one year's active service—battles, sickness, hardship and the various incidents of warlike life, had now reduced the regiment to about three hundred and fifteen men fit for duty, and these were weary, ragged, many of them barefooted and without overcoats or blankets—only the tattered remains of their shelter tents. With only one day allowed to rest, we marched

52. John Sedgwick (1813–1864) commanded the Second Division of Sumner's Second Corps. Ibid., 430–431.

to Arlington Heights, and the next day, about 2 o'clock, received orders to march without shelter tents or blankets, as rapidly as possible, to the front to re-enforce General Pope.[53] We marched twenty-three miles without halting but once, and then laid down in a rain on the wet ground to rest. More than twenty of the men had no shoes, and their feet were blistered and bleeding. The next day we were marched to the front and formed the skirmish line in front of the enemy, which position we held without relief until the entire army moved away, when we fell back and joined the main body at Fairfax Court House, being the last regiment that left Centreville, from which place we marched the same day to within a short distance of Chain bridge, twenty-six miles, without a single straggler, even among the barefooted. This was a hard march. Many officers and men fell asleep as they walked along, and tumbled down. All were exhausted. The next day we marched across the Potomac and camped at Tennallytown, where we hoped for a few day's rest, but in vain.

By dint of hard efforts, a few shoes and some clothing were here obtained, and on the 4th of September we marched for Frederick, Md. The weather was very hot and the roads dusty. After passing through Frederick we camped near the battle-ground of South Mountain but were held in reserve during the battle. On the 15th of September Richardson's Division[54] crossed South Mountain in pursuit of the enemy. The Fifth was ordered to the front and deployed as skirmishers. In this position, we drove in the cavalry and light troops of the enemy, and discerned the rebel line of battle beyond Antietam river. In the pursuit the regiment captured sixty prisoners. We might have taken more, but I could not spare men to pursue them. All the remainder of the day and until late at night, the Fifth engaged the enemy's sharpshooters, driving them from a strong position. We were not relieved until nearly exhausted. The next day four companies were sent to fight the enemy's riflemen, and prevent their destroying an important bridge over the Antietam. Other companies were sent to destroy obstructions in the river. On the 17th, the day of the great battle, the Fifth went into the fight with three hundred rifles and nineteen commissioned officers. The regiment behaved nobly; in the language of the official report, "was entitled to the sole credit of discovering and defeating the attempt of the enemy to turn the left flank of Richardson's Division." The large state colors of the Fourth North Carolina Regiment, which we captured, are now in the war department. We remained in the field where we fought; assisted to carry off the wounded and bury the

53. General John Pope (1822–1892) and his Army of Virginia were threatened and eventually overrun by Confederate forces at the Second Battle of Bull Run. Ibid., 376–377.

54. Israel Bush Richardson commanded the First Division of the Second Corps.

dead; gathered up over four hundred rifles from the field; had no stragglers; nor did we leave behind a man able to march. Arriving at Harper's Ferry we forded the Potomac and went into camp at Bolivar Heights. My men fought in the Battle of Antietam very ragged, more than forty of them without shoes, and I was compelled to equip thirty recruits from the bodies of the slain.

On reaching Bolivar Heights, the regiment was at once placed on active duty, and we formed a portion of the advance on Hancock's[55] reconnoissance.

Great trouble has been experienced on obtaining supplies. My men have been sent out on picket, even within the past ten days, without overcoats, coats or blankets. So it has been with half of the army. At the time this report is written the regiment has just received a portion of its winter clothing, but is ready for march or battle. Men have come in from the hospital and from detached service, until three hundred can be taken into the field. I now invite your attention to a few figures in reference to the regiment.

ORIGINAL STRENGTH OF THE REGIMENT

Officers and men		1010
Recruits during the year,		146
	Total,	1156

LOSSES DURING THE YEAR

	Officers.	Enlisted men.
Killed in battle	1	40
Died of wounds received in battle,	1	20
Wounded in battle,	17	240
Missing,		16
	19	316
Total casualties in battle,		335

DEATHS

In the hospitals of the regiment during the year,	23
In other hospitals,	46
Total deaths from disease during the year,	69

55. Winfield Scott Hancock (1824–1886) was transferred to command of the First Division, Second Corps, on September 17, 1862, during the Battle of Antietam. Boatner, *Civil War Dictionary*, 372.

DISMISSED THE SERVICE

Captain Edmund Brown, Company B;[56] Captain Richard Welch, Company K;[57] Lieutenant E. W. Johnson, Company I;[58] Lieutenant J. B. David, Company K.[59] Total 4.

Resigned.—Major William A. Cook,[60] Captain R. R. Davis,[61] Chaplain E. R. Wilkins,[62] Lieutenant S. E. Twombley,[63] Lieutenant R. R. Somes,[64] Captain Thomas J. Rice,[65] Captain Ira McL. Barton,[66] Lieutenant D. G. Reed,[67] Lieutenant S. F. Varney,[68] Lieutenant M. W. Rand,[69] Captain Charles H. Long.[70] Total, 12.

Promoted during the year.—Captain E. E. Sturtevant to be major; First Lieutenant T. J. Rice to be captain; First Lieutenant R. E. Cross to be captain; First Lieutenant J. W. Keller to be captain;[71] First Lieutenant James E.

56. Edmund Brown, 40-year-old resident of Lancaster, N.H., mustered in as captain of company B, but he was discharged from service in February 1862. Child, "Complete Roster," 23.

57. Richard E. Welsh, of Plaistow, N.H., was mustered in as captain of Company K. Ibid., 192.

58. Elijah W. Johnson, of Canaan, N.H., mustered in as a 34-year-old first lieutenant in Company I in October 1861, but he was discharged the following January. Ibid., 98.

59. James B. David, a 26-year-old resident of Amherst, N.H., was mustered in on October 12, 1861, and appointed first lieutenant of Company K. Ibid., 49.

60. Cook resigned as the result of injuries received at the Battle of Fair Oaks.

61. Richard R. Davis, of Wolfeborough, N.H., was appointed captain of Company H in October 1861, but he resigned from service on July 25, 1862. Child, "Complete Roster," 50.

62. Elijah R. Wilkins, a printer, Methodist Episcopal minister, and resident of Lisbon, N.H., joined the Fifth upon it organization in the fall of 1861. He resigned as chaplain on June 18, 1862. Ibid., 195.

63. Stephen E. Twombly, from Milton, N.H., was appointed second lieutenant of Company A in October 1861, but he resigned May 10, 1862. Ibid., 186.

64. Rinaldo R. Somes, of Laconia, N.H., was a first lieutenant in Company I when he resigned in June 1862. Ibid., 170.

65. Thomas J. Rice, resident of Boston, Mass., mustered in as a first lieutenant in Company E, but he resigned his commission as captain of Company B on September 10, 1862. Ibid., 151.

66. Ira McL. Barton was a resident of Newport, N.H. Even though he was appointed captain of Company E in October 1862, Barton did not get along with Cross and resigned on September 6, 1862. Ibid., 13.

67. First Lieutenant Dexter G. Reed, of Newport, N.H., was wounded at Fair Oaks and resigned in November 1862. Ibid., 150.

68. Samuel F. Varney, of Rochester, N.H., mustered in as second lieutenant of Company D and resigned April 1862. Ibid., 187.

69. Moses W. Rand was a resident of Gorham, N.H. A first lieutenant in Company F, he resigned on April 26, 1862. Ibid., 149.

70. Captain Charles H. Long, of Claremont, N.H., was wounded at Antietam in September 1862 and resigned two months later. Ibid., 114.

71. Jacob W. Keller, resident of Claremont, N.H., was originally a first lieutenant in Company G and was promoted to captain of Company H in July 1862. Ibid., 102.

Larkin to be captain;[72] First Lieutenant W. A. Crafts to be captain; First Lieutenant W. A. Moore[73] to be captain; First Lieutenant G. W. Ballock[74] to be captain in the United States commissary department.

To be First Lieutenants.—Second Lieutenants J. W. Graves, C. O. Ballou,[75] D. G. Reed, F. W. Butler,[76] J. W. Bean, S. S. Quinn,[77] D. K. Cross, James W. Parks, J. S. Ricker,[78] W. A. Moore.—10.

Sergeants promoted to be Lieutenants.—J. W. Lawrence,[79] A. G. Cummings, Sumner F. Hurd, Thomas L. Livermore, George W. George, George W. Goodwin, Samuel B. Little, O'Neil R. Twitchell, Charles W. Bean, Charles F. Liscomb, George A. Gay, Henry B. Rendell.[80]—12.

Commissioned officers absent, wounded, sick and on detached service, 18. Enlisted men absent, wounded, sick and on detached service, 18. Enlisted men absent, wounded, sick and on detached service, 307; total, 325. Discharged for various causes during the year, 135. Dropped from the rolls by orders of the war department, for absence without leave, 51. Present for duty: Officers, 21; enlisted men, 323. Total, present and absent: Officers, 89; enlisted men, 663. Total strength during the 26th of October, 1862, 707. Total strength during the year, officers and men, 1156. Total losses by death, discharged, dismissed, desertion, etc., etc., including the band (21) mustered out during the year ending October 26, 1862, 449.

I have thus presented you a narrative of my regiment for its first year.

72. James E. Larkin of Concord, N.H., was appointed first lieutenant of Company A October 12, 1861. He went on to serve as captain of Company A, major, and lieutenant colonel and was discharged October 12, 1864. Ibid., 108.

73. William A. Moore mustered in as a twenty-year-old second lieutenant in Company C. He was appointed first lieutenant in Company E prior to his promotion as captain of Company H. Moore was killed at Fredericksburg on December 13, 1862. Ibid., 130.

74. George W. Ballock came from Claremont, N.H., and had been appointed first lieutenant of Company D. He left in July 1862 to accept a commission in the Commissary Department. Ibid., 12.

75. Charles O. Ballou, of Claremont, N.H., was promoted from second lieutenant of Company G to first lieutenant of Company K in February 1862. Ibid., 12.

76. Francis W. Butler, of Bennington, N.H., served as second lieutenant of Company K prior to his promotion to first lieutenant of Company I. He later returned to Company K as captain. Ibid., 28.

77. Samuel S. Quinn, of Swanzey, N.H., mustered in as 21-year-old second lieutenant in Company F. He was promoted to first lieutenant of Company D in August 1862. He was appointed captain in December, but he was never mustered in at that rank prior to his resignation in February 1863. Ibid., 148.

78. John S. Ricker, then sergeant in Company D. Ibid., 153.

79. John W. Lawrence, of Claremont, N.H., mustered in as a sergeant of Company E and was appointed second lieutenant of Company C. He resigned October 1862. Ibid., 109.

80. Henry B. Rendel, resident of Wolfeborough, N.H., enlisted as first sergeant of Company H. He was promoted to second lieutenant in February 1862, but he resigned September 1862. Ibid., 151.

I have no hesitation in saying it has had fewer recruits, performed more labor and made more severe marches, than any other regiment from the state, in the same time, and, to say the least, has fought as well. In whatever position placed, in battle or in march, enduring hunger, cold or heat, the regiment has never faltered, never failed to do its duty. A sense of obligation to my officers and men for their patience, courage and fortitude, constrains me to bear this testimony to their worth and their character as brave soldiers. It is my earnest wish that those who are left of us may live to see the skies of our country no longer darkened with the clouds of war, but radiant and glorious in the sunshine of peace; and I can but feel confident that our native state will honor and cherish the names of those gallant soldiers who have so nobly sustained her military renown.

I am, very truly,

Edward E. Cross,

Col. 5th N. H. V.

To Hon. N. S. Berry,
Governor of New Hampshire

PUBLISHED REPORT OF THE BATTLE OF FREDERICKSBURG, DECEMBER 15, 1862[81]

♣ ♣ ♣ ♣ ♣

The men held their ground and endeavored to whip the enemy, instead of skulking or shamefully leaving the field, as many of the new regiments did.

No. 58.
Report of Col. Edward E. Cross, Fifth New Hampshire Infantry.

HOSPITAL NEAR FREDERICKSBURG, VA.,
December 15, 1862.

CAPTAIN: In reference to the part taken by my regiment at the Battle of Fredericksburg, on the 13th instant, I have the honor to report that my regiment formed the extreme right of Caldwell's brigade[82] in the third line. It marched to its place in the order of battle under a severe fire of round shot and shell;

---

81. OR, vol. XXI, 234–235.

82. John Caldwell (1833–1912) took command of the First Brigade, First Division, of the Second Corps on June 4, 1862, and would remain with the Second Corps until March 1864. Warner, *Generals in Blue*, 63–64.

remained in line some moments, when orders came to move forward to the attack. My regiment started slightly in advance of the rest of the brigade, and almost instantly encountered a storm of shell, canister, and rifle balls. No man faltered or straggled. We were moving rapidly and steadily on, when I was unfortunately disabled by the explosion of a shell directly in front of me. Major Sturtevant immediately took command, but soon fell, and is supposed to be killed. By this time the regiment had reached a position as near the rifle-pits of the enemy as it was possible to get, owing to the squads and groups of troops (mostly new regiments) in very disorderly condition, who were firing wildly at the enemy. My officers endeavored to form line of battle in such manner as to move forward and carry the enemy's rifle-pits; the rest of the brigade endeavored to accomplish the same result, but were unable to do so, owing to the confusion and the terrible fire of the enemy. My regiment advanced farther than any regiment of the division, and held its place as long as there was any organization left. When all my officers were disabled but 3, not more than 30 men for duty, and they completely out of ammunition, orders came to withdraw. Capt. James E. Larkin brought off all that were left who were able to walk.

The regiment went into action with 247 bayonets and 19 commissioned officers. Its loss was as follows: Commissioned officers — killed, 4; wounded, 12; missing, 1 (Maj. E. E. Sturtevant). Enlisted men — killed, 15; wounded, 142; missing, 12; making a total of 186 men killed, wounded, and missing.[*][83]

Allow me to state here the reason why the loss of my regiment was so heavy was, the men held their ground and endeavored to whip the enemy, instead of skulking or shamefully leaving the field, as many of the new regiments did.

In regard to Major Sturtevant, he was seen badly wounded; his body cannot be found. It is supposed that he died on the field. He was a brave and faithful officer, and his loss is greatly regretted by the regiment.

Captains Murray, Perry, Moore, and Lieutenant Ballou, who were killed while bravely encouraging their men, were among the best officers in the service. Captain Perry was shot with the colors of the regiment in his hand. Captain Murray fell dead in the front rank. Captain Moore was first shot in the arm, and soon afterward received a mortal wound. The other officers present were Captains Pierce, Larkin, Keller, and Crafts; First Lieutenants Graves, Cummings, and Bean, and Second Lieutenants Goodwin, Liscomb, Sanborn,[84] and Nettleton. All were wounded except Captains Pierce and

---

83. List of casualties not included.

84. Augustus D. Sanborn, of Franklin, N.H., mustered in as a corporal in Company E. He was appointed sergeant of Company E in October 1861, second lieutenant of Company H in October 1862, and first lieutenant of Company B in December. Child, "Complete Roster," 158.

Larkin and Lieutenant Sanborn, and all behaved with prudence and bravery. Justice to the dead, the wounded, and the few unscathed of my regiment constrains me to express the opinion that no soldiers on any battle-field ever exhibited greater bravery or devotion.

At the time of writing this report I have 3 officers and 63 enlisted men for duty. They are in their places in line of battle, and I greatly regret that I am not able to be with them.

I herewith inclose a list* of the killed, wounded, and missing of my regiment.

> Very respectfully,
> EDWARD E. CROSS,
> Colonel Fifth New Hampshire Volunteers.

Capt. GEORGE H. CALDWELL,
   Assistant Adjutant-General

---

* But see revised statement, p. 129.[85]

MANUSCRIPT REPORT OF CHANCELLORSVILLE CAMPAIGN (MAY OR JUNE 1863?)[86]

♣ ♣ ♣ ♣ ♣

Hooker has not the amount of brains *necessary to manage a vast army.*

Hooker's Campaign

On the 27th of April, after more than five months of inaction, the main body of infantry comprising Gen. Hooker's[87] Grand Army commenced its movement. Great preparations had been made. No army in the world was better armed, clothed or equipped. The force consisted of 150,000 men with not less than 300 pieces of artillery, Pontoon trains; Engineers, Battalion ambulance trains, wagons and pack mules were in the greatest abundance. All the vast resources of the nation—intellect, money, skill and everything which could be suggested to make an army strong, and confident, was lavished without stint. All through the winter drills, reviews, Schools and Mili-

85. Not attached.
86. Edward E. Cross Papers, Milne Special Collections and Archives, University of New Hampshire, Durham, N.H.
87. Major General Joseph Hooker, then commander of the Army of the Potomac.

tary ~~Boards~~ had been kept up. The discipline of the troops & their general bearing was excellent. No one can dispute this.

The plan, evidently, was to make a strong feint on the enemy's left, & then to attack on the centre and right. The 1st 6th ~~3d~~ & a part of the 2d Corps remained to make the feint and centre attack while the 5th, 11th ~~3d~~ 3d & 2d Corps & a very large force of cavalry moved up the river to cross at Banks Ford, United States Ford & Kelley's Ford.[88]

The 2d Corps, with the exception of Gen Gibbons Division[89]—marched out of camp about sunrise on the of the 2~~7~~8th—the troops appearing in fine spirits. I am sure that the 5th Reg't was never in better fighting condition. Each man carried five day's rations of sugar, coffee bread & salt, in his knapsack, and three days full rations in haversacks. The weight of the knapsacks averaged about 23 pounds. 60 rounds of ammunition was carried by *each* man. No wagons or tents were taken by Regts.

About 4 miles from ~~the~~ camp the Corps halted. I was sent out with my own Regt & the 81st Pa to picket houses and roads to United States ford, in order to prevent information going to the enemy. In this way, we kept up a constant communication from Gibbons Division to United States Ford—about 8 miles. My command after a severe march in the rain, finished its position. My Reg't occupied 27 dwelling houses, Col McKean's Reg't[90] 14 houses & some roads. We found the people very generally full of smothered rebellion, but ~~very~~ quite Civil. The 5th, 11th, & 12th Corps in the meantime pushed on. The 2d Corps sent out heavy details to open and repair roads.

I remained with my command until the afternoon of the 30th when I received orders to move on after the Division which had crossed the rivers, and guard the corps supply trains and ambulances. The day before, two men came into my lines, saying they were spies of Gen Hooker. They stated that they had just come from the other side of the river—that the enemy were fully informed of our movements, & prepared for us; they also stated that Gen Hooker would find himself in a "tight place"—that no fight would be made until we were five or six miles from the river, and then Stuart[91] would try to cut us off. These statements proved true.

I reached the wagon in the evening & was joined by the 88th ~~66th~~ New

88. Kelly's Ford.

89. John Gibbon (1827–1896), once commander of the Iron Brigade, rose to command of the Second Division of First Corps. After recovering from wounds received at Fredericksburg, he was transferred to command of the Second Division of Hancock's Second Corps. Warner, *Generals in Blue*, 171–172.

90. Henry Boyd McKeen was colonel of the Eighty-first Pennsylvania. Walker, *Second Corps*, 144, 172.

91. Confederate general James Ewell Brown ("Jeb") Stuart.

York—a portion of the Irish Brigade.[92] I found the corps had moved on across the river, so my command bivouacked. At 9 o'clock next day, May 1 I started, crossed the river and made the best of the way to the front. The road was very bad—mostly through woods, & blocked by trains and artillery. About ~~4~~ 12 o'clock fighting commenced, & increased until 3 when it ~~stack~~ slackened. My command arrived on the ground about 4 o'clock—just as orders were given to the reserve artillery to move back and cover Banks ford. We found Hancock's position was in the front line, & were at once [illegible] to join him. After considerable marching we halted to get supper & instantly after marched up to a road leading from Gen Hooker's headquarters to Fredericksburg, & placed in order of battle. General Geary's Division[93] on my right had just repulsed a strong attack of the enemy.

I formed my line with the 88th on my right 81st in the centre & 5th NH on the left. The enemy soon opened a complete enfilading fire on us, but fired too high. About 2 o'clock in the morning orders came to move, we marched about 800 yards to the right into an open field fronting a piece of forest, & again formed line of battle—this time the 5th NH on my right. Our line then was as follows

Hill occupied by the enemy

Woods   woods   woods

. . . . .

edge of the woods   federal pickets

open field, undulating

145th 6120—
Gen Caldwell   *66th*

55th / 5100 / 55th
Col Hou

Gen Hancock ordered me to draw

---

92. Cross was given command of a temporary brigade in the First Division during the Chancellorsville campaign and reported to Winfield Scott Hancock. This Fifth Brigade consisted of the Fifth New Hampshire, Eighty-first Pennsylvania, and Eighty-eighth New York. And Lieutenant Charles Hapgood commanded the Fifth. Pride and Travis, *My Brave Boys*, 205, and Stephen W. Sears, *Chancellorsville* (Boston and New York: Houghton-Mifflin, 1996), 455.

93. John White Geary (1819–1873) was appointed brigadier general in April 1862 for his distinguished service. He became commander of the Second Division of the Twelfth Corps shortly before the Battle of Chancellorsville. Warner, *Generals in Blue*, 169–170.

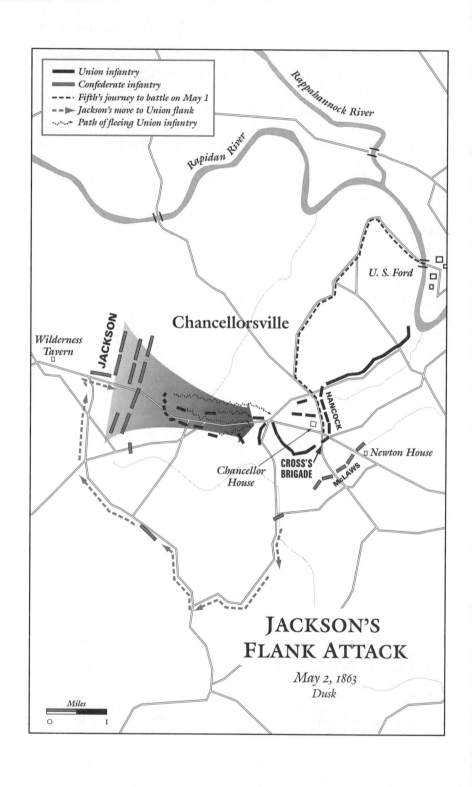

Union infantry
Confederate infantry
Fifth's journey to battle on May 1
Jackson's move to Union flank
Path of fleeing Union infantry

Rappahannock River

Rapidan River

U. S. Ford

Chancellorsville

JACKSON

Wilderness
Tavern

HANCOCK

Newton House

Chancellor
House

CROSS'S
BRIGADE

McLAWS

JACKSON'S
FLANK ATTACK

May 2, 1863
Dusk

Miles

O   I

Gen Hancock ordered me to throw up a rifle pit and sent me 89 shovels and 50 picks and one dozen axes—for about 1000 ~~600~~ men to work with. However, we went to work in earnest and completed our fortification in just 40 minutes by the watch! We were scarcely done when the rebel batteries opened, throwing shell, solid shot, iron wedges, and bundles of rasps! Several balls passed through our breastworks and two men were ~~badly~~ wounded.

The day wore away with occasional shelling, until about 3 o'clock when Williams Division[94] of Slocums Corps[95] pressed into the woods in good style, but was soon driven out in disorder. Gen Slocum sat on his horse near where I was standing and as some of the green troops came out, broken & scared, Slocum turned to an aid & said—"for God's sake send in some three year troops!". So the 7th Ohio & 28th Pa vols of Geary's command was sent in. They remained until ordered out. The rebels followed but were checked by our artillery.

About five o'clock a furious attack was made on the 11th Corps (formerly Siegels) ~~by~~ commanded by Maj Gen Howard.[96] Now occurred one of the most disgraceful scenes of the war. The 11th Corps made only a feeble resistance—broke, and officers and men ran shamefully. A perfect panic took place and thousands of fugitives came back on my lines. I ordered my men to fix bayonets and drive them back, & we did stop & turn back more than 1000 officers, & men. Still, a vast number escaped into the woods. The shells of the enemy at this time came in from front and rear. At this moment the enemy attacked my pickets very briskly, but were driven off. So I had the rebels on my front and the rebels and our stragglers on my rear. The cowardice of the German troops was ludicrous. They hid in the woods—forced their way into our rifle pit. In fact, they seemed half scared to death.

94. Alpheus S. Williams (1810–1878) was appointed brigadier general in August 1861 and served in John Pope's Army of Virginia. After the death of J. K. F. Mansfield, he commanded the Twelfth Corps briefly at the Battle of Antietam. He later commanded the First Division of the Twelfth Corps. Ibid., 559–60, and Sears, *Chancellorsville*, 464.

95. Henry W. Slocum (1827–1894) in May 1861 was colonel of the Twenty-seventh New York and served in the Sixth Corps under William B. Franklin. He was promoted to brigadier general in August 1861 and then major general in July 1862. He commanded of the Twelfth Corps after the Battle of Antietam. Warner, *Generals in Blue*, 451–453, 559–560; Sears, *Chancellorsville*, 464.

96. Franz Sigel (1824–1902) had been commissioned brigadier general in August 1861 and was promoted to major general in March 1862. He replaced John C. Frémont as commander of the First Corps of John Pope's Army of Virginia. After the Army of Virginia was incorporated into the Army of the Potomac, he commanded the new Eleventh Corps but resigned for health reasons in February 1863. Howard had commanded the Second Division of the Second Corps at the Battle of Antietam. He was promoted to major general in November 1862 and appointed as commander of the Eleventh Corps at the end of March 1863. Warner, *Generals in Blue*, 237, 447–448; Boatner, *Civil War Dictionary*, 761.

I have no hesitation in saying that had our line broke at that time the army would have been ruined! The commander of Knapps battery[97] came to me and said "what are you going to do?" "*Stay here, Sir,*" said I ~~told him~~. "Then I'll stay with you," said he. I tied my red silk handkerchief around my head & went along my lines, exhorting every man to stand firm, & the men answered with loud cheers, which had the effect to shame some of the fugitives & ~~then~~ & they halted. Sickles Corps[98]—the 3d checked the rebels & held them though they several times attacked fiercely during the night, which was one of constant alarms. During the night Reynolds Corps[99] came up & occupied a position to hold our right & prevent the enemy turning our right flank.

Early Sunday morning the rebels attacked fiercely front flank & rear— for about two hours the fighting was desperate but they slowly drove our men slowly back. French's Division of the 2d Corps & Caldwells Brigade & Brooke[100] fought nobly, driving back the rebels in disorder, until the latter came on in overwhelming numbers. While the battle in the rear was going on we had constant attacks on our front & flank. Several times we were taken out of our rifle pit to reinforce weak points in our line, & marched over the field under fire. The Brigade was perfectly cool and steady.

Our forces were now falling back along the whole line, & the rebels came on shouting furiously. My command was again ordered from its position; We faced by the rear rank, and marched back some 200 yards to the crest of a little hill. Geary's Division was now on my left ~~right~~ flank, engaged with the enemy, & in my front was two brass batteries & Petits [illegible] bat-

97. This was likely Captain Joseph E. Knap. Knap was commanding two companies, E and F, of the Pennsylvania Light Artillery in the Second Division of the Twelfth Corps. Sears, *Chancellorsville*, 239, 465.

98. Daniel E. Sickles (1819–1914) received his commission as brigadier general in September 1861 and major general in November 1862. After serving in brigade command in the Third Corps in the Peninsula campaign, he commanded the Second Division, Third Corps, at Fredericksburg. He then succeeded Hooker in the command of Third Corps. Warner, *Generals in Blue*, 446–447.

99. John F. Reynolds (1820–1863) was appointed brigadier general in August 1861 and served under Fitz-John Porter in the Fifth Corps during the Peninsula campaign until his capture by Confederates. He returned to the Army of the Potomac as commander of the First Corps after commanding Pennsylvania militia during the Antietam campaign. He was promoted to major general in November 1862. Ibid., 396–397.

100. John R. Brooke (1838–1926) was appointed colonel of the Fifty-third Pennsylvania in November 1861 and commanded the Third Brigade, First Division, Second Corps, during the Battle of Antietam. He commanded the Fourth Brigade, First Division, under Winfield Scott Hancock at Chancellorsville. Boatner, *Civil War Dictionary*, 88, Sears, *Landscape Turned Red*, 361, and Sears, *Chancellorsville*, 455.

tery[101] of ten pd Parrotts all firing rapidly except one Brass battery which was badly officered. The rebels deployed from the woods in a line of double columns closed in mass. They halted, fronted & commenced to deploy but were driven back by a severe fire of grape & shell. I sighted one gun after helping shove it to the front. In a few moments the enemy got a splendid rifle battery into position, which fired with wonderful accuracy. So heavy was the fire that Capt Petit was compelled for the first time during the war to limber up & leave—but was instantly ordered back. For about 40 minutes my command was under the heaviest fire it ever experienced. Every instant some one in each Regt was hit. The air seemed full of bursting shell. From our rear from the left from the front came a storm of missiles. Three times I sent Lieut Fay[102] to tell Gen Hancock that our left was defeated. Geary's Division, being whipped out, was retreating in disorder. All the others had gone, and our situation was perilous in the extreme. The artillery limbered up & ran away, and not until a heavy line of the enemy, cheering and firing as it came on was within 300 yards of my flank and already engaged with the 5th Reg't did orders come to fall back. We faced to the right & marched off—but the fire of the enemy from three directions made a slight confusion, but only for an instant. We marched steadily after reaching the woods, though our ranks thinned and shattered by grape, canister & rifle balls. Had we delayed *five* minutes more we should have been taken prisoners or cut to pieces.

I do not understand why Geary was not supported or reinforced. The day was not lost if fresh troops & artillery and been thrown in. I had no idea that a retreat had been ordered. While lying under that awful fire my belief was that a fresh division & some artillery would soon be sent to aid us, & I so stated to our men. The enemy might have been greatly injured if not entirely checked by a little vigorous action.

The conduct of Maj Gen Couch[103] was splendid. Both he and Gen Hancock remained until the batteries limbered up. Gen Couch was slightly wounded and Gen Hancock's horse killed.

101. Rufus D. Pettit was captain of Company B of the First New York Light Artillery and also commanded the artillery unit of the First Division, Second Corps. Sears, *Chancellorsville*, 363, 455.

102. Joseph B. Fay, of Amherst, N.H., mustered in as a sergeant. He was promoted to second lieutenant of Company F in March 1862 and to first lieutenant on July 3, 1863. He would be wounded during the Battle of Chancellorsville. Child, "Complete Roster," 63.

103. Darius Couch (1822–1897) was appointed brigadier general in August 1861 and major general in July 1862. He commanded a division in the Fourth Corps in the Peninsula campaign. He served in the Second Corps after his promotion, eventually commanding the Second Corps from Fredericksburg until his resignation after the Battle of Chancellorsville. Warner, *Generals in Blue*, 95–96.

We might, in my opinion have fallen back on the Fredericksburg road and connected with Sedgwick. The 2d Corps formed near the front line to cover the retreat of the army, & only fell back about half a mile. The other corps were previously in position—showing that a retreat had been ordered early in the day—our position was now as follows:

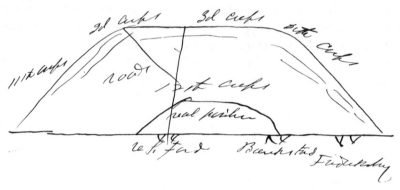

Such was the position but not so far down the river. We only held from ~~to~~ US ford to Banks [Ford]—I have only made the circle large to show the position of the troops. We had barely formed line when the artillery of the enemy opened upon us—throwing shell or shrapnel—doing great damage. Men sent for water were knocked over, & the trees stripped of their limbs over our heads. Our position was too strong, however to be successfully assailed by infantry. The instant shelling ceased, we commenced to throw up field works along the entire line, & by dark we were well situated.

From this time until orders came to fall back we were in constant alarms —picket firing and shelling every ~~short~~ few hours. The enemy had excellent range, but fired to high for the front line. The reserves, however, in the woods back were greatly injured. Several ~~strong~~ attacks were made at different points but in each case beaten off. About midnight of the 6th orders came to move. We did not get away until 4 oclock, but where once ~~in~~ on the move pushed rapidly along. The mud was half leg deep most of the way. All along the forest which extended about 4 miles to the river were columns of troops looking dirty, fatigued and anxious.

Let me here record that on the afternoon of the 6th, during a furious shelling Brig Gen T. F. Meagher lay among the enlisted men of Company G of my regiment—evidently badly scared. As soon as the firing ceased, he ran as fast as possible to the left rear where he had a private fortification constructed.

Thousands of troops were massed at the bridges over the Rappahannock. We crossed and marched the same night to our old camp—weary, sad and almost [illegible]. Our guard had failed. Gen Hooker was completely—his magnificent army badly handled—his artillery not massed—not half of it used and could not be, on account of the woods. The 9 mos & two years troops whose time drew near a close could not be made to stand fire. They wavered, broke—in some cases threw away their arms, in all cases the stragglers told the old stories—that they were "all cut to pieces![") The amount of straggling was fearful, especially in the 11th & 12th Corps.

My own Reg't lost 27 in all, Maj Cross was badly wounded—My Brigade lost about 200.

Hooker has not the amount of *brains* necessary to manage a vast army. In generalship we fall far behind the rebels, & since McClellan left the Army of the Potomac, its organization has been extremely defective. Hookers popularity lay chiefly in the soft bread, potatoes & onions he issued. The army never believed him to be a great commander—never. His failure was predicted by thousands of officers & soldiers—from the first day he started.

I have endeavored in the above narrative to state only *facts*, with as few opinions as possible.

> E. E. Cross
> Col 5th NHV

MANUSCRIPT NOTES OF CHANCELLORSVILLE CAMPAIGN (MAY OR JUNE 1863?)[104]

♣ ♣ ♣ ♣ ♣

The women—terrified

The burning house Gen. Hooker's headquarters—the wounded in the woods. The flames bursting from the roof. The wounded in the yard. The women—terrified

---

Failure of the Gov't to reinforce Sedgwick with 25000 men as might have been done, & thereby held Fredericksburg & greatly assisted Gen Hooker.

Gen Heintzelman[105] mustered in & around Washington not less than 80,000 men at muster for payment on the 1st of May.

Idle until the enemy repaired all the damages in their rear

104. Edward E. Cross Papers, Milne Special Collections and Archives, University of New Hampshire, Durham, N.H.

105. Samuel P. Heintzelman (1805–1880) graduated from West Point in 1826 and served with distinction in the Mexican War. During the Civil War, Heintzelman proved ineffective as a division and corps commander. After the Second Bull Run campaign he became commander of a portion of the defenses of Washington. Warner, *Generals in Blue*, 227–228.

Part Three

Civil War Letters of
Colonel Edward E. Cross

LETTER TO HENRY KENT, JULY 3, 1861[1]

Have written to the Governor offering myself for any position but prefer mounted service.

San Francisco July 3, 1861

Dear Kent,[2]

I came to this city a few days since *en route* for the "old country." The Apaches, since the withdrawal of the "regulars" have driven us out of Arizona causing me a loss of over ten thousand dollars.

1. Courtesy of M. Faith Kent.

2. Henry O. Kent (1834–1909), of Lancaster, N.H., was Cross's best friend. He owned and edited the local newspaper, the *Coös Republican*, and represented Lancaster in the state legislature. Kent attended Norwich University, a military school in Vermont, yet his Civil War career was less illustrious than that of his friend. In the fall of 1862, Kent became colonel of the Seventeenth New Hampshire Regiment. However, the adjutant general drew from its ranks to strengthen other New Hampshire regiments. In April 1863, Kent transferred remaining volunteers to the Second New Hampshire Regiment, and the Seventeenth ceased to exist. See *Granite State Monthly* 16 (April 1909): 144–145 and Charles N. Kent, *History of the Seventeenth Regiment; New Hampshire Volunteer Infantry, 1862–1863* (Concord, N.H.: Rumford Press, 1898).

I am ready for the wars—have been offered a captaincy in a regiment of Mounted Rifles in this state but declined. Have written to the Governor[3] offering myself for any position but prefer mounted service with which I am familiar as three years of Indian fighting has made me a tolerable partisan officer. Should like to raise a squadron of dragoons from old Coos. Be kind enough to keep the matter secret, but if you can do anything with the Governor, I will thank you.

Shall leave on the next steamer for New York & be in Lancaster by August 12th, if nothing happens. You may say I am coming but not for what end.

Hoping to see you soon, I am

Yours truly,
Edward E. Cross

LETTER TO HENRY KENT, SEPTEMBER 15, 1861[4]

♣ ♣ ♣ ♣ ♣

It is generally conceded that the Fifth is the best organized, officered & equipped Regiment yet raised in this State.

Headquarters 5th Infantry
Concord, Sept. 15, 1861

Dear Kent:

Everything goes on first rate with the 5th. Over 650 are reported. What regiment was ever raised so soon in this State? Every article of equipment is under contract. I shall start the camp at once and order in the men.

My Lieut. Col. is Edward J. Conner,[5] a citizen of N. H. graduated high at West Point, has had 4 years active service on the plains. Is a gallant, accomplished officer. Major—William W. Cook,[6] of Derry. Excellent officer, in every respect a thorough soldier.

Quartermaster Lieut. Webber[7] from Fort Constitution, first rate man.

3. Nathaniel S. Berry (1796–1894), governor of New Hampshire from 1861 to 1862.
4. Courtesy of M. Faith Kent.
5. Edward J. Conner, of Exeter, N.H., never served in the Fifth New Hampshire. He remained in the U.S. Army, rising to the rank of captain prior to his retirement in December 1863. *Soldiers and Sailors of New Hampshire*, 1039.
6. William W. Cook, of Derry, N.H., was mustered in as major on October 26, 1861. Wounded at the Battle of Fair Oaks on June 1, 1862, he resigned from the service the following month. Child, "Complete Roster," 42.
7. Edmund M. Webber, a 40-year-old resident of Somersworth, N.H., was appointed quartermaster in September 1861 and served in that capacity until his discharge in October 1864. He died in Somersworth in April 1891. Ibid., 191.

Captains
Rockingham County
  Richard Welch,[8] of Plaistow
  Experienced officer
Hillsborough
  Charles E. Hapgood[9] of Amherst
Merrimack
  Edward E. Sturtevant,[10] of Concord
  Late Captain 1st Rg't
Strafford
  John Murry,[11] of Great Falls
  Served with credit in the Mexican War
Sullivan
  Charles H. Long,[12] of Claremont
  Graduate of Norwich Mil. Academy
Belknap
  E. W. Johnson[13]
  Graduate of Norwich Mil. Academy
Cheshire
  H. T. H. Pierce[14] of Keene
  Late 1st Lieut in the 1st Rgt

8. Richard E. Welsh enlisted as a 45-year-old resident of Plaistow, N.H. Welsh was mustered in and appointed captain of Company K, but he was discharged the following February. He later served in Company L of the First New Hampshire Heavy Artillery. Ibid., 192.

9. Charles E. Hapgood, a 30-year-old resident of Amherst, N.H., served as captain of Company I. He was appointed lieutenant colonel on December 14, 1862, and assumed command of the regiment on July 3, 1863, the day Cross died. Wounded at the Battle of Cold Harbor in June 1864, Hapgood was discharged the following October. Ibid., 82, and Secomb, *History of Amherst*, 889.

10. Edward E. Sturtevant mustered in as a 33-year-old resident of Concord, N.H. He was captain of Company I prior to his promotion to major in July 1862. He died at Fredericksburg on December 13, 1862. Child, "Complete Roster," 175.

11. John Murray, a 37-year-old native of New York, was listed as a resident of New Castle rather than Great Falls (later Somersworth), N.H. He served as captain of Company D of the Fifth from October 12, 1861, until his death at Fredericksburg on December 13, 1862. Ibid., 134.

12. Charles H. Long, 28-year-old resident of Claremont, N.H., was appointed captain of Company G. Wounded at Antietam on September 17, 1862, Long resigned his commission in November 1862. Ibid., 114.

13. Elijah W. Johnson, of Canaan, N.H., was mustered in as a 34-year-old first lieutenant in Company I in October 1861, but he was discharged the following January. He later joined the Eleventh New Hampshire at the rank of private. Ibid., 98, and *Soldiers and Sailors of New Hampshire*, 577.

14. Horace T. H. Pierce was a 37-year-old resident of Keene, N.H., when appointed captain of Company F. Cross later accused Pierce of tardiness in organizing a detail for guard duty and

Carroll
  R. K. Davis[15] of Wolfeboro
  Excellent officer
Coos
  Edmond Brown,[16] Lancaster
Grafton
  James B. Perry, of Hanover[17]
Four of the 1st Lieutenants are graduates of Norwich.[18] Mr. Richard E. Cross,[19] of this town now in the Engineer Corps, United States Army, as sergeant, will be a lieutenant. It is generally conceded that the Fifth is the best organized, officered & equipped Regiment yet raised in this State. The camp will be near Concord, & the Regiment will leave in 20 days. The 6th Regiment will be immediately called out.

Captain Ira Barton[20] of Newport, Sullivan County has received permission from the War Department to raise a battery of Light Artillery. He has already 40 men recruited.

Don't publish this letter. Extract what you want. Send me a paper to the Phoenix[21]

[no signature]

---

asked for his resignation; Pierce complied on January 29, 1863. Child, "Complete Roster," 145, and Pride and Travis, *Brave Boys*, 158.

15. Richard R. Davis, 37-year-old resident of Wolfeborough, N.H., was appointed captain of Company H in October 1861. He resigned from service on July 25, 1862, and returned to Wolfeborough, where he died in 1885. Child, "Complete Roster," 50.

16. Edmund Brown, 40-year-old resident of Lancaster, N.H., mustered in as captain of company B, but he was discharged from service in February 1862. Ibid., 23.

17. James B. Perry was born in Cabot, Vt. He mustered into service as a 27-year-old captain assigned to Company C and served in that capacity until his death at Fredericksburg in December 1862. *Soldiers and Sailors of New Hampshire*, 260.

18. Norwich University, then located in Norwich, Vt. It was the first private military college established in the United States. See Brian W. Smith, *Norwich University* (Louisville, Ky.: Harmony House, 1995).

19. Richard E. "Dick" Cross (1824–1894), younger brother of Edward Cross, was appointed first lieutenant in Company H in October 1861. He later rose to the rank of captain in Company K, major, and lieutenant colonel. Child, "Complete Roster," 45, and Pride and Travis, *Brave Boys*, 264–265.

20. Ira McL. Barton was a 22-year-old resident of Newport, N.H., at the time of enlistment. He became captain of Company E in October 1862. Barton resigned from the Fifth on September 6, 1862. He later joined the Second Company, New Hampshire Heavy Artillery, as a captain and rose to the rank of lieutenant colonel. Child, "Complete Roster," 13, and *Soldiers and Sailors of New Hampshire*, 914.

21. The Phenix Hotel was located on Main Street next to Concord's stage depot. *History of Concord*, vol. II, 859.

LETTER TO JOSEPH FOSTER, PORTSMOUTH, N.H., SEPTEMBER 27, 1861[22]

I want rank and file more than officers.

Concord Sept 27, 1861
Mr Joseph Foster[23]
Portsmouth

Dear Sir

Your letter received. I want rank and file more than officers.

I can only appoint good competent men who bring from 20 to 30 ~~men~~ soldiers.

Yours truly
Edward E Cross
Col 5th

LETTER TO NATHANIEL S. BERRY, GOVERNOR OF NEW HAMPSHIRE, OCTOBER 17, 1861[24]

I have 15 more men coming to-morrow.

Camp Jackson[25]
Oct 17 1861

Gov Berry

Captain Davis[26] wishes to make a statement in reference to six men en-

22. Spaulding-Foster Family Papers, Milne Special Collections and Archives, University of New Hampshire, Durham, N.H.

23. Joseph Foster, IV (1841–1930), a resident of Portsmouth, N.H., was a clerk for the firm of Edward F. Sise. In October 1862, Foster entered the U.S. Navy as a captain's clerk on the USS *Acacia*, thus embarking on a long and distinguished naval career. *Soldiers and Sailors of New Hampshire*, 1122.

24. Executive Records, Division of Records Management and Archives, Concord, N.H.

25. Camp Jackson, named after President Andrew Jackson, was located on Glover's Hill across the lower bridge from Concord, N.H. *History of Concord*, vol. II, 1175.

26. Richard R. Davis, captain of Company H.

listed for his company, who are detained against their will. It is only a specimen of several such cases. I have 15 more men coming to-morrow.

Edward Cross
Col 5th

LETTER TO GOVERNOR NATHANIEL S. BERRY, NOVEMBER 11, 1861[27]

♣ ♣ ♣ ♣ ♣

The Enfield Rifles I am pained to say, are a swindle.

Headquarters 5th NHV
Camp Casey[28]
Nov 11 1861

Governor

My Regiment had a very hard time on the expedition to Marlborough,[29] marching 4 days in the rain & mud, & sleeping without tents. It was [illegible] hard for the first trial, but the men did nobly, & we received the written thanks of the General.[30]

I am greatly in need of the articles called for in my requisition & beg that they be sent at once. I ~~lose~~ lost 7 blankets on the march, also some canteens.

The Enfield Rifles[31] I am pained to say, are a swindle. They are very poorly made & of bad iron. The locks break, the ramirons bend & the bayonets are brittle as sealing wax. I have reported them to the Government. Besides, I do not believe they were ever proved. Do not buy any more of them.

My Regiment improves every day. We have 5 hours daily drill, & evening school.

27. Executive Records, Division of Records Management and Archives, Concord, N.H.

28. Camp Casey was located outside of Bladensburg, Prince George's County, Md., east of Washington, D.C. It was named after Brigadier General Silas Casey, the brigade commander. Child, *Fifth New Hampshire*, 27–29.

29. The county seat of Prince George's County, Md.

30. Likely Brigadier General Silas Casey (1807–1882), a West Point graduate and native of East Greenwich, R.I. *Encyclopedia of the Civil War*, 118–119.

31. Enfield rifles were patterned after the regulation British Enfield-made rifle musket. Because it wished to remain neutral during the war, the British government refused to sell weapons manufactured at the Royal Small Arms Factory in Enfield to either side. Those used during the Civil War were manufactured by private contractors in London and Birmingham. Unfortunately, poor-quality finishing and the fact that parts were not interchangeable from one Enfield model rifle to the next led to numerous complaints. Ibid., 243–244.

The first day to Marlborough we marched 18 miles, the second 27. Coming home we were two & one half days. The small force of secessionists did not stay to fight. With my remembrance to Tenny[32] & the Hon Council[33]

> I am very truly
> Edward E. Cross
> Col 5th Reg't

LETTER TO HENRY KENT, NOVEMBER 24, 1861[34]

I want 50 good men to fill some vacancies and for extras.

Camp Casey
Nov 24, 1861

Dear Kent,

I thank you for your papers. All the Coos men read them with much interest. Crafts[35] is home on recruiting service. I want 50 good men to fill some vacancies and for extras. If you can conscientiously say a few words for us, pray do so.

I believe we stand A1 hereabouts. Frank Heywood[36] is very sick. I sent you a poor picture taken in Washington. My remembrance to Mrs. K. Where's Tenney?[37]

> Yours truly,
> Edward E. Cross
> Col

32. New Hampshire Secretary of State Allen Tenney.

33. In the State of New Hampshire five executive councilors are elected "for advising the governor in the executive part of government." State of New Hampshire, *Manual for the General Court*, 78.

34. Courtesy of M. Faith Kent.

35. Welcome A. Crafts, a 26-year-old volunteer from Milan, N.H., was mustered in as a first lieutenant in October 1861. By the end of the war, Crafts rose to the rank of colonel, although he was mustered out at the rank of lieutenant colonel. Child, "Complete Roster," 44.

36. Francis Heywood was a native of Guildhall, Vt. He was 22 years old and a resident of Lancaster, N.H., when he volunteered for service. The roster lists his death from disease on November 25, 1861, although Cross put the date as November 24, 1861. Ibid., 87, and Edward E. Cross, manuscript Journal, [p. 9], Edward E. Cross Papers, Milne Special Collections and Archives, University of New Hampshire, Durham, N.H. Hereinafter cited as: Cross, Journal.

37. New Hampshire Secretary of State Allen Tenney. It is possible that Cross was anticipating a visit from Tenney. The secretary of state and governor did visit the regiment on February 2, 1862. Child, *Fifth New Hampshire*, 32.

LETTER TO HENRY KENT, DECEMBER 17, 1861[38]

♣ ♣ ♣ ♣ ♣

By the way, I say it & say it boldly—the Sanitary Commission
as at present managed is a gigantic humbug.

On Edsell's Hill[39]
Headquarters 5th NHV
Camp Sumner,[40] Dec. 17, 1861

Dear Kent,

Your letter received. This attempt to make an abolition war is going to make trouble if not stopped. A little more attention to soldiers and less ~~than~~ to Negroes is what is wanted. If not we shall get whipped.

We learn here that the 3ᵈ is turning out bad, & that Whipple[41] is going to resign. "I tell you, young man," to use the words of the sage of Plymouth— the Fifth regiment is hard to beat.

We occupy the right of Sumner's Division[42]—right in front of the enemy & picket up to their outpost every day. A Gorham fellow killed a "Sesesher" the other night. He was a scout trying to spy out our lines.

I am ranking Colonel in the Brigade, which is some comfort, in that I command the Brigade about half the time. I am suffering for an adjutant.

By the way, I say it & say it boldly—the Sanitary Commission[43] as at

---

38. Courtesy of M. Faith Kent.

39. Edsall's Hill was located in Fairfax County, Va., southwest of Alexandria.

40. The Fifth was assigned to Camp California, named in honor of division commander Edwin "Bull" Sumner, former commander of the Department of the Pacific. The camp lay adjacent to the Little River Turnpike about 3 miles west of Alexandria, Va. Cross named the Fifth's temporary picket outpost on Edsall's Hill "Camp Sumner." Pride and Travis, *Brave Boys*, 51– 52, and Cross, Journal, [p. 12].

41. Cross was mistaken here. Enoch Q. Fellows, not Whipple, was colonel of the Third New Hampshire. Thomas J. Whipple (1816–1889), a lawyer and veteran of the Mexican War, was appointed colonel of the Fourth New Hampshire on August 20, 1861. He resigned his commission in March 1862. Lieutenant Colonel Louis Bell succeeded him as colonel. See D. Eldridge, *The Third New Hampshire and All about It* (Boston: E. B. Skillings, 1893), Waite, *New Hampshire in the Rebellion*, 223–224, and *Soldiers and Sailors of New Hampshire*, 202.

42. The Fifth, one of four regiments in Brigadier General Oliver Otis Howard's brigade, was assigned to Sumner's division of the Second Corps of the Army of the Potomac. Pride and Travis, *Brave Boys*, 51.

43. The U.S. Sanitary Commission was created by citizens in June 1861 to help care for sick and wounded Union soldiers. During the war, the Sanitary Commission raised over $7 million and handed out donated supplies valued at $15 million. *Encyclopedia of the Civil War*, 656.

present managed is a gigantic humbug. Do say so, & caution our people not to send anything to it. We shall never see one cent's worth of all sent from Lancaster. If our mothers, sisters & wives make shirts & mittens for us we want them. The Sanitary Com. have store-houses full *of goods* on hand, & *soldiers* freezing on guard nights. It's a d——d shame.

Come out & see us.

Yours truly,
Edward E. Cross

LETTER TO HENRY KENT, DECEMBER 23, 1861[44]

♣ ♣ ♣ ♣ ♣

The camps are full of mischievous lying fellows who constantly write home trash.

Headquarters 5th NH
Camp California
Dec 23 1861

Dear Kent,

I have a good prospect of securing Frank's[45] appointment to West Point as one of the cadets at large.

I have sent him the regulations for application. Be kind enough to help him make it in "due & ancient form" and I will be obliged.

Do not believe one half you see in the papers about our troops. The camps are full of mischievous lying fellows who constantly write home trash. I have forbidden it in the 5th.

The NH 2d seems to have *literary diarreah* of the meanest sort. They are getting famous for it hereabouts. God is mercy forbid my Regiment should catch it!!

Jesse Mann's son Corporal Harrison J. Mann[46] of Co. A., 5th died a few days ago of fever. His father left camp to-day with the body.

---

44. Courtesy of M. Faith Kent.

45. Probably Cross's youngest brother, Francis L. "Frank" Cross. According to the regimental roster, he joined the Fifth in February 1862 at the age of 18, although a family genealogy suggests that he may have been younger. He was discharged a few months later in August 1862. Child, "Complete Roster," 45, and "Cross Family Genealogy," Lancaster Historical Society, Lancaster, N.H.

46. Harrison T. Mann was a resident of Bath, N.H., when he enlisted at the age of 20. He died on December 21, 1861, at Camp California. Child, "Complete Roster," 118.

Corporal Mann was a good soldier, sober, attentive, and always an example of manly conduct. I have few better men in the regiment.

Up to this date since leaving Concord out of 1010 officers and men, eight only have died, which considering our hardships, exposures & the acclimation we are all going through, is really extraordinary.

I send you a letter from the Sanitary Committee by which you will see that there is a prospect of our getting those boxes sent by out mothers, sisters, sweethearts and wives!

> Yours ever
> Edward E Cross
> Col 5th NHV

LETTER TO HENRY KENT, DECEMBER 27, 1861[47]

♣ ♣ ♣ ♣ ♣

We don't want to make this an abolition war, don't crowd us into it.

Headquarters 5th NHV
Camp on Edsall's Hill
Dec 27 1861

Dear Kent

Yours received. I remember Miss Hackett.[48] It is a wonder she has not hooked some fellow before this—she is "heavy" on the flirtation. I wouldn't wonder if *you* had a "hankering" the way she once spoke of you pathetically, sentimentally, & evidently cherishes divers and kindly feelings "which the world may never know." I have no pictures now. After pay day I am going to try to get over to Washington a few days & will then be "taken" on Miss Hackett's account. Give my love to her, when next you write.

I have a splendid anecdote of Tom Whipple.[49] It seems that the 3d got into the habit of swearing, worse than "our army in Flanders." So one day Gen Sherman[50] meeting with Col Whipple, remonstrated against the profanity of

47. Courtesy of M. Faith Kent.
48. Unidentified.
49. A good story, but Cross confused the two regiments. See note 41.
50. Thomas West Sherman (1813–1879), a native of Newport, R.I., graduated from West Point in 1836. A veteran of various Indian wars and the Mexican War, Sherman was among the first brigadier generals appointed in 1861. At the time, he commanded the Third and Fourth New Hampshire Regiments, among others, along the coast of South Carolina. Warner, *Generals in Blue*, 440–441.

the New Hampshire 3d. Said he, "Col Whipple, why do your men use so much profane language, look at the New Hampshire 4th, it is a moral Regiment. They had 14 men baptized this morning!" The h—ll they did, said Whipple. Then turning around towards his tent he called out in his [illegible] voice "*Adjutant, detail 14 men* to *be baptized at daylight* to-*morrow morning! I'll be damned if any New Hampshire men shall get ahead* of me *in piety!*" About that time Gen Sherman suddenly discerned a sail coming up the bay & hastened to the beach. This is true & would do well to stand in print. It is said that the Col of the N.H. 5th details fatigue parties for church every Sunday!

Come out and see us. You ought to be here. I suppose its no use to offer you the Adjutant but you can have. Do give old [illegible] hell. He is a fanatic. We don't want to make this an abolition war, don't crowd us into it.

Why don't you put up Ira Perly[51] for Governor. Have a gentleman & a scholar once

Yours ever
Edward E Cross

LETTER TO HENRY KENT, DECEMBER 27, 1861[52]

♣ ♣ ♣ ♣ ♣

I don't think the men like me, but the War Department and the Generals have a different opinion.

Edsell's Hill
27th [December 1861]

Dear Kent,

After writing and sending off my letter of the above date, it occurred to me that I have said nothing about "jeems" [illegible][53] and his prize. The $30

51. Ira Perley (1799–1874) graduated from Dartmouth College in 1822. He established a law practice in Hanover three years later. He moved his practice to Concord in 1850. He served as chief justice of the Supreme Judicial Court from 1855 until his resignation in 1859. He was reappointed to that same seat in 1864, serving until he reached the age of 70. Charles H. Bell, *The Bench and Bar of New Hampshire* (Boston and New York: Houghton Mifflin, 1894), 105–108.

52. Courtesy of M. Faith Kent.

53. Unidentified, although the subject may have turned in a deserter; the reward sometimes reached as high as $30 to encourage the arrest of those absent without leave. Child, "Complete Roster," and *Encyclopedia of the Civil War*, 216.

will be paid by the State Treasurer, & I shall deduct it from the prisoner's pay. That is the way the other three cases were settled.

I shall be glad to see Mr. Davis[54]—very glad. I have a ball & chain which is an ornament to any man's leg, all prepared for him.

I want you to come out and see a model volunteer Regiment where there is no drunkenness, no rows—where the men are well fed, clothed, and made to walk up square to martial. I don't think the men like me, but the War Department & the Generals have a different opinion.

Come & see us. Dick[55] is building a stockade. Come & see us.

Yours
E. E. Cross

LETTER TO N.H. REPRESENTATIVE THOMAS M. EDWARDS, JANUARY 13, 1862[56]

♣ ♣ ♣ ♣ ♣

Private Orastus J. Verry, Company F, will be discharged according to orders.

Headquarters Fifth N. H. Volunteers
Camp California, Jan. 13, 1862
Hon. Thomas M. Edwards,[57] Washington:

Dear Sir:

Private Orastus J. Verry,[58] Company F, will be discharged according to orders; but allow me to say that his discharge is an outrage against military custom, against law, and cannot fail to have a bad example. The young man is strong, able-bodied, and if *he* is discharged, with equal reason might one-half our army be discharged.[59]

54. Unidentified, although possibly the subject of the court-martial Cross was serving at that time. See letter to Henry Kent, January 20, 1862, in this volume.

55. Richard E. Cross.

56. Letter reprinted in the *Patriot and Gazette* (Concord, N.H.), February 5, 1862, 2.

57. Thomas McKey Edwards (1795–1875), a graduate of Dartmouth, was a lawyer and businessman from Keene, N.H. He was elected to the U.S. House of Representatives as a Republican in 1858 and 1860. He declined to run for reelection in 1862 and the following spring returned to his business interests in New Hampshire. Bell, *Bench and Bar*, 335–336.

58. Listed as Oratus J. Verry, who joined the Fifth as a 19-year-old resident of Swanzey, N.H., and was discharged on December 13, 1861. Verry later served in Company I of the Sixteenth New Hampshire and Company E of the Eighteenth. Child, "Complete Roster," 187.

59. Because he was under 21, his parents petitioned Edwards for his discharge. Edwards's interference clearly outraged Cross. Pride and Travis, *Brave Boys*, 57.

I shall see that Ortastus Verry is prosecuted for obtaining money and clothes from the United States under false pretenses. It seems to me, *Sir*, with all due respect, that at this crisis of our national affairs, Members of Congress would do better service by attending to public business, retrenching expenses, punishing corrupt officers, and providing means to pay those who are enduring the hardships and dangers of the field, than to spend time and energy in getting able-bodied men discharged from service. Such, sir, is the opinion of

Your obedient servant,
Edward E. Cross
Colonel Fifth N. H. Vols.

LETTER TO HENRY KENT, JANUARY 20, 1862[60]

♣ ♣ ♣ ♣ ♣

Dick went out with 40 men the other night & brought in
one rebel & 10 cows prisoners.

Camp California
Jan. 20, 1862

Dear Kent,

The State refuses to pay the $30. I have written to them. When I advertised the $30, it was with the understanding that it would be paid. But the $30 reward was afterward repealed by the Council. I have been on a court trying Davis today. Crafts brought some good men. I have lots of measles in camp, & in the army generally there is lots of sickness. We have rain and wind every day. Dick went out with 40 men the other night & brought in one rebel & 10 *cows* prisoners.[61] The cows we shall eat—blessed be God—soon. You can be Adjutant any day you want. I have yet made no changes. But there will be changes soon.

Yours truly
Edward E. Cross

I sent Miss H.[62] the "picters."

60. Courtesy of M. Faith Kent.

61. According to the reminiscences collected by William Child, the 100-day stay at Camp California was a time of plenty. Beyond normal food rations, "a raid or foraging party might furnish fresh pig, mutton, chicken, turkey, duck and goose . . . and anything that could be used for the benefit, gratification or delight of men." Child, *Fifth New Hampshire*, 39.

62. Probably the "Miss Hackett" referred to in a previous letter. See letter to Henry Kent, December 27, 1861, in this volume.

LETTER TO HENRY KENT, JANUARY 29, 1862[63]

♣ ♣ ♣ ♣ ♣
You will hear of exchanges in the Rg't soon.

Camp California
Jan 29 1862

Dear Kent,

We have not seen a Republican[64] for an age. Send one occasionally. Are you going to run for Rep?[65] You will hear of exchanges in the Rg't soon—that is, some resignations & promotions. I sent a piece from the Wash. Star[66]—don't know who wrote it.

How is recruiting? Come out. Very niply now, on the Potomac.

Yours Truly
Edward E. Cross
Col

LETTER TO HENRY KENT, MARCH 18, 1862[67]

♣ ♣ ♣ ♣ ♣
We are well & in full possession of the rebel stronghold.

Headquarters 5th N H Vols
Camp near Manassas Junction[68]
March 18 1862

Dear Kent

We are well & in full possession of the rebel stronghold. I have been all over and around it. By the camps and works they have had over 80,000 men

---

63. Courtesy of M. Faith Kent.
64. The *Coos Republican*, the Lancaster newspaper Kent owned and edited. *Granite State Monthly* I (August 1877): 99.
65. Kent was planning to run for a seat in the New Hampshire state legislature.
66. Clipping not located.
67. Courtesy of M. Faith Kent.
68. On the morning of March 10, 1862, the Fifth New Hampshire left the comforts of Camp California and marched toward Manassas Junction. Sumner's division led the Army of the Potomac with the Fifth New Hampshire in the van, followed by the rest of Howard's brigade. Child, *Fifth New Hampshire*, 44.

here. They ~~al~~ only left because their *base* was attacked. They could have held the works against 100,000 men. I write in a Secession hut with their paper & pen just as they left.

I send you one of their letters. We are going South by water in a few days.[69] The rebels had fine log camps and plenty of *everything* all winter.

> Yours ever
> E E Cross Col

LETTER TO ALLEN TENNEY, N.H. SECRETARY OF STATE, MARCH 30, 1862[70]

♣ ♣ ♣ ♣ ♣

My Regiment behaved nobly, *never faltered, never flinched, but marched deployed, and fired, with perfect coolness.*

Headquarters 5th NHV
Camp Niles Warrenton Junction Va[71]
March 30 1862

Dear *Tenney*[72]

We *had* our first fight day before yesterday. We drove the rear guard of the rebels over the Rappahannock River, causing them to blow up the fine railroad bridge we started early in the morning. I had the honor to command the advanced guard, which was—the 5th NH, the rifled 10 pounders & one squadron cavalry. We skirmished all day and shelled the retreating rebels every chance, until they opened on us from their works on the other side after blowing up the bridge. My Regiment behaved *nobly*, never faltered, never flinched, but marched deployed, and fired, with perfect coolness. The enemy fired lots of heavy shot at us, but never hit a man. We shelled them out of sight into the wood. On the road they burned houses barns bridges and haystacks. We had to wade three streams over 3 feet deep and one, under fire. Tell

69. The foray toward Manassas helped McClellan ease his army out of winter camp and prepare it for the transfer to the Virginia tidewater and the prolonged Peninsula campaign that followed. Pride and Travis, *Brave Boys*, 68.

70. Military Records, Fifth Regiment, 1861–1865. New Hampshire Records and Archives, Concord, N.H.

71. The Fifth camped at Warrenton Junction from March 20 until April 1. March 30 was cold and raw, with some snow. The regiment remained in camp on both the thirtieth and thirty-first of March. Child, *Fifth New Hampshire*, 50.

72. New Hampshire Secretary of State Allen Tenney.

Keller[73] Varney[74] has arrived, & I want him, Keller, at once. Why, O why don't you send the commissions! You are certainly in possession of all the dates.

Welch[75] and David[76] can *never* come back, as they are *trying* to do. I won't have either of them, & they cannot be forced on me. I have blocked the game in Washington.

Excuse this paper. I have no other. My regards to the Governor.

Yours truly
Edward E. Cross
Col 5th

LETTER TO HENRY KENT, APRIL 6, 1862[77]

♣ ♣ ♣ ♣ ♣

I feel better now I have seen the men under fire & know they can be depended on.

Headquarters 5th NHV
~~Camp~~ On board the Davidson[78]
Potomac River April 6, 1862

Dear Kent,

I see by the "Republican" that you have won the game,[79] but they haven't

73. Most likely Jacob W. Keller, a 34-year-old native of Germany who resided in Claremont, N.H. Originally a first lieutenant in Company G, he was promoted to captain of Company H in July 1862. Child, "Complete Roster," 102.

74. Unidentified.

75. Richard E. Welsh, of Plaistow, N.H., former captain of Company K. Child, "Complete Roster," 192.

76. James B. David, a 26-year-old resident of Amherst, N.H. David was mustered in on October 12, 1861, and appointed first lieutenant of Company K. He was discharged for "incompetency" on February 15, 1862, the same date as Welsh's discharge. Cross removed both because they failed competency tests that he required only of officers he wished to discharge. Cross's actions were suspect for other reasons. First, his brother, Richard E. Cross, replaced Captain Welsh. Moreover, both Welsh and David were outspoken Republicans. The two tried to block Cross's actions by going to Governor Berry and New Hampshire's all-Republican congressional delegation, but to no avail. Ibid., 49, and Pride and Travis, *Brave Boys*, 65–66.

77. Courtesy of M. Faith Kent.

78. Actually the *Donaldson*. It carried Cross and six of the regiment's companies. The remaining four companies, under Lieutenant Colonel Samuel Langley, made the voyage on the *Croton*. Pride and Travis, *Brave Boys*, 68.

79. Kent was elected to his first term in the New Hampshire legislature in 1862. During that year he served as chairman of the committee on military affairs. He was later elected to the legislature in 1868 and 1869. *Sketches of Successful New Hampshire Men* (Manchester, N.H.: J. B. Clarke, 1882), 22.

given you a very illustrious coadjutor. I want to suggest to you that now that the war fever is on to try to get a State Arsenal at Concord—a handsome capacious building where arms & military equipment could be stored and repaired. You know the troops of each state will bring home a great lot of equipment.

I think you can get the thing through.

After a month of very hard service, night & day in front of the enemy, without tents & only 4 wagons to a Regiment, our Brigade embarked yesterday to join the thousands of brave & good fellows that have "gone before" *towards* Richmond by water. During our past month's service we have carried everything ourselves, officers carrying all their baggage & blankets, men 3 or 4 days bread & pork & 60 rounds of ball. We made some hard marches, once from Union Mills to Fairfax C. H. & back the same day or rather night—30 miles—in rain and mud half leg deep. The men do nobly. I never saw more patient obedient soldiers. I com had the honor to command the advanced guard when we moved on Manassas, and on the 28th of March when Howard's Brigade[80] moved on the Rappahannock & drove the rebels across the river, which we did in good style under a sharp fire of rifles, round shot and shell. My men fired the first and last shots at the enemy. It was new for them to hear the screaming of the conical cannon balls & the bursting of shells but not a man flinched. One big ball struck about ten feet from the front of Co. B throwing the dirt sand on the leading files but not a man wavered. At one time no less than a dozen cannon shots passed over the heads of my men within five minutes. We killed several of the enemy, but had not a man injured. Everybody praised the coolness and bravery of the 5th Regiment. I feel better now I have seen the men under fire & know they can be depended on.

Since the papers are not allowed to send details you miss a great many things.

As you are a military man I give you the other side of my arrangements of the advanced guard, of which I had command. We first encountered Stuart's[81] cavalry and skirmished with them for several miles. I had 50 picked fellows in front & they killed or wounded several of the cavalry. I also had to 2 10 pd. Parrotts with which I pitched shell into every clump of horsemen I saw. Gen. Howard commanded the expedition & it was a complete success. We forced the rebels to burn their RR bridges.

Order of the march for Gen Howard's Expedition to the Rappahannock RR river.

80. General Oliver Otis Howard.
81. Brigadier General James Ewell Brown "Jeb" Stuart.

You see I had no fear of the "masked batteries" or flank attacks. Coming home we captured 400 head of cattle & lots of horses.[82]

We are in good health. I have 900 officers & men with me—the sharpest Regiment in the Division.

Direct mail to Alexandria Va.

> I am
> As ever your friend
> Edward E. Cross
> Col. 5th

82. According to Cross, the men had Howard's permission to forage. In addition to the cattle and horses, "[e]very man had a pig or a chicken. . . ." Child, *Fifth New Hampshire*, 50.

LETTER TO HENRY KENT, MAY 3, 1862[83]

♣ ♣ ♣ ♣ ♣

I have written you lots of contraband information. Don't
say it was from me or it will raise the devil.

Headquarters 5th NHV
Camp Winfield Scott[84]
May 3, 1862

Dear Kent,

I can write you not exactly "by the rocket's red glare," but when you come to "the bursting in air," & in camps, & in the woods, & the parallels the batteries, & in fact everywhere! Where a bomb sees fit to burst, the lines of the port come in. All day and night, the awful booming of the guns shakes the earth, & the still awful screaming of the 10 & 11 inch shells makes the air hideous. We have not opened yet only with one small battery of rifled two hundred pd Parrotts just to silence some very troublesome guns. But the enemy fire day & night from all sorts of guns, rifled & smooth bore, & no locality within 3 & ½ miles is safe. Thousands of our men lay within one mile of this batteries & it is Providential that most of the shells go far over us, cutting away the tree tops & sometimes bursting high in the air. Large shells are now falling within a few hundred yards of where I write & where my whole regiment is making gabions and facines.[85] For be it known, orders from Army Hdqrs detached us a few weeks since, and we are now (temporarily) in the Engineer Brigade, General Daniel P. Woodbury[86] of N. H. in command. Last winter Dick & Rice[87] instructed the men in gabion and facine

83. Courtesy of M. Faith Kent.

84. Named for General Winfield Scott (1786–1866), Virginia native and commander of Union forces prior to his resignation on November 1, 1861. The Fifth occupied these grounds during the siege of Yorktown, Va. *Encyclopedia of the Civil War*, 662–663, and Child, *Fifth New Hampshire*, 56.

85. Gabions are open-ended baskets made of wood or metal, and fascines are bundles of brush or stakes. Both were used in building retaining walls in field fortifications. Boatner, *Civil War Dictionary*, 276, 320, 693.

86. Daniel Phineas Woodbury (1812–1864), a native of New London, N.H., directed McClellan's brigade of engineer troops during the Peninsula campaign and laid the bridges across the Rappahannock River at Fredericksburg. Warner, *Generals in Blue*, 570–571.

87. Most likely Thomas J. Rice. A resident of Boston, Mass., Rice was 33 when mustered in as a first lieutenant in Company E. He resigned his commission as captain of Company B on September 10, 1862. Child, "Complete Roster," 151.

making—somehow it leaked out, & for two weeks we have been hard at work as "Engineers" & I feel bound to say the officers and men have done themselves great credit receiving strong approbation from Headquarters.

Night before last we heard that an attack was contemplated. We turned out at midnight, marched 4 miles through the woods, joined our Brigade—stood under arms til daylight—marched back, & in a few hours were making gabions, or as the boys call them "gabriels," as gay as any of the most fancy soldier men you ever saw. Those who think a "soldier's life is always gay" ought to have been with us for 60 days past. Every moment we have been marching, picketing, skirmishing, or working with not a single tent and only one wagon—officers packing their own blankets & rations—the men their rations & kettles. A few days since we received new shoes & some "shelter tents," after the French pattern—but I left them back in my old camp—the boys preferring to do so.

It is not often that I write you about the Regiment, & you are the only man I do write to, but let me tell you one little fact, known to all officers. A few days before we went into the gabion business, I was taking the Regt out to drill one afternoon when an aid rode up & told me we were to be inspected by one of the Inspectors General of the Army, ~~on~~ in one hour. Well, in one hour we were out, were inspected, & Col Davis, USA,[88] told Gen Howard in my presence that it was "the most perfect Regiment of Infantry he ever inspected." He said other Regiments were better in some *things* but in *all* the 5th N H Vols were the best he ever saw. Now if I had "R" or some other "complete letter writer" this puff would have gone the rounds. This is the same Col. Davis who inspected the 2d.

All things are lovely here. Every 24 hours we lose a few men but I reckon we keep the a/c square. I wish you could be here to see. We have 130,000 infantry, 300 pieces light artillery—100 siege guns & mortars, over 5000 cavalry, & when we open, 8 or ten gun boats will help us.

But *we need every man.* The rebels have works of great strength, well picketed by ditches, bristling with cannon, & full of concealed rifle pits. For thousands of us the end of our lives is at hand. The men do not seem to realize it, but I do for I have seen this thing before. A few days since while one of the Regular sergeants was standing in a battery, smoking & talking, when a 32 lb shot came in & cut him in two parts! I saw the awful spectacle, but every day they happen. Somehow I have an idea that this god abandoned spot is to be my future residence. It matters little. Some one told me you were

---

88. Most likely Major Nelson Henry Davis (1821–1890), a graduate of West Point who was assistant inspector general for the Army of the Potomac (1862–1863). John H. Eicher and David J. Eicher, *Civil War High Commands* (Stanford: Stanford University Press, 2001), 203.

Speaker of the H. of Reps.[89] Good. Don't forget the soldier men when you have a chance. The militia bill ought to be fixed up. We ought to have about 4 Brigades, each with a battery provided for. But you know all about it.

I have written you lots of contraband information. Don't say it was from me or it will raise the d——l. My regards to Mrs K. Write soon.

Yours truly
Edward E Cross
Col

LETTER TO HENRY KENT, JUNE 3, 1862[90]

♣ ♣ ♣ ♣ ♣

The Rgt did nobly, more than nobly, gloriously. *We beat back the enemy, but at fearful cost.*

On board the Steamer "Spaulding"[91]
June 3 '62

Dear Kent,

You have no doubt heard of the great battle.[92] Nelson, Dick, Francis & myself[93] were all there & I only of the 4 was wounded—very severely—shot through the left hip by a Minie ball.

I reached this place this morning & will go to the hospital but cannot tell to which one. The Rgt did nobly, more than nobly, *gloriously.* We beat back the enemy, but at fearful cost. The 5th lost nearly 200 killed and wounded. Co B had 29 disabled mostly from Coos.

Can't you give us a vote of thanks? It is little for the state to do.

Yours ever
E E Cross
Col

89. Kent was not elected Speaker of the House of Representatives. That honor went to Edward A. Rollins of Somersworth. Lyon, *New-Hampshire Annual Register . . . for the Year 1863*, 23.

90. Courtesy of M. Faith Kent.

91. Cross and about 1,500 wounded men took the *Spaulding* from a landing on the Pamunkey River to Philadelphia, Pa. Among those traveling with Cross were General Howard, Major William Cook, and a number of wounded Confederate prisoners. Pride and Travis, *Brave Boys*, 91.

92. The Battle of Fair Oaks, May 31–June 1, 1862. Although a draw in terms of casualties, Union forces at Fair Oaks held the field, thus preserving a tactical victory. *Encyclopedia of the Civil War*, 668.

93. According to Cross, there were seven men from the Cross family at the Battle of Fair Oaks, four brothers and three cousins. Child, *Fifth New Hampshire*, 99.

Say to Persis[94] that I shall be along soon. Major Cook[95] was also wounded. I was acting Brig Gen at the time I was hit & disabled. 3 balls struck me—but only one did the damage.

My regards to all. Especially Tenny.[96]

LETTER TO THE *NEW YORK HERALD*, JUNE 12, 1862[97]

♣ ♣ ♣ ♣ ♣

While advancing the second time on the enemy's line, the 69th fired a volley—one of the "terrific volleys" mentioned by your correspondent—right into the backs of my men.

To the Editor of the Herald:
United States General Hospital
Philadelphia, June 12, 1862

In your paper of to-day appears a detailed account of the battles lately fought near Richmond, including that of Sunday, June 1. I beg your permission to correct several grave errors of your correspondent, who doubtless supposed he was writing facts. In one place he says:

"Soon Col. Cross was wounded in the thigh, and Col. Parker, of the 64th,[98] conducted the regiments through the remainder of the fight."

This is not correct, as I will soon show. Farther down, under the title "Irish Brigade," the 69th has the credit of driving back the enemy.

This, also, is not correct; nor do I believe the gallant officers and men of that regiment will thank any letter-writer for placing them in such a false position. The facts are as follows:

My regiment, the 5th New Hampshire, was detached from Howard's bri-

94. Persis LaFayette Cross (1839–1903) was Cross's younger sister. "Cross Family Genealogy," Lancaster Historical Society.

95. A minié ball had entered Cook's hip and lodged near his sciatic nerve. He never returned to active duty, resigning on July 17, 1862. Pride and Travis, *Brave Boys*, 91, and Child, "Complete Roster," 42.

96. Secretary of State Allen Tenney.

97. Unidentified newspaper clipping. Edward E. Cross Papers, Milne Special Collections and Archives, University of New Hampshire, Durham, N.H.

98. Colonel Thomas J. Parker of the Sixty-fourth New York. Parker was honorably discharged a month later, on July 12, 1862. Walker, *Second Corps*, 4, 88.

gade on Saturday evening, and on Sunday morning occupied the extreme right of the line formed by Gen. French, where we skirmished the enemy and took quite a number of prisoners. The battle had raged some time, when orders came for me to go to the relief of a portion of French's brigade. I moved quickly down the railroad track, passed General French, and halted on the track, face to the enemy, in rear of the position just occupied by Howard's two regiments, the 61st and 64th New York. Being in command of the brigade, I sent an order by Adjutant Gregory,[99] of the 61st, for the two regiments to clear my front as soon as possible and I would take their place. This was done at once; and, while the movement was going on, the Irish Brigade did come up in my rear. The 69th formed on the right of my line, and the 88th on my left, but in rear of my line, and there they remained. The 5th New Hampshire then entered the woods, solitary and alone, the regiments on the right and left remaining in their places. About two hundred yards from the track we came upon the dead and wounded of the 61st and 64th, and a few yards further we met the enemy. Twice we drove back their line and it rallied; the third time it broke. Most of the firing took place at twenty yards' range. While advancing the second time on the enemy's line, the 69th fired a volley—one of the "terrific volleys" mentioned by your correspondent—right into the backs of my men, for I had obliqued my line to the right, to prevent being flanked. That volley mortally wounded some of my best men; fortunately, being on the railroad track, the aim was high. I expected the two regiments on my flanks would enter the woods with me; but they did not. Why, I have never learned.

When the enemy ceased firing, my regiment broke by the right of companies to the rear, and fired out to the railroad. Being shot through the thigh, I was carried to the track in front of the regiment. On the track we found the two regiments, and some soldiers of the Sixty-Ninth kindly relieved my men and carried me to the rear. The Irish brigade on the track lost four men killed and twenty-seven wounded. The Fifth New Hampshire lost within a fraction of two hundred killed and wounded, among the latter the Colonel, Major and several other officers—yet the regiment has scarcely been mentioned as present, and even then grossly misrepresented.

No other regiment was sent into the woods. The Battle of Sunday was ended. The Fifth played its humble part in the closing scene. Then, and not till then, did I turn over the command of the First brigade to Colonel Parker, of the Sixty-Fourth New York. All this statement I made in substance to a reporter for some Boston paper, the evening of the battle, at his request; and I would never have troubled you, sir, had not the very incorrect report of

99. Unidentified.

your correspondent appeared. It is a fact that the brigade of the lamented and gallant Howard bore the brunt of Sunday's battle, and the official reports will cer[t]ainly do tardy justice to the brave Sixty-first and Sixty-fourth regiments, which left so many men on the battle-field, and faced the enemy with such stubborn bravery. All we ask is simple justice; no fulsome flattery, no distorted praise. The facts will suffice for Howard's brigade.

EDWARD E. CROSS
Colonel Fifth New Hampshire regiment

LETTER TO GOVERNOR NATHANIEL S. BERRY AND THE GOVERNOR'S COUNCIL, JULY 9, 1862[100]

♣ ♣ ♣ ♣ ♣

I think 150 of my men will join for duty with me in a few days.
I make this statement so that if there is a draft my share of
men may be secured.

Lancaster July 9, 1862
Hon Governor & Council
of New Hampshire

Gentlemen

I beg to call your attention to the importance of filling up the well drilled, disciplined, and tried Regiments of troops now in service to this State. Their organization is perfect, their officers and non-commissioned officers experienced, and recruits placed in such organizations soon become equal to the veterans of the campaign.

It is the desire of the General Government & the chief officers of the Army, that the old Regiments be at once recruited, in preference to having new Regiments sent into the field.

I have now on my rolls over 700 men. Of this number 300 are disabled, (many temporarily) so that 250 or 300 men will bring my forces to the standard. I think 150 of my men will join for duty with me in a few days. I make this statement so that if there is a draft my share of men may be secured.

I respectfully submit my opinion that a *Brigade of three* Regiments under proper officers can be raised in this State.

Very truly
Edward E Cross
Col 5th NHV

100. Executive Records, Division of Records Management and Archives, Concord, N.H.

LETTER TO HENRY KENT, JULY 24, 1862[101]

♣ ♣ ♣ ♣ ♣

Please send word to Long that if he does not report in Concord as soon as possible after notice he will be advertised as a deserter.

Concord N H
July 24 '62

Dear Kent,

Arrived here safe. Find that passes can be had. Send one for Mr. M'Carty[102] & for Long.[103] Please send word to Long that if he does not report in Concord as soon as possible after notice he will be advertised as a deserter. Ditto M'Carty. I am sent Cummings[104] letter in reference to Long so that [there] can be no mistake as to the man.

Shall remain here for the present. My men will leave Monday.

Be kind enough to see this.

Yours
E E Cross

Who do you think I found in the cars!! The two pretty girls of the wagons in the Pinkham woods![105] They are Babcocks from Boston.[106] ~~An~~ Got acquainted.

LETTER TO HENRY KENT, JULY 28, 1862[107]

♣ ♣ ♣ ♣ ♣

The two girls aforesaid live in Jamaica Plains—father a clergyman—both educated refined & "smart." If I had time should "prospect" the diggings.

101. Courtesy of M. Faith Kent.
102. Thomas McCarty, a 35-year-old private from Stratford, N.H. Like Cross, he had returned home to recover from wounds suffered at Fair Oaks. Child, "Complete Roster," 121.
103. Captain Charles H. Long, of Company G.
104. Unidentified.
105. While in Lancaster, Cross, Kent, and several others toured the White Mountains. They took a red wagon to the top of Mount Washington, via the carriage road that originates near Pinkham Notch. Pride and Travis, *Brave Boys,* 111.
106. Unidentified.
107. Courtesy of M. Faith Kent.

Concord July 28 1862

Dear Kent,

Burbank's[108] document received. He cannot be paid here. Must go in *person* to the paymaster at Boston—No. 25 Duane Street—who will pay him. Therefore I send back the papers.

The two girls aforesaid live in Jamaica Plains—father a clergyman[109]—both educated refined & "smart." If I had time should "prospect" the diggings. The other *individual* was here the day before I came. Promised Dumas[110] she would come back. We expect her. The notice will be served. Other parties are here including the fair ones of Concord so well known to fame. Also one other, fair but frail. Have enlisted 7 new men & to-morrow start off 20 of my veterans & the new ones—the Lord bless them. Am getting on slow, collecting my men and sending them on. Gov. and Council models of politeness. Shall be here a week or more at least.

'O won't you come down?

Yours truly
E. E. Cross

LETTER TO HENRY KENT, AUGUST 5, 1862[111]

I thank God we are to have a draft and a big one.

Concord Aug 5th 1862

Dear Henry,

We had a splendid meeting last evening at this place.[112] Gen. Howard[113]

---

108. Probably Isaiah W. Burbank, who enlisted as a 30-year-old private assigned to Company B. A resident of Gorham, N.H., he also received wounds at Fair Oaks. Child, "Complete Roster," 25.

109. Possibly Reverend Samuel Brazer Babcock (1808–1873), an Episcopal minister who served as rector of the St. Paul's Society for 41 years. A graduate of Harvard, Babcock received additional theological training in New Hampshire. *New York Times*, October 27, 1873, 5:4.

110. Unidentified.

111. Courtesy of M. Faith Kent.

112. The aim of the meeting was recruitment, a subject of great interest to Cross. Pride and Travis, *Brave Boys*, 111.

113. Howard lost his right arm but recovered in time to rejoin the Army of the Potomac and lead a division at Antietam in September. In his well-received speech at the meeting, Howard voiced support for the creation of black regiments, a sentiment that received mixed reviews in the New Hampshire newspapers. *Encyclopedia of the Civil War*, 373, and Pride and Travis, *Brave Boys*, 111–112.

of Maine was present and made a fine speech. Also Walter Harriman.[114] I shall start on the 12th for the Reg't. I thank God we are to have a draft and a big one. I feel confident *now* that we can do something.

If you write Gen. Howard & invite him, I think he would speak in Coos —Jefferson, for instance, where they better volunteer and get their bounty than be drafted and get nothing. Can't you arrest Long? Five dollars & *all expenses* on his delivery.[115] I hope you will publish Sec. Stanton's order about absentees.[116]

I am to have 350 drafted men to fill up. My health is improving. One squad of ~~300~~ 30 of my old soldiers has gone & 25 others will start to-morrow. Also about a dozen new ones. Wrote a note to Miss ——[117] the other day. Had a very polite answer. Think the bait took.

Yours truly

E. E. Cross

LETTER TO HENRY KENT, AUGUST 12, 1862[118]

I am off on the 10 o'clock train with 44 recruits & 17 convalescants for the 5th and about the same number for the Second.

Concord Aug 12 1862

Dear Henry,

I am really sorry that you cannot do anything with the papers—but don't give it up.

I am off on the 10 o'clock train with 44 recruits & 17 convalescants for

---

114. Walter Harriman (1817–1884), of Warner, N.H., worked as a teacher, minister, and small businessman before entering politics as a Democratic state representative in 1849. In 1861, Harriman became editor and part owner of the Manchester *Weekly Union*. A leader of the "War Democrats," he later had a falling-out with the Democrats and aligned himself with the Republicans. As a Republican, Harriman later served two terms as governor of New Hampshire. *Successful New Hampshire Men*, 74–78, and Waite, *New Hampshire in the Rebellion*, 449–452.

115. Five dollars was the standard reward for returning deserters to service. *Encyclopedia of the Civil War*, 216.

116. Secretary of War Edwin M. Stanton responded to a growing problem in the Union army. Although formal leaves from service were permitted, some historians have estimated that absenteeism in the Union army was as high as one-third. Ibid., 216–217.

117. Unidentified.

118. Courtesy of M. Faith Kent.

the 5th and about the same number for the 2d. The 11th is officered. Harriman,[119] Col. Barker, Lieut. Col.,[120] & Marston's Law partner, Major.[121] The 9th goes slowly—the 2d Reg't seems to be absorbing all of the officers.

Col. Eastman[122] is sick & I have been recruiting officers for the two days past.

I sent Ned[123] some papers & wish him to enlist for me. In an old Reg't the recruit gets $10 additional from the state & $44 do from the US. The men have choice of company. Send them to Col Eastman as fast as enlisted. I go in good spirits—Hoping to hear from you soon. I am

Yours ever

E. E. Cross

P. S. The mare is with John Lindsey.[124]

LETTER TO GOVERNOR NATHANIEL S. BERRY AND THE GOVERNOR'S COUNCIL, AUGUST 13, 1862[125]

♣ ♣ ♣ ♣ ♣

I respectfully suggest that some of the line officers and sergeants of the 5th are equally deserving of promotion.

119. Harriman became colonel of the Eleventh New Hampshire in August 1862. He led his regiment in the assault on Marye's Heights at Fredericksburg and was captured while leading a charge at the Battle of the Wilderness in 1864. Harriman survived four months in various Confederate prisons before leading the Eleventh into Petersburg, Va., in April 1865. Appointed brigadier general for "gallant conduct during the war," Harriman mustered out as a colonel on June 4, 1865. Waite, *New Hampshire in the Rebellion*, 444, and *Successful New Hampshire Men*, 74–78.

120. Thomas E. Barker, of Barnstead, N.H., actually served as lieutenant colonel of the Twelfth New Hampshire. Waite, *New Hampshire in the Rebellion*, 462.

121. Moses N. Collins (1820–1864), of Exeter, N.H., was a law partner of Gilman Marston, congressman and colonel of the Second New Hampshire. He was elected to the state legislature in 1855, 1861, and 1862. He entered service following the Union defeat at the Second Battle of Bull Run. He died at the Battle of the Wilderness in May 1864. Ibid., 452–453.

122. Lieutenant Colonel Seth Eastman (1808–1875), a native of Brunswick, Maine, graduated from West Point in 1829 and served in the U.S. Army for most of his life. Eastman was superintendent for recruiting in New Hampshire from 1861 until January 1863. He is best remembered as an artist who specialized in Native American subjects. Eicher and Eicher, *High Commands*, 221.

123. Unidentified.

124. Cross had taken a mare, known thereafter as the "Rebel mare," from a Confederate courier during the Battle of Fair Oaks. John Lindsey, of Lancaster, was manager of the Lancaster House hotel. See Cross, Journal, [p. 39]; and A. N. Somers, *History of Lancaster, New Hampshire* (Concord, N.H.: Rumford Press, 1899), 515–516.

125. Executive Papers, Division of Records Management and Archives, Concord, N.H.

Concord Aug 13, 1862
To the Hon Governor & Council

Gentlemen

I have the honor to state that I have in the 5th Rg't officers and men that deserve promotion, having earned it by long & arduous service in the field, and brave conduct in battle.

As the 2d Rg't NHV has received a larger share of promotions—having received two Lieut Colonelcys & one Majority in the 9th & 10th, I respectfully suggest that some of the line officers and sergeants of the 5th are equally deserving of promotion.

Very resp'y
Edward E. Cross
Col 5th NHV

LETTER TO HENRY KENT, AUGUST 22, 1862[126]

♣ ♣ ♣ ♣ ♣

My men look rough but they have become good soldiers.

Headquarters 5th N H V
Newport News Aug 22 '62

Dear Kent,

I am with my Reg't, & a great time we had. But O! the disastrous effects of this retreat. A great battle would not have damaged us more—the officers dispirited, men tired and homesick & the whole army shattered & discouraged. All McClellan's generals opposed the movement & Mc himself offered to advance on Richmond at a day's notice. But Pope was in danger![127] Washington exposed, and off we are trundled to the old war path of the Rappahannock.

My men look rough but they have become good soldiers. Dick is pretty well & sends regards.

Yours truly
Edward E Cross
Col 5th

126. Courtesy of M. Faith Kent.

127. In August 1862, Lee dispatched Confederate troops under Major General "Stonewall" Jackson and Major General James Longstreet to threaten Washington, D.C. The scheme halted McClellan's advance on Richmond and resulted in the defeat of Major General John Pope's Army of Virginia at the Second Battle of Bull Run. *Encyclopedia of the Civil War*, 92–93.

LETTER TO HENRY KENT, SEPTEMBER 5, 1862[128]

♣ ♣ ♣ ♣ ♣

*"Pope told a flattering tale"—but he played out quick
& is now a ruined and disgraced man.*

Headquarters 5th NHV
Camp near Washington[129]
Sept 5 1862

Dear Henry

"Pope told a flattering tale"—but he played out quick & is now a ruined and disgraced man.[130] He was completely out generalled by Jackson & Lee, defeated, with a loss of 10,000 killed & wounded, & was saved by McClellan & his Army from utter destruction. As it was, Pope lost half a million worth of property & all his own baggage & papers. McClellan sent three Army corps to help him. Sumner's Corps[131] marched at ten minutes notice without anything but arms—leaving all our camp equippage and blankets. The first day we marched from Alexandria to Centreville 24 miles, & arrived in rear of the battle field soon after daylight. As we came up Pope's stragglers & fugitives poured through our lines. The 5th happened to be in the reserve, but the 2d & 6th went in & caught *hell*.[132] McDowell made his usual *awful blunders*[133] & our men were mowed down by ranks. Sumner's Corps formed

128. Courtesy of M. Faith Kent.

129. On September 3, 1862, the Fifth crossed the Potomac River and entered the District of Columbia via the Chain Bridge. Cross described the action as "evacuating Virginia in the most inglorious manner." The Fifth camped near the defenses of Washington at Fort Gaines and Tennallytown before advancing toward Frederick, Md. The pause also enabled the regiment to resupply in anticipation of the Antietam campaign. Pride and Travis, *Brave Boys*, 120–121, and Cross, "Diary."

130. Cross used this same phrase and assessment of Pope's abilities in his journal. Cross, Journal, [p. 50].

131. Sumner was appointed commander of the Second Corps of the Army of the Potomac in March 1862. Under this organization, Israel Richardson commanded the First Division, which included the First Brigade under Howard. The brigade consisted of the Fifth New Hampshire, Sixty-first New York, Sixty-fourth New York, and Eighty-first Pennsylvania. Warner, *Generals in Blue*, 237, 403, 489–490.

132. The Second and Sixth New Hampshire Regiments.

133. Irwin McDowell (1818–1885) graduated from West Point in 1838 and taught tactics at his alma mater in the early 1840s. Appointed brigadier general of volunteers in May 1861, McDowell will forever be remembered as the Union commander at the First Battle of Bull Run. Replaced by McClellan, McDowell, now a major general, was left with a force to protect Washington during the Peninsula campaign. He was paralyzed by Stonewall Jackson's Shenandoah Valley campaign and never applied pressure on Richmond from the north. His indecision

the rear. ~~I was~~ My Command was the best. I commanded the pickets & after the army had been gone two hours I drew them in & silently followed. We were shelled but no one hurt.

Oh but we had a hard time of it. Five days and nights on the move—the days hot & the nights bitter cold. We only had hard bread, & little of it to eat.

Now McClellan is going to be Com in Chief of all the Army & we had a grand pow wow over it.

I have been recommended for Brig Gen by five Generals & lots of Colonels. You might say so.

Yours ever
E. E. Cross
vol

LETTER TO HENRY KENT, SEPTEMBER 20, 1862[134]

This has been for the Rebels a Waterloo defeat.

Headquarters 5th N H V
Camp on the Battle field of Sharpsburg
Sept 20 1862

Dear Kent

This has been for the Rebels a Waterloo defeat. I think 4 or 5 thousand of them are dead on this field.[135] The bodies of six colonels & two generals have been found. The rebel wounded cannot number less than 10,000 with several thousand prisoners. Our loss is about 7000 killed and wounded. The battle commenced early in the morning, & lasted all day. At one time we had 800 pieces of artillery in full play, with almost as many more in reserve. Richardson's Division[136] played a proud part in the fight, and our Brigade

---

contributed to the debacle at Second Manassas, and he was removed from field command. *Encyclopedia of the Civil War*, 459–460.

134. Courtesy of M. Faith Kent.

135. Actual Confederate losses have been put at about 2,700 dead, Union forces about 1,800. *Encyclopedia of the Civil War*, 20.

136. Major General Israel Bush Richardson (1815–1862) rejoined the Second Corps of the Army of the Potomac just prior to the commencement of the Antietam campaign. While directing Union artillery during his division's attack at "Bloody Lane," Richardson was hit by an enemy shell. He died from his wounds on November 3, 1862. Ibid., 629.

captured six stand of colors. My Regt took the large blue silk flag of the 4th North Carolina Vols, and saved the whole Division from being outflanked. By the time I had changed front to the rear, and formed my line, the centre of ~~the~~ Wilcox'[137] Brigade the 8th 9th & 10th Regt of Alabama troops was within 100 yards of us coming through the tall corn with leveled bayonets. My boys brought down their rifles as cool as on parade, & our volley ~~hard~~ tore them into fragments. The three mounted officers of ~~w~~ the Regt in our front ~~all~~ fell at the fire. They rallied, but we held them until help came & then we hurled them back capturing their flags & many prisoners. They struck the wrong crowd when they ran against my brave men.

I went into battle with just 300 bayonets & 19 com. officers, lost one Lieut. killed, 10 officers wounded—some very badly, 6 enlisted men killed outright, and one hundred wounded—many dangerously.

Gen McClellan fought this battle, & it is a specimen of what ~~we~~ his veterans can do on a fair field. I hope this great victory of the favorite General of the Army, will put to shame the cowardly ~~sne~~ envious sneaks who stay at home & abuse him. There is a day of retribution coming for all such when the Army gets home.

Capt Cross was hit on the foot ~~a little~~ very slightly by a spent ball.[138] I got a fragment of shell over my right eye, ~~& a~~ ditto on the left cheek & ~~left~~ right arm, but not enough to keep me from duty a moment. The 5th slept in the field of battle & picketed beyond it. All night long we carried off rebel wounded & the next day picked up over 400 rifles. I changed all my Enfield for Springfield Rifles in the field. I think not less than 15000 stand of arms have already been picked up. The rebels fought with perfect desperation, & many of their prisoners owned that this defeat was ~~their ruin~~ the ruin of their cause.

The battle field was ~~m~~ several miles in extent & in some places the rebel dead ~~were~~ lay in two ranks, & in files, the most awful spectacle ever presented while the wounded strewing the earth at every step were fast dying for want of attention. O, it was a dreadful *dreadful* battle field.

The day before, while getting ready for the fight, while my Regt was deployed as sharpshooters, one of the enemy's riflemen came near ending my soldiering. He sent a ball right through my coat at the point of the shoulder—half an inch more & the shoulder joint would have been smashed to

137. Brigadier General Cadmus Marcellus Wilcox (1824–1890), whose Alabama troops were a mainstay of Longstreet's division. Ibid., 825.

138. Richard Cross's injury was minor enough that it did not appear on muster records. Child, "Complete Roster," 45.

pieces. Serg't Rhodes[139] is badly wounded but doing well. Howard[140] is also badly wounded. Joe Hart[141] safe. Send me the papers.

Yours

E E Cross Col 5th

LETTER TO EDWIN STANTON, SECRETARY OF WAR, SEPTEMBER 26, 1862[142]

♣ ♣ ♣ ♣ ♣

I respectfully ask that the colors of the 4th North Carolina Regiment, captured by my Rg't at the Battle of Antietam be restored to my Rg't.

Headquarters 5th NHVols
Camp on Bolivar's Heights
Sept 26, 1862
To the Hon Secretary of War[143]
Washington DC

Sir

I respectfully ask that the colors of the 4th North Carolina Regiment, captured by my Rg't at the Battle of Antietam be restored to my Rg't that I may send them to the Governor of New Hampshire.

I believe that similar requests to this have been granted in several instances.

I have the honor to be

Very respectfully etc.

Edward E. Cross

Col 5th NHVols

139. Eldad A. Rhodes was mustered in as a 20-year-old private from Lancaster, N.H. Appointed sergeant in January 1862, Rhodes received wounds at Antietam severe enough to lead to his discharge in February 1863. Ibid., 151.

140. Leonard W. Howard enlisted as a 19-year-old resident of Lancaster, N.H. He was wounded at Fair Oaks, but the wounds he received at Antietam put him out of service for a year and a half. He rejoined the Fifth in February 1864, serving for the remainder of the war. Ibid., 92.

141. Joseph Hart was English by birth. A 31-year-old resident of Lancaster, he joined the Fifth as a musician in August 1862. Ibid., 84.

142. Executive Records, Division of Records Management and Archives, Concord, N.H. Cross attached a copy of this to a letter written to Governor Nathaniel Berry on November 10, 1862.

143. Edwin M. Stanton (1814–1869) served as Secretary of War in the administrations of both Abraham Lincoln and Andrew Johnson. President Ulysses S. Grant appointed him to the Supreme Court in 1869; however Stanton died four days after the Senate confirmed the nomination. *Encyclopedia of the Civil War*, 712–713.

LETTER TO HENRY KENT, OCTOBER 2, 1862[144]

I begin to believe that hard work, hard times & danger
don't amount to anything.

Headquarters 5th NHV
Camp on Bolivar Heights[145]
Oct 2 1862

Dear Henry

I hear you are to have a 9 mos Rg't. If so, I can let you have some good officers. Let me know.

The enclosed paragraph is from the New York Argus.[146]

Yours truly
Edward E. Cross
Col 5th

PS. They say Col Marston[147] has been appointed Brig Gen—but he declines. He wants to be US Senator in place of Clark.[148] I have the next chance I suppose. I begin to believe that hard work, hard times & danger don't amount to anything.

144. Courtesy of M. Faith Kent.

145. On September 22, 1862, the Fifth New Hampshire left the Antietam battlefield and marched to Harper's Ferry, where it camped on Bolivar Heights, a ridge on the Maryland side of the Potomac River. The Fifth remained there for 36 days. Child, *Fifth New Hampshire*, 131–132.

146. Clipping not found.

147. Gilman Marston (1811–1890) was a graduate of Dartmouth College and Harvard Law School. A former Whig and committed abolitionist, he was elected to Congress as a Republican in 1858, 1860, and 1862. Marston returned to New Hampshire in 1861 to recruit and lead the Second New Hampshire Regiment. He led the regiment at First Bull Run, the Peninsula campaign, at Second Bull Run, and at Fredericksburg. Marston was promoted to the rank of brigadier general in the fall of 1862, but he remained with his regiment until reassigned in April 1863. After leaving the Second, he established the Point Lookout prison camp in Maryland. As a brigade commander in the Eighteenth Corps, he led a disastrous attack during the Battle of Cold Harbor. Marston intermittently returned to his seat in the House but was nevertheless reelected to Congress in 1864. He served in the U.S. Senate for four months in 1889. Waite, *New Hampshire in the Rebellion*, 116–123, and Warner, *Generals in Blue*, 312.

148. Daniel Clark (1809–1891) was a prominent Manchester attorney and politician before the legislature chose him to fill out the U.S. Senate term of James Bell, who died in 1857. He was elected to another term in 1860. Afterward, he was appointed judge of the U.S. District Court for New Hampshire. Bell, *Bench and Bar*, 269–272.

LETTER TO HENRY KENT, OCTOBER 14, 1862[149]

♣ ♣ ♣ ♣ ♣

You can have the following officers.

Headquarters 5th NH Vols
Camp on Bolivar Heights
Oct 14 1862
Dear Kent
    Yours received. I handed the documents to Merrill & he says he will pay —on pay day—
    You can have the following officers

Capt RE Cross for major
Serg't E A Rhodes[150]
    "   Lyford[151]
    "   Humphrey[152]
    "   Hale[153]
    "   Low[154]
    "   Marston[155]
    "   Gove[156]
    "   Nettleton[157]

149. Courtesy of M. Faith Kent.

150. Sergeant Eldad A. Rhodes, who was wounded at Antietam and discharged the following February. Child, "Complete Roster," 151.

151. William O. Lyford, mustered in as an 18-year-old private. He rose to the rank of first lieutenant in the Fifth prior to his discharge for disability in November 1863. Ibid., 116.

152. Mason W. Humphrey was a 20-year-old resident of Waterbury, Vt., who mustered in as a sergeant in Company B. He eventually rose to the rank of first lieutenant in Company G prior to his death at the Battle of Cold Harbor in June 1864. Ibid., 94.

153. Charles A. Hale, of Lebanon, N.H., mustered in as a 20-year-old corporal in Company C. Wounded at Fredericksburg and Chancellorsville, Hale was promoted to first lieutenant of Company E during the Battle of Gettysburg. Hale became a resident of Gettysburg after the war. Ibid., 79.

154. Probably Nathaniel F. Lowe, of Randolph, N.H., who mustered in as a 19-year-old corporal in Company B. He eventually rose to the rank of first lieutenant before his discharge in October 1864. Ibid., 115

155. Elias H. Marston, of North Hampton, N.H., began service as an 18-year-old private. He rose to the rank of sergeant major prior to his discharge in October 1864. Ibid., 119.

156. George S. Gove was a 20-year-old recruit from Raymond, N.H. He mustered in as a sergeant and eventually rose to the rank of first lieutenant in Company C. Ibid., 75.

157. A native of England, George Nettleton was a 29-year-old resident of Claremont, N.H., upon muster. He was appointed sergeant of Company G shortly thereafter. Despite being

"   Hubbard[158]
"   Walker[159]

for Lieutenants. Also Lieut Livermore[160] for Adjutant. That is the best I can do for you. They are all *fire proof* men & know their duty.

I hope you will get the Reg't. If they appoint anybody over me I shall at once quit the Service. Everybody says I ought to have the place. No man from N H has the recommendations that I have. Griffin[161] has not been heard of. I have no political recommendations to offer. Six generals have signed my recommendations, including Richardson, Sedgwick,[162] and Sumner. Also I have been three times mentioned in orders for "gallant and meritorious conduct under fire."

If they don't give me the place it is an act of gross injustice.

Yours ever

Edward E. Cross

The appointments of the Sergeants named, secures their discharge from my Rg't. Dick will make you a good major.

---

wounded, he captured the flag of the Fourth North Carolina at the Battle of Antietam. Nettleton was promoted to second lieutenant of Company E on November 10, 1862, but died from wounds received at Fredericksburg a month later. Ibid., 135.

158. Either Charles L. Hubbard, of Wakefield, N.H., or George Hubbard, of Winchester, N.H., although neither ever rose to the rank of sergeant in the Fifth. Both were discharged on account of disability in early 1863. Ibid., 93.

159. Thomas H. Walker was a 23-year-old resident of Durham, N.H., upon enlistment. He was promoted from sergeant to second lieutenant in Company K in December 1862, but he resigned his commission in June 1863. Ibid., 189.

160. Thomas L. Livermore was a 19-year-old enlistee from Milford, N.H. He rose from sergeant, Company K, to second lieutenant in June 1862 and to first lieutenant in December 1862. He was appointed captain of Company E in March 1863, but he left the Fifth on June 30, 1863, to become chief of ambulance for the Second Corps. In January 1865 Livermore became colonel of the Eighteenth New Hampshire. Ibid., 113.

161. Simon Goodell Griffin (1824–1902), of Nelson, N.H., was a captain in the Second New Hampshire prior to becoming lieutenant colonel of the Sixth New Hampshire in November 1861. He became colonel of the regiment in 1862 while serving along the Carolina coast with General Ambrose E. Burnside. The Sixth was part of Burnside's Ninth Corps at Second Bull Run and at Antietam. At the Battle of Fredericksburg, his regiment lost a third of its men. He later served at Vicksburg and in the campaign against Richmond and Petersburg. Griffin was promoted to the rank of brigadier general in May 1864. Waite, *New Hampshire in the Rebellion*, 306–311, and Warner, *Generals in Blue*, 191–192.

162. John Sedgwick (1813–1864) graduated from West Point in the class of 1837. He fought against the Seminoles in Florida, in the Mexican War, and out West prior to the Civil War. By mid-1862, he had achieved both the rank of major general and a reputation for gallantry under fire. He died at the Battle of Spotsylvania in May 1864 after being struck in the face by a sharpshooter's bullet. Warner, *Generals in Blue*, 430–431.

LETTER TO HENRY KENT, OCTOBER 24, 1862[163]

♣ ♣ ♣ ♣ ♣

Do not take many people from Coos. They will watch you
like cats & be the first to find fault. — Mark my word.

Headquarters 5th N H Vols
Camp on Bolivar Heights
Oct 24 1862

Dear Kent

I am glad you have a Regiment—but it should have been a three-year
instead of a 9 mos militia. In Long you have a good & brave soldier. I have
been trying for a long time to secure his appointment. *Barton* is *nowhere*
compared to Long.[164] Go to the State House and ask to see the papers in
Long's favor. I do not care about sparing many of my boys. They are tried &
true, & would rather have their promotion in the Reg't with which they have
so long been identified. Our tattered colors now bear the names of Eight battles & it is an honor to march under them.

Dick's ambition is to go into the regular cavalry, and he will have ample
recommendations.

Leave all your prejudices at home. Do just; & strive to preserve discipline
among officers and men or you are a *goner*. There will be but two or three
successful colonels out of all the lot appointed from NH. The friends to
which you should go for advice, and on which you should rely, are the *Articles of War*. Do not take many people from Coos. They will watch you like
cats & be the first to find fault. — Mark my word.

I thank God constantly that I have as few as I have from my own vicinity.
I hope & trust that you nine months men will have the front of the battle &
let the old Reg'ts rest. The new troops here are very unpopular on account of
their grumbling & inefficiency. My regards to Long.

Yours truly
E. Cross

About my appointment I can only say that I am entitled to it. And let me say
also—that after one year's service ⨍ & what I have seen & what I *know*—let

---

163. Executive Records, Division of Records Management and Archives, Concord, N.H.
164. Cross advised Kent to appoint Charles H. Long rather than Ira McL. Barton as major
of the Seventeenth New Hampshire. Long received the appointment, although both Long and
Barton later served in New Hampshire artillery units. Waite, *New Hampshire in the Rebellion*,
535, and Child, "Complete Roster," 13, 114.

me tell you, I can get along without the service better than the service can get along without me! If we mean to whip the South, we must keep our old officers & old troops. If I am not appointed I shall quit the service & go back to the Land of the Hidalgos.

LETTER TO GOVERNOR NATHANIEL S. BERRY, NOVEMBER 10, 1862[165]

*I have endeavored to get the large State colors captured by
my Rg't at Antietam, to send them home.*

Headquarters 5th NHVols
Camp near Warrenton Nov 10, 1862
Hon N. S. Berry
Gov of NH
Concord

Dear Sir

By the enclosed letter to the Secretary of War[166] & its endorsements, you will see that I have endeavored to get the large State colors captured by my Rg't at Antietam, to send them home.[167] The War Department however declines. I think if you were to apply the Secretary of War would allow the flag to go. I should like to have it placed in the Council Chamber, along with the torn & battle worn colors of the state.

I am very truly
Edward E. Cross
Col 5th NHV

LETTER TO ELIJAH C. WILKINS, NOVEMBER 10, 1862[168]

*I tell the boys we have just space on our colors for the name of
one more big battle and just men enough to fight one.*

165. Executive Records, Division of Records Management and Archives, Concord, N.H.

166. See letter to Edwin Stanton, Secretary of War, September 26, 1862.

167. Cross received his wish following the Battle of Fredericksburg and presented the captured flag at a Republican assembly in Concord, N.H., on New Year's Day 1863. Pride and Travis, *Brave Boys*, 182.

168. Published as part of the appendix, Child, *Fifth New Hampshire*, 217–219.

Headquarters Fifth N. H. Volunteers
Camp near Warrenton,[169] Nov. 10, 1862

Rev. E. R. Wilkins:[170]

Dear Friend: Your kind letter reached me yesterday. We were all glad to hear from you, officers and men, and there is no one in the state from whom we should be more pleased to receive a visit. If we should happen to go into winter quarters you must come and spend a week with us. You would miss many familiar faces. The hard labors of the past year have told heavily on us, and we have received only 127 recruits. Yet no regiment from the state holds its own better. For example we went into Antietam with 300 rifles, lost 107 killed and wounded. Two months have passed, months of hard labor, skirmishing, picketing, guards, and long marches, and to-day we have again just 300 rifles for duty! All the gain since Antietam is from old soldiers returned. I tell the boys we have just space on our colors for the name of one more big battle and just men enough to fight one.

The regiment is very healthy, though we need clothes and shoes very much. The shoes and clothes, as a general thing, are very poor. The shoes do not wear over twenty days and the clothing is not half sewed. As for pay, it is now going on five months since the men have had a cent. It is so all through the army. Be assured my dear friend, I do not write these things in a complaining spirit, but only to let you know how the old regiment gets along, while the new ones seem to have everything. If there is a dangerous post, an important picket or a place of responsibility, an old regiment is sent. This is very natural, but at the same time rather hard, under the circumstances.

A year has passed. The Fifth has fought in eight battles, half a dozen skirmishes, six times advanced in front of the enemy. First at Antietam and Fair Oaks, last to leave the bloody field of Malvern Hill; rear guard on the retreat from Centreville; first to drive the enemy through Snicker's Gap a few days since—bronzed, scarred, ragged, diminished, but not dismayed. Our works, too, has been heavy—roads, bridges, facines and gabions used at Yorktown, the big observatory of the Signal Corps; the great bridge over the Chickahominy, built in water and mud from two to six feet deep and seventy rods

169. When the Fifth left Harper's Ferry, it was assigned to guard a wagon train en route to Warrenton, Va. The army encamped at Warrenton for a final review by McClellan, who had been replaced as commander of the Army of the Potomac by Ambrose Burnside. Pride and Travis, *Brave Boys*, 154–155.

170. Elijah R. Wilkins, a printer, Methodist Episcopal minister, and resident of Lisbon, N.H., joined the Fifth upon it organization in the fall of 1861. He resigned as chaplain on June 18, 1862. Child, *Fifth New Hampshire*, 320.

long; the rifle-pits at Fair Oaks, and the redoubts at Harrison's Landing; New Hampshire muscle, you know, many a hard day's labor. When I think of our work, out fights and our marches, our days and nights in mud and rain without tents and on short allowance, I feel that what is left of us have verily "Come up out of great tribulations."

In all the year past many, very many times, have I admired the courage, patience and fortitude of my officers and men; for new troops—citizens turned suddenly into soldiers—these qualities were exemplified in an extra-ordinary degree. I feel proud of the regiment, of its good name and high standing in the army, for we all know it does stand high, and for its noble and steady bravery under fire. You know "Old Richardson,"[171] as we called him, styled us the "Fire Proofs," and the boys have earned the title."

Come and see the boys if you can. You will find lots of changes, some promotions, but only two deaths of commissioned officers, Lieutenants Bean[172] and Gay.[173] Both received their mortal wounds at Antietam—fine young men, both of them, promoted the same day from sergeants. You remember George Gay, tall, straight, fine looking young man, a perfect young soldier. At Antietam he was the first to discover the flank movement of the enemy. We were in the tall corn firing to the front, when suddenly Gay came running up, seized me by the arm and shouted in my ear "Colonel, the enemy are trying to outflank us!" I ran with him and being pretty tall I saw more than he did—I saw five battle-flags of the enemy waving in the corn on our left, and in an instant the gray-backs raised their well-known battle yell and came on. I tell you brother Wilkins, it was a big moment just then. We changed front "double quick" and met them full in the centre, bang!! At thirty paces. It was beautiful to see how those devils piled up, and when we raised the war-whoop and tumbled them back over the rail-fence they had not a single color left! But poor Gay was struck down—a piece of shell right in the top of his head, paralyzing the brain in an instant. We buried him near the battle-field, but his body has since been carried to Boston and buried with his father.

Yours ever,
E. E. Cross, Col. 5th

171. General Israel Bush Richardson.

172. Second Lieutenant Charles W. Bean died a month later as the result of wounds received at Antietam. Child, "Complete Roster," 14.

173. Lieutenant George A. Gay was commissioned second lieutenant of Company D six days prior to his death at Antietam on September 17, 1862. Ibid., 70.

LETTER TO WILLIAM H. HACKETT, PORTSMOUTH, N.H., NOVEMBER 26, 1862[174]

♣ ♣ ♣ ♣ ♣

Captain Murray served in the regular army during the Mexican War & has no superior in the service for bravery & capacity to command.

Headquarters 5th NHVols
Camp near Fredericksburg[175]
Nov 26 1862

W. H. Hackett Esq[176]
Dear Sir

There will be a vacancy in my Rg't soon for the post of Major. I desire a citizen of your city to have it, namely John Murray,[177] 2nd Capt of my Rg't. he is one of the best officers in the service. You can help him with the Gov & Council. I shall recommend him. My 1st Captain is unfit for a field officer.[178]

Captain Murray served in the regular army during the Mexican War & has no superior in the service for bravery & capacity to command.

Yours truly
Edward E. Cross
Col 5th NHV

LETTER TO MRS. JAMES B. PERRY, DECEMBER 20, 1862[179]

♣ ♣ ♣ ♣ ♣

He fell in front of the enemy with the colors of the regiment in his hand.

174. Military Records, Fifth Regiment, 1861–1865. New Hampshire Records and Archives, Concord, N.H.

175. The Fifth had reached Falmouth, across the river from Fredericksburg, on November 17, 1862. Pride and Travis, *Brave Boys,* 164.

176. William Henry Hackett (1827–1891), of Portsmouth, N.H., was a lawyer, politician, and journalist. During the war, he served on the Portsmouth City Council and was elected to the state legislature in 1864 in and 1865. Bell, *Bench and Bar,* 410.

177. John Murray, captain of Company D of the Fifth from October 12, 1861, until he was killed at Fredericksburg on December 13, 1862. Child, "Complete Roster," 134.

178. Cross was probably referring to Captain James E. Larkin, who along with Captain James B. Perry had been charged with inciting mutiny. Both survived court-martial and were reinstated as company commanders on December 10, 1862. Pride and Travis, *Brave Boys,* 157–162.

179. Unidentified newspaper clipping. Edward E. Cross Papers, Milne Special Collections and Archives, University of New Hampshire, Durham, N.H.

Washington, D. C.
Dec. 20, 1862

Mrs. James B. Perry
Dear Madam:

I take the first opportunity afforded me by the state of my wounds, since the disastrous Battle of Fredericksburg, to address you a few words in relation to your lamented husband, the brave, faithful and accomplished soldier, so long a Captain in my regiment.[180]

He fell in front of the enemy with the colors of the regiment in his hand.[181] He was not instantly killed, but to those around spoke of his family—of his regret that he could not see them—that he was not afraid to die, and hoped to meet all his friends and comrades in the spirit world. His last act was to press the colors to his lips, and the brave soul passed calmly to his Maker.

Captain Perry was greatly esteemed for his soldierly and manly qualities, by the whole regiment, and his country has lost a faithful and fearless defender.

I believe that he has only "gone before"—a little sooner than the rest he is permitted to view the glories of a better world, which are secure to the true patriot, the good citizen and one who falls in his country's cause.

Accept, Madam, my cordial sympathy for yourself and little one, and if I can ever be of any service to the family of my brave comrade, do not fail to write me.

> Very truly, &c
> Edward E. Cross
> Col. 5th. Reg't N.H.V.

LETTER TO MRS. JOHN MURRAY, DECEMBER 21, 1862[182]

♣ ♣ ♣ ♣ ♣

He fell in the front rank of battle—killed instantly—probably suffering no pain.

---

180. Captain James B. Perry of Company C. Just days before, he and Captain James E. Larkin had been cleared of charges of mutinous behavior brought against them by Cross. Child, "Complete Roster," 143, and Pride and Travis, *Brave Boys*, 156–162.

181. Perry was hit by a minié ball shortly after he took the flag from Corporal Jacob Davis, who lay mortally wounded. Pride and Travis, *Brave Boys*, 174–175.

182. Unidentified newspaper clipping. Edward E. Cross Papers, Milne Special Collections and Archives, University of New Hampshire, Durham, N.H.

Washington
Dec. 21 [1862]

Mrs. John Murray
Dear Madame:

I avail myself of the first opportunity since the Battle of Fredericksburg—allowed by my wounds,—to address you a few lines in relation to your lamented husband, Capt. John Murray, who was one of the bravest and most faithful officers in the army.—Certainly he had no superior in my regiment. Captain Murray was one of my best friends. I loved him for his sterling honesty, his frankness, and the dependence which could always be placed in him; for his brave and soldierly character.

He fell in the front rank of battle[183]—killed instantly—probably suffering no pain.—Accept, Madame, for yourself and children, my kindest sympathy, and if ever I can be of service to the family of my beloved comrade, do not fail to call on me.

I am, Madame, with much respect, your ob't serv't,

Edward E. Cross
Col. 5th N. H. Regt.

LETTER TO EPHRAIM CROSS, DECEMBER 21, 1862[184]

♣ ♣ ♣ ♣ ♣

I am not half as badly hurt as the papers say.

Washington Dec 21, 1862

Dear father[185]

I am in this city doing well. Mr Chase[186] is with me. I am not half so badly hurt as the papers say.

183. Murray assumed command of the Fifth after Cross and Major Sturtevant had fallen and continued the advance for 200 yards more. When he fell, shot through the head, the Fifth's advance began to falter. Pride and Travis, *Brave Boys,* 172–174.

184. Edward E. Cross Papers, Milne Special Collections and Archives. University of New Hampshire, Durham, N.H.

185. Ephraim Cross (1795–1876), although trained as a hatter, was listed as a farmer in the census of 1860. He had been a lieutenant colonel in the town militia and was commonly addressed as Colonel Cross. "Cross Family Genealogy," Lancaster Historical Society, and Pride and Travis, *Brave Boys,* 7.

186. Cross's brother-in-law, Dexter Chase. "Cross Family Genealogy," Lancaster Historical Society.

As soon as I am able I shall go to Concord, for a few days—but not to Lancaster—the weather is to cold.

You need not be in any apprehension about me. I hope the Democrats will carry the State next spring.

You probably received the money Dick & I sent.

> In haste
> Yours
> E E Cross
> Col 5th
> NHV

LETTER TO FRANKLIN PIERCE, FEBRUARY 19, 1863[187]

I find that everything I said or done as a democrat is known here to Rollins and his fanatiks.

National Hotel
Washington DC
Feb 19, 1863

Dear General,[188]

I have been here *some* days quite lame on account of the cold damp weather.

You will observe that the new conscription bill passed the Senate without opposition. I am told that the President has assured the opposition party in the Senate that he will not adhere to his radical policy. At all events Seward[189] was on the floor of the Senate all the time the bill was up, &

---

187. Franklin Pierce Papers, New Hampshire Historical Society, Concord, N.H.

188. Franklin Pierce, fourteenth president of the United States and a New Hampshire native.

189. William Henry Seward (1801–1872), of New York, secretary of state under both Abraham Lincoln and Andrew Johnson. While sometimes heavy-handed and prone to meddling in military decisions, Seward successfully kept foreign nations from siding with the Confederacy for the duration of the war. *Encyclopedia of the Civil War*, 668–669.

appeared very busy. Butler[190] is here very active at the War Department. Gen Fremont[191] is urging his claims for a command.

The Senate was so disgusted at the conduct of the President in sending in such a batch of military appointments (& many of them so unworthy) that they sent the entire lot back with a resolution requesting him to send in none but *soldiers*, recommended by the General in Chief. They all tell me that I shall have my appointment, but I think Harriman[192] has been *hired* to stand by the promise of a Brig Genship. My senior officers oppose my resigning and my Reg't is in great trouble about it. I shall wait a few days. I find that everything I said or done as a democrat is known here to Rollins[193] and his fanatiks. I had a long talk with [illegible] Forney.[194] He asked very particularly after you. He looks careworn & old.

I should be glad to hear of the prospects at home. Very truly etc

Edward E. Cross

Gen Franklin Pierce
Concord, NH

190. Benjamin Franklin Butler (1818–1893), born in Deerfield, N.H., rose to prominence as a lawyer and politician in Massachusetts. As a Democrat, Butler championed the unsuccessful candidacy of Jefferson Davis at the Democratic convention. A few years later, Butler had aligned himself with the radical wing of the Republican Party. Butler began his military career as brigadier general in the Massachusetts militia. Lincoln promoted Butler to volunteer major general in May 1861. Butler offended many Southerners with his strict administration as the military governor of New Orleans. He was removed from New Orleans in December 1862 and given command of the Army of the James later in 1863. Warner, *Generals in Blue*, 60–61.

191. John Charles Frémont (1813–1890), the mercurial explorer and California pioneer, served one term in the U.S. Senate before becoming the Republican Party's first candidate for president in 1856. Lincoln appointed him a major general in the regular army, yet his performance during the Civil War was poor. In the spring of 1862, he had asked to be relieved from duty after he had been assigned to the command of General John Pope. Ibid., 160–161.

192. Walter Harriman (1817–1884), of Warner, N.H., colonel of the Eleventh New Hampshire.

193. Edward Henry Rollins (1824–1889), of Rollinsford, N.H., served three terms in the U.S. House of Representatives (1861–1867). He left the American or Know-Nothing Party in the mid-1850s to join the newly formed Republican Party. He became the state party's first chairman and later represented New Hampshire in the U.S. Senate (1877–1883). *New Hampshire Men: A Collection of Biographical Sketches*, George H. Moses, ed. (Concord, N.H.: New Hampshire Publishing Co., 1893), 72.

194. John Wien Forney (1817–1891), Pennsylvania-born journalist and politician, was secretary of the U.S. Senate and founding editor of the *Sunday Morning Chronicle* during the Civil War. Although a longtime Democratic operative and James Buchanan supporter, Forney joined the Republicans in 1860. Nevertheless, he gave Cross a strong letter of recommendation and later wrote a biography of General Winfield Scott Hancock. *American Authors, 1600–1900: A Biographical Dictionary of American Literature*, Stanley J. Kunitz and Howard Haycraft, eds. (New York: Wilson, 1938), 282, and Pride and Travis, *Brave Boys*, 198.

LETTER TO JOHN HATCH GEORGE, CONCORD, N.H.
FEBRUARY 25, 1863[195]

I am quite sick—unable to go to my Rg't.

Washington Feb 25 1863

John H. George, Esq[196]
    Dear Sir
    W H Farrar[197] formerly of ~~Oregon~~ NH now of Oregon, a splendid speaker, is now here. He wants to visit NH—especially Lancaster where he was born —he will speak in each Congressional District if invited. His address is Kirkwood House Washington DC.
    Farrar was Attorney Gen of Oregon under Pierce.
    How are the prospects?
    I hope for the best. I am quite sick—unable to go to my Rg't.
    The Prest[198] will soon call for *500,000 men* as soon as the conscription bill passes.

Yours truly
E. E. Cross
National Hotel

195. New Hampshire Historical Society, Concord, N.H.

196. John Hatch George (1824–1888), a Concord native and three-time Democratic candidate for Congress. He practiced law with Franklin Pierce, later serving as U.S. Attorney for the District of New Hampshire (1854–1858), as chairman of the New Hampshire Democratic Committee, and as a member of the Democratic National Committee (1852–1856). Bell, *Bench and Bar*, 393–394.

197. William H. Farrar (1826–1873) practiced law in Massachusetts prior to his appointment as territorial district attorney for Oregon in 1853. A delegate to Oregon's Constitutional Convention in 1857, Farrar practiced law in Portland, Oregon, and served as that city's mayor from 1862 to 1863. In 1863, Farrar moved to Washington, D. C., where he practiced law until his death ten years later. *Dictionary of Oregon History*, Howard McKinley Corning, ed. (Portland: Binfords and Mort, 1956), 82.

198. Abraham Lincoln (1809–1865), sixteenth president of the United States.

LETTER TO FRANKLIN PIERCE, APRIL 14, 1863[199]

♣ ♣ ♣ ♣ ♣

Did any one ever hear or know of anything equal to the malice of Niggerism!

5th NHV
Head-Quarters Right Grand Division
Army of the Potomac
Camp near Falmouth April 14, 1863

Dear General

I thank you for the kind opinion you were pleased to express of my military services, in your letter lately received. The President promised me my promotion, and Gen Sumner[200] applied for me to be assigned to Arizona. In fact, the orders to that effect were in my hands, when they were countermanded by the War Department, on the account of Gen Sumner's death. Otherwise, it would have been my fortune to join the destinies of a New Territory. This hope kept me in the service, together with the natural reluctance which a commander feels to leave the tried, true, & brave men of his command, who have so nobly acquitted themselves in this war.

Since the adjournment of Congress the President has appointed several Colonels Brig Gens—and had the Army been searched for that purpose he could not have selected more unworthy men. For instance, Col Owens[201] of Pa., was tried and convicted before Gen Court Martial of "drunkenness & attempt at rape," & afterwards restored by political influence. Gen Carr,[202]

199. Franklin Pierce Papers, New Hampshire Historical Society, Concord, N.H.

200. Major General Edwin Vose Sumner, the oldest active corps commander during the Civil War, left the Army of the Potomac during the winter of 1863. Exhausted and besieged by criticism of his command decisions at Antietam, he was assigned to the Department of Missouri. He died in Syracuse, N.Y., on March 21, 1863, while en route to his new post. *Encyclopedia of the Civil War*, 733.

201. Joshua Thomas Owen (1821–1887) was nicknamed "Paddy" despite his Welsh birth. He served as colonel of the Sixty-ninth Pennsylvania prior to his promotion to the rank of brigadier general on November 29, 1862. Warner, *Generals in Blue*, 353–354.

202. Joseph Bradford Carr (1828–1895), born in Albany, N.Y., of Irish parents, commanded the Second New York Infantry and rose to brigade command during the Peninsula campaign. Nevertheless, the U.S. Senate refused to act upon his commission. In late 1863, he rose to division command in Hancock's Second Corps but officially remained junior to his brigade commanders as the result of Senate inaction. An official commission notwithstanding, he later commanded a division of Negro troops in the Army of the James and was brevetted major general at the close of the war. Ibid., 71–72.

whom the Senate refused to confirm on the ground of "unfitness to command" has also been re-appointed, while such noble and well tried officers as *Cowdin*[203] are allowed to go home, through the spleen & malice of John A. Andrew[204] & Associates. Did any one ever hear or know of anything equal to the *malice* of *Niggerism!*

Again, the Army is full of Abolition spies, under the guise of tract distributors, State Agents—chaplains & Sanitary Commission Agents. The correspondents of the Abolition papers are also among the most malignant spies of the administration. Every opinion an officer privately expresses in social conversation is liable to appear against him when he least expects it. All the 2d & 3d rate officers, the Sneaks, the Malingers, the *Cowards*, have found this out, & cover their deficiencies by the cloak of Abolitionism. That is why so many of this lot are coming up to be Colonels, Generals &

The order for the mustering out of all Colonels & Majors & all officers not needed for five Companies in each Reg't having less than 500 men was either devised by a *traitor* or a *fool*. ⊞ Clean the Army of all the experienced Colonels, & leave in service only those of the nine mos Reg'ts & issue few of the new 3 yr. No more effectual blow could have been struck for the destruction & demoralization of the Army. The injustice & bad policy of this order will be apparent to you, at once Colonels of 12 & 18 month's service, who have been in 6 or 8 battles, all sent away, & all the reputation, the *Esprit de Corps* of the Rgt lost. Such was the feeling of astonishment and indignation expressed by Division and Corps Commanders, that Gen Hooker[205] has returned the order, as "totally impracticable."

The cause of this order is said to be—that the War Dep't desires to call out the conscripts in new Rg'ts—one of the most *insane* & foolish ideas that could be entertained at this time. We should have another lot of armed *mobs* for the next year to secure defeat & disgrace. In God's name why don't the

203. Robert Cowdin (1805–1874), a native of Jamaica, Vt., who served as colonel of the First Massachusetts, the state's first three-year regiment. General Joseph Hooker recommended him for promotion to brigadier general for his bravery at Williamsburg. He received that appointment in September 1862 and led a brigade in the defense of Washington during the fall and winter of 1862. The Senate chose not to confirm his appointment, and on March 30, 1863, Cowdin was relieved of command. He subsequently returned to his home in Massachusetts. Ibid., 96–97.

204. John Albion Andrew (1818–1866), a native of Maine, was governor of Massachusetts from 1860 to 1866. Andrew's abolitionist sympathies and public support of insurrectionist John Brown made him a controversial figure. As war governor of Massachusetts, he pushed for the state to meet volunteer quotas, raised the famous Fifty-fourth Massachusetts, the state's first African-American regiment, and fought for the defense of the commonwealth against possible Confederate sympathizers in Canada. *Encyclopedia of the Civil War*, 17.

205. Major General Joseph Hooker, then commander of the Army of the Potomac.

people protect against such miserable management. Again—Gen Hooker has *Wilkes*[206] of the spirit of the times as a chief sutler[207] at headquarters. His real business is to cheat gov't—manage the newspaper correspondents —keep the *Hooker* sentiment up, by the aid of *whiskey* and *champaign*.

These points, General are all good ones. You can use them, but keep the authority secret for the present.

I am always glad to hear from you, in relation to State matters.

With much respect etc
Edward E. Cross

Gen F Pierce
Concord NH

LETTER TO ANTHONY OR DANIEL COLBY, ADJUTANT GENERAL OF NEW HAMPSHIRE, APRIL 21, 1863[208]

♣ ♣ ♣ ♣ ♣

The order to muster out all the Colonels, Majors, & surplus Line and non com officers of Rgts less than 300 men would strip the Army of its best officers.

Headquarters 5th NHVols
Camp near Falmouth
April 21 1863

General[209]

206. George Wilkes (1817–1885), journalist and founder of both the *National Police Gazette* and *Wilkes' Spirit of the Times*. During the war, Wilkes used his vigorous editorials and other publications to attack George McClellan. His wartime coverage and praise for Ulysses Grant made him one of Secretary of War Edwin Stanton's favorite writers. Sam G. Riley, "George Wilkes," *Dictionary of Literary Biography* (Detroit: Gale Research, 1989), vol. 79, *American Magazine Journalists, 1850–1900*, Sam G. Riley, ed., 302–305.

207. Sutlers were civilian merchants who sold approved items to soldiers in camp. There was usually one sutler per regiment. In many cases, sutlers were the only source for such goods, and soldiers often felt cheated by this monopoly. Although alcoholic beverages were not among "approved" items, sutlers clearly played a role in this illegal trade. *Encyclopedia of the Civil War*, 738.

208. Military Records, Fifth Regiment, 1861–1865, New Hampshire Records and Archives, Concord, N.H.

209. Probably Daniel E. Colby (1815–1891), who officially succeeded his father as adjutant general on August 21, 1863. Anthony Colby had resigned as adjutant general at the beginning the year. *A History of the Town of New London, Merrimack County, New Hampshire, 1779–1899* (Concord, N.H.: Rumford Press, 1899), 336–337; and Waite, *New Hampshire in the Rebellion*, 601.

Your letter with the three commissions enclosed received. Dame[210] goes to Co K—Duren[211] to Co B. The others are not yet assigned. As soon as the assignment is made you will be notified. I did not intend to put in the letters of the Co.

My Rg't was never in so good condition. I have the veterans of ~~th~~ nearly two years service. None sick in Regimental Hospital and only 10 in quarters —of this ten 5 are laid up from old wounds—but will be soon on duty. The other five have slight camp ailments. I have 200 bayonets for duty—total present 240 officers & men. We are in good spirits and ready to march on a moment's notice.

The order to muster out all the Colonels, Majors, & surplus Line and non com officers of Rgts less than 300 men would strip the Army of its best officers. Gen Hooker declines issuing the order & threatens to leave if it is issued. Such is the report here. I am perfectly willing to go. If the gov't can stand it we can. Still, I do not believe such an injudicious order will be carried out. The enemy are in strong force in front of us. With regards to the Gov & Council

> I am
> Very truly
> Edward E. Cross
> Col 5th NHV

Gen Colby
A A Gen
NH

LETTER TO GOVERNOR NATHANIEL S. BERRY, MAY 16, 1863[212]

We are worn down—we feel entitled to a little rest.

Washington May 16 1863

Hon N S Berry
Dear Sir

---

210. Robert S. Dame, of Concord, N.H., was promoted from second lieutenant of Company B to first lieutenant of Company K on March 3, 1863. Child, "Complete Roster," 48.

211. John A. Duren, also of Concord, replaced Dame as second lieutenant of Company B on April 1, 1863. Ibid., 58.

212. Executive Records, Division of Records Management and Archives, Concord, N.H.

I came up yesterday to the Sec of War[213] about the 5th going home for a short time, now the 2d is ordered back. I lost severely in the late great battle, & have only 190 for duty.[214]

I desire to fill up with drafted men, & in behalf of the Rg't ask that an effort may be made to get us home. We have hard service, more so than any Rg't from the state. We are worn down—we feel entitled to a little rest. I earnestly entrust the action of the State authorities in the matter. We only ask 30 days,[215]

Very truly,
Edward E. Cross
Col 5th NHV

LETTER TO COLONEL J. B. FRY, MAY 31, 1863[216]

I beg leave to state that Capt Barton has received
no recommendation from me.

Headquarters 1st Brigade
May 31 1863

Colonel[217]

I understand that Capt Ira M' L Barton,[218] formerly Captain in my Rg't has applied to be appointed Major or Colonel in the Invalid Corps.[219]

---

213. Edwin M. Stanton.

214. Actually, the Fifth's casualty list at Chancellorsville was shorter than what had become customary: 5 killed and 28 wounded. Pride and Travis, *Brave Boys*, 220–221.

215. The Fifth returned to New Hampshire for leave in August 1863, a month after the Battle of Gettysburg and Cross's death. Ibid., 251.

216. Barton Papers, Rauner Special Collections Library, Dartmouth College, Hanover, N.H.

217. James Barnet Fry (1827–1894), a West Pointer who spent most of his military career in staff positions. As director of the Bureau of the Provost Marshal General, Fry worked to stem the tide of deserters, reorganized recruiting, and enforced the conscription acts. He rose to the rank of brevet major general. Warner, *Generals in Blue*, 162–163.

218. Ira McL. Barton, of Newport, N.H., formerly captain of Company E, prior to his resignation on September 6, 1862. Child, "Complete Roster," 13.

219. Created in April 1863, the Invalid Corps enabled disabled soldiers a chance to serve in noncombatant roles, thus enabling fitter soldiers to serve at the front. *Encyclopedia of the Civil War*, 383.

I beg leave to state that Capt Barton has received no recommendation from me nor from the Brigadier under which he served; nor *can he receive any*.

> Very truly &
> Edward E Cross
> Col 5th NHV
> Com 1st Brig

Col J B Fry
[illegible]
USA

LETTER TO MURAT HALSTEAD, *CINCINNATI COMMERCIAL*, JUNE 1, 1863[220]

♣ ♣ ♣ ♣ ♣

For if I am to die on the battle field, I pray it may be with the cheers of victory in my ears.

Headquarters 1st Brigade
Hancock's Division. June 1, 1863

Fredericksburg came near being my last battle. As we were advancing to those fatal heights in line of battle, I was near my colors. A twelve-pounder shell from the Washington battery burst in front of me. One fragment struck me just below the heart, making a bad wound. Another blew off my hat; another (small bit) entered my mouth and broke out three of my best jaw teeth, while gravel, bits of frozen earth and minute fragments of shell covered my face with bruises. I fell insensible, and lay for some time when another fragment of shell striking me on the left leg below my knee, brought me to my senses.—My mouth was full of blood, fragments of teeth and gravel, my breast bone almost broken in, and I lay in the mud two inches deep. My brave boys had gone along. I always told them never to stop for me. Dead and wounded lay thick around. One Captain of French's Division

220. This letter was reprinted in several, mostly Democratic, papers. This extract is taken from the *Granite State Free Press* (Littleton, N.H.), August 15, 1863, 2. The original was most likely addressed to Murat Halstead, editor and correspondent of the *Cincinnati Commercial*. His friendship with Cross dated back to Cross's time at the *Cincinnati Times*. As a war correspondent, Halstead gained access to the front prior to the Battle of Fredericksburg, thus enabling him to spend a few hours in camp with his old friend. Pride and Travis, *Brave Boys*, 165.

was gasping in death within a foot of me, his bowels all torn out.—The air was full of hissing bullets and bursting shells. Getting on my hands and knees, I looked for my flag. Thank God, there it fluttered right amid the smoke and fire of the front line. I could hear the cheers of my brave men. Twice the colors dropped, but twice they were up in an instant. I tried to crawl along, but a shell came and struck the steel scabbard of my saber, splitting it open and knocking me flat. Dizzy and faint, I had sense enough to lay myself out decently, "feet to toe." Two lines passed over me, but soon they swayed back, trampling on the dead and dying. Halting about thirty yards in the rear, one laid down and commenced firing. Image the situation. Right between two fires of bullets and shell, for our own artillery fire from over the river was mostly too short, and did great damage to our own troops. I lay on the field for hours—the most awful moments of my life. As the balls from our line hissed over me within a foot of my head, covered my face with both hands, and counted rapidly from one to two hundred, expecting every moment my brains would spatter the ground. But they did not. My guardian angels (if there are such personages) or my destiny saved me. The end of my days was reserved for another, and I hope more fortunate occasion. For if I am to die on the battle field, I pray it may be with the cheers of victory in my ears. When it became dark some of my men found me, and I was carried to the hospital.

You remember the evening of our little festival. Out of the gay crowd of officers, three assembled; death has made a painful muster. Of the nineteen officers of the Fifth New Hampshire, in the battle, seven were killed and ten wounded.—Only our mounted officer was left in the brigade, which left half its numbers dead and wounded on the field.

Thank Heaven, that the old "Fire-proof" added to its glorious names that day. The same colors that were in front at Fair Oaks, Malvern Hill and Antietam, were planted nearest to those inaccessible batteries. Out of two hundred and forty-nine of my regiment, one hundred and eighty were killed and wounded. Capt. Perry, and Capt. Merrey,[221] were shot with the colors in their hands.—Major Sturtevant and Capt. Moore[222] fell within thirty or forty yards of that stone wall at the foot of the hill. But I have no heart to go over details. The scenes of that battle added ten years to my existence. I suppose we are now in summer quarters.

When are the *conscripts coming?* The enemy are very strong in front of

221. Captains James B. Perry and John Murray.
222. Major Edward E. Sturtevant and Captain William A. Moore of Littleton, N.H. Mustered in as a 20-year-old second lieutenant, Moore became captain of Company H only weeks before his death. Child, "Complete Roster," 130.

us. I want to fight this thing out. My life, my all, is at the service of this country, but let me tell you, it is *hard fighting* against *stupidity foolishness* and *treason* at *home.*

I now command the old 1st Brigade. I have often been recommended for promotion, and by no less than twelve Generals. Yet, so it goes.

Yours truly,
Edward E. Cross
Commanding 1st Brigade

Part Four

Civil War Poetry of
Colonel Edward E. Cross

Cross likely penned the following verses while recovering from wounds received at Fredericksburg. These words are reminiscent of the heroic fiction that Cross had published years before he became a witness to war. More important, they reflect the pride he held for his regiment. Walter Holden arranged the verses from Cross's draft; editorial additions are bracketed, while Cross's strike-throughs from the original have been retained.

TRAMP AND HURRAH FOR THE FIFTH[1]

Come gather around ~~in the mellow moonlight~~ while the campfires are bright;
    Let your voices go out on the wings of the night.
We've arms tried in battle and ~~the~~ hearts ~~that will dare~~ without fear;
    Let the rebels find in battle that the old Fifth, it is ~~there~~ here.
And it's tramp & hurrah for the fifth.

1. Edward E. Cross Papers, Milne Special Collections and Archives, University of New Hampshire, Durham, N.H.

At Fair Oaks we formed in the silence of the night.
  With Howard to lead us we opened the fight.
O, we entered the woods & with no one to aid
  We drove out & whipped a whole rebel brigade.

Again at Antietam we charged through the foe,
  Their colors were captured their leaders laid low.
O, we ~~stoppe~~ paused on the field where the bullets flew thick
  And gave a salute to our brave Fighting Dick.[2]
Tramp & [hurrah for the Fifth; it was there!]

"Close up," cried the Colonel. "Close up and fire low.
  If you fall, die like men with your hearts to the foe."
And it's tramp & hurrah for the 5th it was there;
  Huzzah for McClellan, the 5th it was there.

On the red field of Fredericksburg see us again
  As we faced the grape shot & the bullets like rain.
"Close up," cried the Colonel, "close up & fire low—
  If you die fall like men with your hearts to the foe—"
And its tramp, & hurrah for the 5th it was there;
  Huzzah for McClellan, the 5th it was there!

---

2. A reference to division commander Israel "Dick" Richardson, who was mortally wounded at Antietam. Richardson had received three cheers from the Fifth on the morning of battle. Cross, Journal, [p. 58].

Afterword

The Final Adventure

The retreat from Chancellorsville brought gloom to Cross and the men of the Fifth New Hampshire. It represented a missed opportunity. In the face of a divided and outnumbered opponent, Hooker had not brought his full strength to bear. And the men who bore the brunt of such fighting knew it. Years later, regimental surgeon William Child would write, "Antietam had been indecisive, Fredericksburg was a disaster and Chancellorsville an inglorious defeat."[1]

Cross felt the disgust more acutely than others. He had watched as McClellan's caution, Burnside's bungling, and Hooker's indecision compromised a powerful and well-equipped army and emboldened the enemy. Cross could not bring himself to criticize McClellan, but Burnside, Hooker, Pope, and other generals were targets of his scorn. All the while, Cross waited for the star, the promotion to brigadier general, which would not come.

Cross was growing weary of the war and his campaign for promotion. He had commanded a brigade temporarily and soon would do so officially, but in spite of numerous well-placed recommendations, his promotion languished. His intemperate pen and the New Hampshire congressional leadership that he loathed represented major obstacles. Moreover, he perceived

---

1. Child, *Fifth New Hampshire*, 195.

political maneuvering in the commissioning of other general officers. On top of the ineptitude and intrigue, Cross despaired that the war to preserve the Union had become, as he put it, "an abolition war."[2]

Whether from revulsion or wanderlust, Cross increasingly spoke of returning to Arizona. He had sought a promotion and transfer to the Southwest, but General "Bull" Sumner's sudden death made the task more difficult. In several letters, he alluded to resigning, but his commitment to his regiment, albeit tempered, was unmistakable. For perhaps the first time in his adult life, Cross felt trapped.

On May 5, 1863, the Fifth and much of Hooker's Army began marching toward their old camp at Falmouth, across the Rappahannock River from Fredericksburg and Marye's Heights. They arrived at Falmouth the following day. Several days of rain helped expose leaky roofs, and men set about to repair cabins and get some much-needed rest. Drills, inspections, and camp life filled the remainder of the month. In spite of the break, Cross recognized that his regiment was tired, undermanned, and dispirited. He began a campaign with the War Department and Governor Berry to have the regiment sent back to New Hampshire on leave. Camp life and thoughts of returning home ended in early June when Lee and his army began moving northward toward Maryland.[3]

Ahead of the Army of Northern Virginia, Rebel cavalry began massing in the vicinity of Culpeper Court House. Hooker sent his cavalry, with infantry support, to meet the threat. General Hancock selected Cross to lead three hundred men from the Second Corps in support of the Union cavalry; Cross drew half of the detachment from his own regiment; Captain James Larkin commanded one half of the force and Captain Thomas Livermore the other half. They moved upstream along the Rappahannock and guarded fords for the eleven thousand Union cavalry under Major General Alfred Pleasonton. On June 9, 1863, Pleasonton's troopers confronted Rebel pickets on the southern bank at Beverly Ford. The Union force moved toward Culpeper Court House and surprised Major General J. E. B. Stuart and his Confederate cavalry at Brandy Station. Union losses totaled nearly one thousand in relentless fighting marked by repeated cavalry charges. Stuart lost about half that number and held the field, in part because Confederate infantry began approaching the battlefield. Despite the losses, Pleasonton's force had held its own against the legendary Stuart, and the Union cavalry emerged from the fight with much-needed confidence. In their supporting role, Cross's forces

2. See letter to Henry Kent, December 17, 1861.
3. Child, *Fifth New Hampshire*, 193–194.

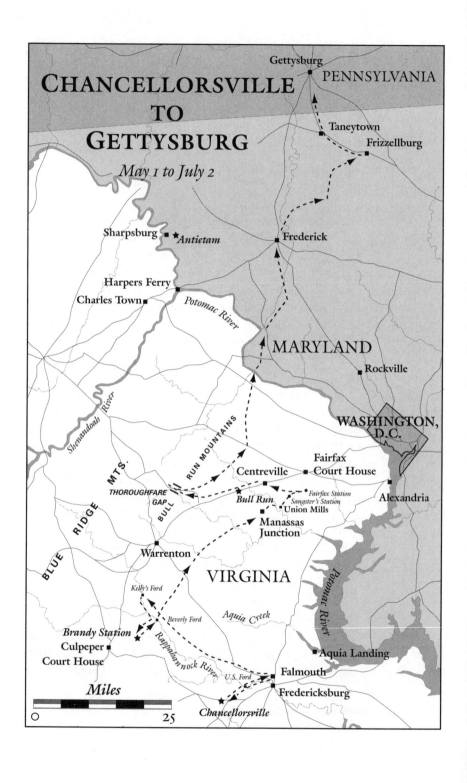

CHANCELLORSVILLE
TO
GETTYSBURG
May 1 to July 2

PENNSYLVANIA

Gettysburg

Taneytown

Frizzellburg

Sharpsburg ★*Antietam*

Frederick

Harpers Ferry

Charles Town

Potomac River

MARYLAND

Rockville

Shenandoah River

WASHINGTON, D.C.

Fairfax
Court House

Centreville

Fairfax Station

Sangster's Station

Alexandria

MTS.

THOROUGHFARE
GAP

Bull Run

Union Mills

Manassas
Junction

BULL

Warrenton

VIRGINIA

BLUE

Kelly's Ford

RIDGE

Aquia Creek

Potomac River

Beverly Ford

Brandy Station ★

Culpeper
Court House

Rappahannock River

Aquia Landing

U.S. Ford

Falmouth

Miles

Fredericksburg

○   25

Chancellorsville

suffered no casualties but had the opportunity to witness the largest cavalry battle of the Civil War.[4]

The battle provided Hooker with hard evidence that Lee was on the move. As Cross's detachment remained near Beverly Ford, the Union Third Corps and First Corps left Falmouth to stay between Washington and the Army of Northern Virginia. Cross's detachment joined the pursuit on June 14 and three days later reunited with the rest of the Union Second Corps at Sangster's Station. In the interim, Major General Darius Couch, still smarting from Hooker's poor leadership at Chancellorsville, asked for reassignment. Couch was transferred to the newly formed Department of the Susquehanna, and Major General Winfield Scott Hancock became commander of the Union Second Corps. Cross returned to the command of the First Brigade, and Lieutenant Colonel Hapgood led the Fifth. On June 20, the Second Corps marched west through Bull Run to guard Thoroughfare Gap, a passage in the Bull Run range. From there, the Fifth and the rest of the Second Corps marched northward to Edward's Ferry on the Potomac River. The corps crossed over into Maryland on the night of June 26.[5]

Lee's Army crossed farther upstream, and the chase was on; the next few days would offer little rest. In two days of marching, the Second Corps would reach the rail yards of Frederick, a distance of twenty-seven miles. On Sunday morning, June 28, Cross rode with Second Lieutenant Charles A. Hale, who was on assignment from the Fifth to the colonel's brigade staff. As they passed Sugar Loaf Mountain, near Boonsboro, Maryland, the conversation turned to the fight ahead. Cross turned to his aide and said, "It will be my last battle." Hale protested, but recalled that his commander had been somewhat preoccupied of late. Then Cross instructed, "Mr. Hale, I wish you to attend to my books and papers. That private box of mine in the headquarters wagon—you helped me to re-pack it the other day. After the campaign is over, get it . . . and turn it over to my brother Richard."[6]

That evening, while camped near the Antietam battlefield, Cross and his men learned that Lincoln had replaced Hooker with Major General George Meade. The following day, Hancock, under orders from the new commanding general, drove the Second Corps over thirty miles in fourteen hours. Thomas Livermore complained that the men were not given enough time to remove their shoes and socks when fording streams en route. Cross, ever the disciplinarian, took his orders from Hancock seriously. The 148th Pennsyl-

4. Livermore, *Days and Events*, 216–221, and Child, *Fifth New Hampshire*, 196–197.

5. Child, *Fifth New Hampshire*, 201–203.

6. Ibid., 203–204, and Charles A. Hale, "With Colonel Cross at the Wheatfield," *Civil War Times Illustrated* 13 (August 1974): 30–38.

vania, a new regiment in Cross's brigade, drew the lion's share of his attention and scorn. As the Pennsylvania regiment slowly and carefully crossed a stream, Cross drew his sword and struck one of the infantrymen with the flat of the blade. He embarrassed the regiment further by placing it under the command of Boyd McKeen, the young colonel of the Eighty-first Pennsylvania. The brigade made its destination by sundown, but Cross would forever be a tyrant in the eyes of its newest regiment.[7]

On June 30, the Second Corps rested near Uniontown, Maryland. The break from marching gave regiments a chance to collect stragglers, maintain quarterly muster rolls, and distribute pay. The brigade broke camp early on the morning of July 1. Thirty miles lay between them and a major battle brewing outside of the town of Gettysburg, Pennsylvania. By midday, the Second Corps had reached Taneytown, Maryland, just south of the Mason-Dixon Line. It was there that the men learned of the great battle underway. The men undoubtedly strained to hear the sounds of battle too far distant. Tangible proof of the fighting came when the column met a southbound ambulance containing the body of Major General John Reynolds, commander of the First Corps. He had been shot and killed on the outskirts of Gettysburg earlier in the day while deploying his troops. Around sunset and after marching some thirty miles, Cross and his men made camp three miles from the fighting.[8]

Hancock gave the order for his corps to move out early in the morning. He had already surveyed the battlefield with Meade and approved of the defensive positions along Cemetery Ridge. Cross and his men awakened at 3:00 A.M. and broke camp just over an hour later. As the Second Corps approached the battlefield, Cross once again turned to his aide and said, "Mr. Hale: attend to that box of mine at the first opportunity."[9]

About 6:00 A.M. the column crossed Taneytown Road and moved into position. Cross's brigade, at the southern end of the ridge closest to Little Round Top, would anchor the Second Corps' left. Not surprisingly, Cross positioned the Fifth on the far left flank. Once deployed, the corps line occupied about one-half mile of Cemetery Ridge. Major General Daniel Sickles's Third Corps filled the low-lying gap between Cemetery Ridge and Little Round Top. The rest of the Union line did not know that Sickles was fuming over Meade's placement of his corps. Sickles's efforts to improve its position would involve them all by day's end.[10]

---

7. Livermore, *Days and Events*, 234, and Pride and Travis, *Brave Boys*, 229–230.

8. Pride and Travis, *Brave Boys*, 231.

9. Hale, "Wheatfield," 32.

10. Harry W. Pfanz, *Gettysburg: The Second Day* (Chapel Hill: University of North Carolina Press, 1987), 137–148.

For a while, the fact that Cross's troops were not deployed along the line led to speculation that they were being held in reserve. Cross rode forward to identify Union forces occupying the wheat fields in front of the line. He returned with full knowledge of the units deployed and an account of the previous day's fighting. Hale noted that the "grave manner of the previous days had entirely disappeared; he was now full of fire, showing the sharp, impulsive manner that had always possessed him on former battlefields."[11]

While the brigade waited for events to unfold, Cross consulted with Colonel McKeen, now commander of both the Eighty-first and 148th Pennsylvania Regiments. The latter's colonel was still recovering from wounds, and Cross chose to put the new unit in the hands of a known and trusted commander. McKeen was younger than the thirty-two-year-old Cross and next in line in seniority. When they returned to within earshot, Hale heard Cross say of McKeen, "to-day, before night, he will probably be commanding the brigade."[12]

Cross's men, with a view across a small stream named Plum Run and an expanse of fields beyond, waited for events to unfold. They heard an occasional cannon and the intermittent sound of skirmishers' rifles. By ten o'clock the early morning mist had given way to July heat. As they waited, the men prepared lunch, filled their canteens, and cared for the horses. The men along the line tried to relax by talking, smoking, and playing cards, but the wait was hard on these veteran troops. Hale recalled, "Our impatience was great and the strain intense."[13]

About 2:00 P.M., General Sickles began moving the Third Corps forward from its position between Cemetery Ridge and Little Round Top. Although the movement impressed those watching from the ridge, it was contrary to Meade's orders. While conferring with Brigadier John Gibbon, Hancock commented on the "splendid advance" but predicted that Sickles's corps would not hold its position for long. Sickles had advanced a half mile beyond the rest of the Union line, thus exposing the left flank to attack. As it turned out, a renewed Rebel attack by Major General Lafayette McLaw's division was under way. Thus, Sickles's advance left his corps exposed to Rebel artillery and infantry alike.

Meade brought the Fifth Corps from reserves to support Sickles's besieged force. One brigade rushed to Little Round Top before onrushing Confederates from Major General John Bell Hood's division could turn the Union army's left flank. That brigade contained the Twentieth Maine under

11. Hale, "Wheatfield," 32–33.
12. Ibid., 33.
13. Pride and Travis, *Brave Boys*, 234, and Hale, "Wheatfield," 34.

Joshua Chamberlain; that regiment and its commander would become legendary for their actions that day. Meade also called for support from Hancock's First Division, now under John Caldwell. Because of its position on Cemetery Ridge, it could move up and support the crumbling Union line.

Cross knew the time of battle was near. He handed Hale his hat and tied a folded black scarf around his head. He twice instructed Hale to tie it tighter. Hale had been amused with this ritual "on other fields with a red bandanna," but in light of his discussions with Cross as they marched northward, Hale found the colonel's actions and the color of his headdress disturbing. Child reported that Cross hurriedly gave him a ring, some papers, and other valuables, and then said, "Good-by! It will be an awful day. Take care of yourself, I must go into the fight, but I fear I shall be killed."[14]

Both Child and Hale wrote of Cross's last conversation with Hancock, his champion and corps commander. According to Child's account, Cross said, "General, I will never live to obtain that star." Hale remembered Hancock riding up with his staff and saying to his battle-tempered brigade commander, "Colonel Cross, this day will bring you a star," to which Cross reportedly responded, "No, general, this is my last battle." Cross then saluted and rode forward, erect as a ramrod, with his eyes on the battle developing before him.[15]

About 5:00 P.M., Caldwell ordered his division forward; it advanced down the west slope of Cemetery Ridge. The Fifth had been dispatched for guard duty, but the regiment soon rejoined the First Brigade and the division's left flank. The 148th Pennsylvania, simmering from Cross's perceived tyranny days before, was next in line, followed by McKeen's Eighty-first Pennsylvania and the Sixty-fourth New York. Cross's brigade was followed, in order, by Colonel Patrick Kelly's "Irish" or Second Brigade, General Samuel K. Zook's Third Brigade, and Colonel John R. Brooke's Fourth Brigade. The First Brigade moved down the slope toward the fighting. They splashed across Plum Run and passed through the woods to the west of the wheat field where much of their fighting would take place. Cross brought his brigade up to the fence along Wheatfield Road, positioned them in three lines facing west toward the enemy.

One of Caldwell's aides rode up and informed Cross that the enemy was moving through the woods to the brigade's left. Cross moved the brigade forward; the Fifth and the left wing of the 148th moved through the woods east of the wheat field. The rest of the brigade advanced through the ripening

14. Hale, "Wheatfield," 34–35, and Child, *Fifth New Hampshire*, 217.
15. Child, 217; and Hale, 34.

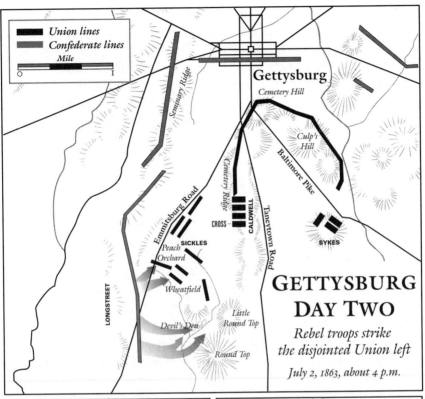

Seminary Ridge

Gettysburg
Cemetery Hill

Culp's Hill

Baltimore Pike

Emmitsburg Road

Cemetery Ridge

Taneytown Road

CROSS   CALDWELL

SYKES

SICKLES

Peach Orchard

LONGSTREET

Wheatfield

Little Round Top

Devil's Den

Round Top

GETTYSBURG DAY TWO

*Rebel troops strike
the disjointed Union left*

July 2, 1863, *about 4 p.m.*

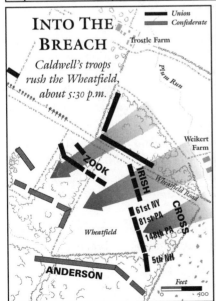

INTO THE BREACH

Trostle Farm

*Caldwell's troops
rush the Wheatfield,
about 5:30 p.m.*

Plum Run

Weikert Farm

ZOOK

IRISH

Wheatfield Road

CROSS

61st NY
81st PA
148th PA
5th NH

Wheatfield

ANDERSON

Feet
0   500

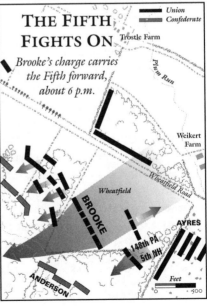

THE FIFTH FIGHTS ON

Trostle Farm

*Brooke's charge carries
the Fifth forward,
about 6 p.m.*

Plum Run

Weikert Farm

Wheatfield

Wheatfield Road

BROOKE

AYRES

148th PA
5th NH

ANDERSON

Feet
0   500

wheat. Cross gave some contradictory orders at first, leading to some confusion, but Hale remembered them "advancing as steadily into the wheat field as though on parade." The Confederates on the edge of the woods on the other side of the field began firing; the men could see puffs of smoke coming from the enemy rifles, and some recalled seeing minié balls clipping the tops of the ripening wheat around them. Most of the shots seemed high; initially the Fifth suffered few casualties. Nevertheless, about halfway through the wheat field, Cross dismounted and ordered his staff and officers to do the same. Orderlies took the horses to the rear. When the brigade reached a rise in the field, the Rebel fire grew heavier. The First Brigade halted along the crest of the rise and returned the fire. Impressed by the sight, Hale wrote with pride: "The entire brigade moved with the mobility of a single battalion. . . . Just in the nick of time, it was hurled against the enemy and it struck a tremendous blow. That was the very way the brigades of the First Division had been trained to fight." [16]

As it advanced though the woods, the Fifth encountered skirmishers in front of the Fifteenth Georgia and First Texas. The rest of Cross's command faced a brigade of Georgians positioned behind a stone wall. As they advanced at a march, the line overtook a group of Rebel skirmishers lying in the wheat field. Cross put Hale in charge of them and pointed out others to be captured. One Confederate officer broke his sword and flung it at Hale's feet. Colonel McKeen recognized Hale's growing difficulty and dispatched three men to help him. Within a few minutes, they had taken twenty prisoners. [17]

Cross, now walking among his men, surveyed the Confederate line and began organizing his men to charge the Confederate positions in the woods and behind the stone wall. According to Hale, Cross looked back to his men and ordered: "Boys—instruct the commanders to be ready to charge when the order is given; wait here for the command, or, if you hear the bugles of the Fifth New Hampshire on the left, move forward on the run." Cross then turned and entered the woods, his old regiment on his left and the 148th Pennsylvania, the brigade's newest regiment, on his right. Hale, still guarding the prisoners, stood behind the advancing brigade and "looked after him [Cross] sort of regretfully as he vanished among the trees." Hale would never see him again. [18]

Cross and his men had advanced to within forty-five yards of the enemy lines when a Rebel sharpshooter, hiding behind a large boulder, took aim

16. Pfanz, *Gettysburg*, 268–271, and Hale, "Wheatfield," 35–36.
17. Pfanz, *Gettysburg*, 273, and Hale, "Wheatfield," 36.
18. Hale, "Wheatfield," 36.

and fired at Cross. The ball found its mark, entering through Cross's abdomen and exiting near his spine. The oft-wounded colonel fell instantly. Lieutenant Colonel Charles Hapgood, commanding the Fifth, had witnessed the event and ordered Sergeant Charles Phelps to shoot the sniper. Phelps lay in wait and, when the Rebel rose to fire again, shot him dead. Later that afternoon, Phelps was shot in the back and died. Hapgood then ordered Cross taken to the edge of the wheat field to a waiting ambulance.[19]

The brigade continued the attack. Across the wheat field, General Zook was felled by a mortal wound to the abdomen. The 148th Pennsylvania, still chafing under Cross's strict discipline, fought side by side with the Fifth. Caldwell sent in Brooke's brigade to relieve the First. Brooke's men cleared the wheat field, but the Fifth and the Pennsylvanians in the woods were on their own. They fought valiantly but ran out of ammunition, and were forced to search for rounds among the wounded. To make matters worse, the remnants of the Third Corps finally gave way, leaving the First Brigade and any reinforcements in the area exposed to Confederate counterattack. As Confederates surged forward, the brigade broke and fled back up the ridge. About 7:30 P.M., two hours after it had led the brigade into battle, members of the Fifth were among the last of the division to cross Plum Run and clamber up Cemetery Ridge. Later that night, Hapgood could not count one hundred officers and men. It would be hours before order was restored to the brigade and its regiments.[20]

Cross did not witness the disorder. He had been taken a mile away northward, near Culp's Hill, to a recently mowed wheat field. He was placed on bound sheaves of wheat to make him more comfortable. Sunset came late, but gloom had already enveloped the vigil surrounding Cross. Some men from the regiment made their way to Cross's side. His brother Richard was there, along with regimental surgeons J. W. Bucknam and William Child. They were helpless to do anything but to make him comfortable. Cross had foretold his death, but it nevertheless came slowly and forlornly. He said his good-byes to his men and, through his brother, to his family. In his delirium he kept repeating, "My brave men." According to Child, his last words were: "I did hope I should see peace restored to our distressed country. I think the boys will miss me. Say goodbye to all."[21]

The following day, Lee massed his troops to attack Union defenses on Cemetery Ridge. Longstreet's Corps, tired and depleted from fighting the day before, would lead the way with their reserves from the previous day.

19. Pfanz, *Gettysburg*, 273, and Pride and Travis, *Brave Boys*, 239.
20. Pride and Travis, *Brave Boys*, 241–242.
21. Child, *Fifth New Hampshire*, 208.

The Fifth was held in reserve, but the deafening cannonade that preceded the charge threatened men up and down Cemetery Ridge. Hancock, among thousands of others, was wounded; however, after fierce fighting, the Union line held. There was a break in fighting on July 4, 1863, the eighty-seventh anniversary of the nation's founding. That night, Lee began a retreat toward the Potomac and his home state of Virginia. Cross was returning home as well.[22]

Captain Welcome Crafts accompanied the body home. Although most of the Fifth's dead were buried on the battlefield, Cross's body had been sent to Baltimore for embalming. Traveling by train, Crafts and the body reached Lancaster on Tuesday, July 7. The funeral took place the following Thursday at the family homestead, on a long porch that stretched the length of the house. A Union flag draped the coffin; a sword and soldier's cap rested on the flag. The North Star Lodge of Masons was responsible for the ceremonies and interment. Cross's best friend and confidant, Henry O. Kent, wrote the following account of his friend and of the ceremony:

> The national flags drooped at half-mast, the band played solemn dirges, the fraternity, in large numbers, assisted in the solemn ceremonies, and, amid a throng of friends who had known him from boyhood, the brave soldier, the true friend, the impulsive and honorable man, was borne to his final resting place in the valley he loved so well, amid all his wanderings, where he now sleeps unmindful of the din of battle or the shouts over the victory for which he laid down his gallant life."[23]

Weeks later, the Fifth would return home for much-needed rest and recruiting. It would then return to the Army of the Potomac for long months of fighting, leading up to Lee's surrender at Appomattox Court House, but without Cross and the many others who had fallen, it would never be quite the same. For Cross, the war, the final adventure, was over.[24]

---

22. Pride and Travis, *Brave Boys*, 244–246.
23. Child, *Fifth New Hampshire*, 212–213.
24. Pride and Travis, *Brave Boys*, 247–248.

Bibliographical Note

This volume belongs to Edward E. Cross. The main task of the editors has been to transcribe, annotate, and illuminate Cross's often powerful words. His published and manuscript writings, scattered throughout the Granite State and beyond, are the primary texts from which the editors have worked. No published source could assist in deciphering Cross's handwriting, but many works proved useful in placing documents in context and in identifying the people, places, and things mention in Cross's diary, reports, and letters.

First and foremost, the editors are indebted to Mike Pride and Mark Travis, authors of *My Brave Boys: To War with Colonel Cross and the Fighting Fifth* (Hanover, N.H.: University Press of New England, 2001). They not only updated the story of the Fifth and its colonel; they gave the editors a broader view of people, places, and events mentioned in Cross's wartime writings. Their well-researched synthesis made work on this volume much easier. Moreover, their bibliography of sources eliminated the need for a full bibliography in this work.

For annotating Cross's journal, reports, and selected letters, the editors drew heavily on the first-person accounts of William Child, in his *History of the Fifth Regiment New Hampshire Volunteers, in the American Civil War, 1861–1865,* and of Thomas L. Livermore, in his *Days and Events, 1860–1866.* Their eyewitness accounts provide the reader with a depth and texture that are unavailable from secondary sources. Added to their work is Charles A. Hale's "With Colonel Cross at the Wheatfield." This unpublished manuscript is probably the single best primary source on Cross's last days. The afterword in this volume, which describes Cross's last campaign, relies heavily on these three primary sources, a fact that was intended to complement Cross's own eyewitness accounts.

Also important are a number of secondary sources. The myriad of fine works by Stephen W. Sears were particularly helpful, including his *To the Gates of Richmond,* which covers the Peninsula campaign; *Landscape Turned Red,* on Antietam; and, finally, *Chancellorsville.* Add to that General Francis W. Palfrey's *The Antietam and Fredericksburg* and Harry Pfanz's *Gettysburg: The Second Day,* and one has an excellent crash course in campaigns involving Colonel Cross. Older histories such as Otis F. R. Waite's

New Hampshire in the Great Rebellion and Francis A. Walker's *History of the Second Army Corps* also proved extremely helpful. All such sources provided the editors with much-needed background, factual information, and context for the actions of Cross and the Fifth New Hampshire.

Annotating carries with it a requisite amount of sleuthing, and a number of fine reference books make the work of the editor easier. Those used include, but are not limited to, the following: Patricia Faust's *Historical Times Illustrated Encyclopedia of the Civil War*; Mark Boatner's *Civil War Dictionary*; E. B. Long's *Civil War Day by Day: An Almanac 1861–1865*; John and David Eicher's *Civil War High Commands*; and Ezra J. Warner's *Generals in Blue*. For more obscure references, the editors used a number of different sources, including local histories of New Hampshire; the New Hampshire Adjutant General's *Soldiers and Sailors of New Hampshire*; *The Granite State Monthly*; and a large number of nineteenth-century political almanacs, collected biographies, newspapers, and professional guides.

Index